UNIVERSITY OF MIAMI CRITICAL STUDIES NO. 5

THE

The Liars by Henry Arthur Jones

NEW

The Notorious Mrs. Ebbsmith by Sir Arthur Wing Pinero

DRAMA

INTRODUCTION BY CARL M. SELLE

UNIVERSITY OF MIAMI PRESS

Second Printing, 1968

ACKNOWLEDGEMENTS

Acknowledgement is made to the Walter H. Baker Co. for permission to reprint Pinero's *The Notorious Mrs. Ebbsmith*; to Samuel French, Inc. for permission to reprint Jones's *The Liars*; to *The Public Trustee* and *The Society of Authors* (London) for permission to quote from Shaw's *Dramatic Opinions and Essays*.

Acknowledgement is also made to the following for permission to quote from their publications: E. P. Dutton and Co. for Clayton Hamilton's critical introductions and prefaces to *The Social Plays* of Pinero; Dodd, Mead, and Co. for William Archer's *The Old Drama and The New*; *Encyclopedia Britannica* for Archer's article "Recent English Drama."

Mrs. Clayton Hamilton has graciously given permission to quote from her husband's criticism of Jones and Pinero.

INTRODUCTION

I

The New Drama, though the twentieth century's catastrophic changes may seem to have pushed it into distant history, is really a recent development. It flourished and spread only a short time ago. Henry Arthur Jones died in 1929 and Sir Arthur Wing Pinero in 1934: hence a present-day student has grandparents who could, in the course of the usual American trip abroad, have attended premières of the later plays of either dramatist, or could have seen an initial production of Jones in New York (*The Hypocrites*—1906). Henrik Ibsen, the chief foreign influence of the era, died in 1906, and so persons who today are in their seventies could have seen the colossus (it was not so easy to speak with him) when he was a European attraction of a piece with Big Ben, the Eiffel Tower, and the Pope: the regularity of his walks to his favorite café had the part broadcloth, part olympian tone of the age. Somerset Maugham, the "durable old party," is still alive, a breathing reminder that in 1908 he established a theatrical record of having four original plays presented in London concurrently.* George Bernard Shaw lived and held forth until 1950, and reaches out from his roiled Victorianism to touch the present world in a thousand ways, including the gathering in of royalties on *My Fair Lady*. John Galsworthy died in 1933; far from merely staring upright in Madame Tussaud's, he is remembered, read, and occasionally seen. Harley Granville Barker lived until 1946; his stress on the "interior action" of person and plot, his co-managership of the Court Theatre, and his stern realistic plays give him firm rank in the New Drama. Augustus Thomas died in 1934; his use of native American material assures his position among the figures of the emergent drama.

---

* *Lady Frederick, Jack Straw, Mrs. Dot, The Explorer.*

The death dates alone of these authors place them close to our time. More significantly, the ways in which they built on antecedent or current material, the kinds of plays they wrote, and the critical theories sustaining them are very much alive, partly to be sure as historical study, but partly as the enduring stuff of highest dramatic accomplishment. This appraisal deals with Jones and Pinero as individual dramatists and as rooted parts of a well-defined literary composite.

II

The term New Drama became one of the important designations in English literary history. Jones conferred on the movement the title *Renascence of English Drama,* and he and Pinero were conscious, and indeed sometimes over-assertive, of their firm place in the unity of purpose and brave-new-world achievements of the time. Even hostile critics felt that the totality of new plays published and produced merited historical classification. The following terms arose, among others: *the modern movement, the higher drama* (undoubtedly in imitation of the higher criticism), *the new live theatre, the era of the problem play, modern realistic drama, the free theatre, the modern social drama, the new school of thinker-dramatists, the theatre of ideas, the modern English school, the new style of writing and acting, the great revival, the literary drama, the rejuvenation of drama, the drama of social significance.* The critical pieces that analyzed the New Drama were occasionally called *New Journalism* and *New Criticism* (not of course to be confused with the New Criticism of the 1930's and 1940's). The term *New Woman* is frequent, but *New Man* is scarce. Shaw jests about the *New Humor.*

The New Dramatists in England were Jones, Pinero, Gilbert, Wilde, Shaw, Galsworthy, Barker, Barrie, Maugham, and less familiar figures such as Hadon Chambers — who enriched the language with the phrase "the long arm of coincidence," R. C. Carton, Israel Zangwill, Elizabeth Baker, Sydney Grundy — who probably invented the phrase "problem play," H. H. Davies, Alfred Sutro, Clemence Dane, and others.

The New Drama embraced the Irish dramatists Edward Martyn, Lady Gregory, (William Archer called her plays "drolls"), William Boyle, T. C. Murray, Lennox Robinson, and others, not only out of English vigor and certitude but because it felt itself vast and irresistible both in the present and for the future. It recognized Yeats as "the first Irish poet" rather than as a dramatist. The New Drama's belief in itself as *fons et origo* of the drama of the time was stated with customary zeal by Clayton Hamilton, friend to both Jones and Pinero:

> . . . in judging the dramatic work of Sir Arthur Pinero [and of] Mr. Henry Arthur Jones—it seems only fair to emphasize the fact that these two men were pioneers, and that—in a period which by most observers was dismissed as hopelessly unpromising— they responded nobly to a faint-hearted call and created a worthy drama out of nothing.

> Their rivals and contemporaries in more recent years [*circa* 1910] have enjoyed the manifest advantage of writing for a theatre whose ideals had been already pointed in the new direction of "high seriousness" by [Pinero and Jones]. Mr. George Bernard Shaw, who has done so much to enliven the modern English drama, did nothing to initiate it, except in his contributive capacity as a practicing dramatic critic. The plays of Mr. John Galsworthy, Mr. Harley Granville Barker, and many other earnest authors of the younger generation, could never have been undertaken except for the established fact that a serious theatre was already waiting to receive them. The programme of the Irish National Theatre Society — which was

formulated . . . to further an insurrection against the
technical formulas made popular by Pinero and Jones
— owed its very inception to the pre-existence of a
power against which it elected to rebel . . . Pinero and
Jones have not only aided those successors who have
chosen to follow in their footsteps, but they have also
aided those successors who have chosen to attempt
another path . . . .[1]

The New Drama was reluctant to come thoroughly to
grips with plays that were non-realistic in its terms. John
Millington Synge was gingerly conceded to be "endowed with
the eloquence of angels." Maeterlinck was dispensed with by
damning him with excess praise — the "Order of the Swan"
was conferred on him and he was thus known as the "Belgian
Shakespeare,"—or with sharper insight as "a Webster who
had read Alfred de Musset."

Of course there also was New Drama in America, but it
was acknowledged with occasional touches of condescension
and critical largess. Such attitudes were related to the fact
that America became a source of solid income for British
dramatists (Jones frankly acknowledged this in his Harvard
lecture in 1906) particularly after the International Copyright
Agreement of 1887 and the American Copyright Bill of 1891:
these regulations enabled an author of plays to obtain the
double profit of acting fees and publication.

It is not our purpose to analyze the unfolding of American
drama along lines that parallel those of the English New
Drama. To the extent that realism was a world movement,
American plays belonged within it (as cisatlantic problem
plays, comedy, farce, melodrama), but certainly not with the
high creativity of English drama. In the first place, America
simply had no playwrights of the stature of the British, and
in the second place, this country had native social mobility
and personal aspiration that flourished in, and shaped, a
quite different milieu, including both the melting pot and

the relentless power of the *robber barons* and the industrial and financial potentates for whom the lodestone land of unlimited opportunities meant neo-feudalism. A comparison of the tones and overtones of the city of London and those of the city of New York reveals many of the significant differences: Buckingham Palace and Gracie Mansion.*

---

* One of the most significant analyses of the differences between the city of Hyde Park and Belgravia and the city of Central Park and Park Avenue is William Dean Howell's *London Films*, published by Harper and Brothers in 1905. See Appendix for further discussion of American New Dramatists.

III

One of the chief characteristics of the New Drama is its relation to the novels that were at the apex of nineteenth-century English literature until the end of the century.* The most important influence of the novel on the drama was a pervasive general one (somewhat analogous to the general dramatic influence of Ibsen): the sheer excellence of the novel's character delineation, its realistic story-telling (often entertainingly picaresque), and its ability to establish varieties

---

* The following dates suggest inevitable influences: Scott wrote *The Heart of Midlothian* in 1818; Balzac wrote *Le Père Goriot* in 1835; Thackeray wrote *Vanity Fair* in 1847; Dickens wrote *Hard Times* in 1854; Trollope wrote *The Warden,* the first of the Barsetshire series, in 1855; Zola wrote *Thérèse Raquin* in 1867 and turned it into a play in 1873; George Eliot wrote *Middlemarch* in 1871, but her earlier translation of Strauss's *Life of Jesus* marked her as a disseminator of the "free thought" and "advanced" analysis that contributed to the mentality of the later New Drama; Tolstoy wrote *Anna Karenina* in 1875; Hardy wrote *The Return of the Native* in 1878; Meredith wrote *The Egoist* in 1879. The student who wishes to see into the English playwrights and plays of 1880 and later can hardly do better than to read Galsworthy's *Forsyte Saga,* just as he will find Thomas Mann's *Buddenbrooks* an avenue of insight into Continental drama.

of tone and texture of person and place by means of artistry in words were noted everywhere. The dialogue in page after page of many novels needed only a few stage directions or a few easy changes to read like true drama. Jones and Pinero, who read widely and enthusiastically, freely acknowledged the influence of novelistic story-telling on the playwright's imagination as he set in motion a plot. Apart from their creation of realistic and naturalistic fiction, the novelists at times discussed their works and theorized about them in a way that was useful to dramatists: for example Dickens, Hardy, Flaubert, Zola. The last-mentioned, both novelist and dramatist, expressed the following literary ideal: ". . . the action resides not in some plot, but in the inner conflicts of the characters; the logic used is not one of facts, but of sensations and sentiments." To be sure, no dramatist could wholly live up to such fine tenet (plot and facts can be suppressed only to a certain point), but it was an antidote to dramatic bombast, cliché, and veneer.

In England polite society, until fairly late in the century, usually preferred novel-reading to play-going. The dramatists were aware that Dickens's thrusts against prudery and hypocrisy, and the high seriousness of the problems (the phrase *problem novel*, to match "problem play," constantly suggests itself) treated in his novels were beyond the drama and the theater of the time. But with the success of drama after 1880, English playwrights equalled or surpassed the novelists in their themes, insights, and forthright revelations, so much so that Shaw could state that *Vanity Fair* and *Middlemarch* were "pretty old prim stories now."

Earlier in the century, dramatists adapted novels in such a way that the development of true drama was scarcely advanced, if not downright hindered. William Schwenck Gilbert's *Dan'l Druce, Blacksmith* (1876) was a sentimental costume play based on George Eliot's *Silas Marner*: it was merely a lush vehicle for the "character actor." But as drama achieved the stature of the novel, dramatists were increasingly secure in their ability to reject unusable aspects of fiction and to accept the usable. Even as an advanced New Dramatist, Shaw based his Mrs. Dudgeon (*The Devil's Disciple*, 1897) on Dickens's Mrs. Clennam (*Little Dorrit*) and on Mrs. Gargery (*Great Expectations*). English dramatists raised their form of verbal art above the mere devices of theatricality to literature worthy to be ranked with novels and poems.

In fact, as the New Drama gathered momentum it began to argue that the novelist had a far easier task than did the dramatist, who had to cope with problems that did not ruffle the novelist. The dramatist had to combat the accumulation of many years of indifference or hostility, as he had to combat the dead-end notion that stagecraft was superior to philosophical and social insight and conviction, and to aesthetic excellence. Persons of sense and sensibility scorned the theater, and therefore the New Dramatists and their sustaining or carping critics made much of the fact that drama as literature and drama as plays for the boards arose from two separate sources, the former of crystalline purity, the latter of theatrical pandering and ranting. Thus we need to grasp the New Dramatists' fervent desire to have plays read widely and eagerly, as we need to grasp their desire to uphold the dramatist as a devoted and profound man of letters. Henry James asserted: "The anomalous fact is that the theatre, so called, can flourish in barbarism, but that any drama worth speaking of can develop but in the air of civilization."

The New Dramatists stressed that serious authors who write plays are, to begin with, persons of a definite cast of thought and temperament, are citizens who take a visible position on the good life, and are men who act on an ascertainable set of values. To be sure, the dramatists of the era were fully aware that worthy theme and effective treatment must coalesce: they readily aired ideas on stage setting, exposition, the *raisonneur*, the confidant, exits and entrances, obligatory scenes, verisimilitude, and so on. They further had strong respect for the statistics of the box office: witness their eager-ness for lucrative long runs, particularly as these permitted subsequent experimentation that might result in financial loss — a run of a hundred performances was regarded as failure or near-failure; *The Dancing Girl* (1891) ran for 310 nights. The New Dramatists asserted their autonomy as authors of worth and dignity, remembering the years of their youth when notions of entertainment and of catering to unschooled audi-ences stifled an entire art form. They wanted to shape, in their own terms, more than to be shaped.

The American critic Brander Matthews pointed out that as late as 1915 the reading of plays in Great Britain and the United States was almost a lost art. He went on to say:

> In the eighteenth century and even in the earlier years of the nineteenth century, before the overwhelm-ing popularity of the Waverly novels led to the enormous expansion of prose-fiction and to the con-sequent decline of the English drama, plays were as freely read as novels. A successful comedy or tragedy went through edition after edition. Hazlitt dwelt on the delight of reading a comedy in which the cleverest things are said and the most amusing hap-pen. But as the novel slowly but surely crowded out the play, the mass of readers became accustomed to the amplitude of description and to the superfluities of analysis in which the novelist was wont to in-dulge; and they came in time to find the bare dialogue of a play, supported only by sparse stage directions, a little too bare for comfortable perusal. They became too lazy to make the effort needed to picture the action for themselves. In other words, the art of reading a play was lost by the immense majority of those whose faculties were weakened by the often excessive amount of detail provided in the more leisurely and less condensed narratives of the novelist.[2]

Jones steadfastly held that the wide reading of plays could hinder "The divorce of the English drama from English literature." Yeats said in the introduction to his *Collected Plays*: "The plays in this book are intended for hearers and for readers." Shaw said: "My plays are literary plays." The critic Thomas H. Dickinson said: "The playwright of powerful personality can mould public demand, can even modify the machinery of the theater."

IV

Plays leading up to and penetrating the era of the New Drama were English in origin and tone, or were imported from across the Channel. The importations were often adapted and distorted with little respect for the values of the original and for the needs of native drama to push on to realistic treatment of contemporary matters. An anecdote relates that a hack who had mistranslated and otherwise manhandled a French melodrama came forth at the opening night to take a bow in response to the audience's call for the author.

The emergent drama often expressed pride in the essentially native and domestic nature of plays and their presentation. Such plays can be divided into two categories: the established English classics (Shakespeare; the Elizabethans in general; the Restoration authors, particularly Congreve; Goldsmith; Sheridan) and the plays, beginning with those, say, of Douglas Jerrold (1803 - 1857), which, however chained to mere theatricality, helped make possible the realism that flowered in the New Drama.

The New Critics gave Shakespeare all due honor (this of course holds for Shaw in particular, whose conclusions on the Bard are the soundest of the lot), but some of them severely assailed Marlowe, Jonson, Middleton, Ford, Beaumont, Fletcher, and the rest. The target of their criticism was not only the Elizabethans but also the adulatory judgments of Lamb, Hazlitt, Swinburne, Rupert Brooke, Lytton Strachey and other earlier or later bardolators and "Elizabethanisers," some of them at the very heartbeat of the New Drama.

Hazlitt called Shakespeare "the tallest and strongest of a race of giants." Lamb's *Tales* and his *Specimens* contributed substantially to the fulsome praise of Elizabethan verse dramatists. Swinburne asserted: ". . . Except in Aeschylus, in Dante, and in Shakespeare, I, at least, know not where to seek for passages which in sheer force of tragic and noble horror . . . may be set against the subtlest, the deepest, the sublimest passages of Webster." Rupert Brooke reached a feverish defense of Dekker and Webster in response to Professor F. E. Schelling's reasonable judgment that the authors of *Westward Ho* and *Northward Ho* had created ". . . figures we would fain believe, in their pruriency and outspoken uncleanliness of speech, represent an occasional aberration, if not an outrageous exaggeration, of the manners of the time." The Georgian poet laid bare one of the central critical issues concerning the New Drama in his protest against Schelling's (and others') ". . . impudent attempt to thrust the filthy and degraded standards of the modern middle-class drawing-room on the clean fineness of the Elizabethans. . . ."[3] Lytton Strachey spoke of "that noble band of Elizabethans, whose strong and splendid spirit gave to England . . . the most glorious heritage of drama that the world has known." Even Jones, at the center of the new realism, held that "Surely the crowning glory of our nation is our Shakespeare; and remember he was one of a great school." All this was too much for some of the sustaining critics of the New Drama, whose frontal or oblique attacks on the Elizabethans amount to a major characteristic of the age. We need to examine one such assault before we deal with Shakespeare himself.

Because Lamb placed excessive value on John Ford's *The Broken Heart*, we can use the New Criticism's "realistic" appraisal of this Elizabethan verse drama as representative. William Archer argued as follows:

> *The Broken Heart* . . . enjoys a reputation only second to that of *The Duchess of Malfy*. Ford's spirit was, indeed, more subtle than that of Webster. He loved the abnormal more than the merely brutal. We breathe in his writings a heavy atmosphere of morbid, sometimes monstrous, passion . . . in point of constructive art he is as much to seek as any of his contemporaries.

> *The Broken Heart* opens very languidly. Orgilus has been betrothed to Penthea, whom he loves; but the tyranny of her brother, Ithocles, prevents their marriage, and gives Penthea to the insanely jealous Bassanes. Orgilus pretends to go to Athens, but in fact remains disguised in Sparta, where the scene is laid. This disguise leads to nothing that matters, and is apparently adopted simply because the Jacobean audiences loved disguise for its own sake. Meanwhile the tyrannous brother, Ithocles, comes back victorious from the wars, and falls in love with Calantha, daughter of the king, Amyclas. [Penthea now dies insane.] Orgilus lures Ithocles into seating himself in a chair with . . . movable arms which imprison him, and then murders him in his helplessness. Now Calantha is at this moment dancing at a wedding, at which the king, her father, is too ill to be present: and here occurs the most admired incident of the tragedy. . . .

They dance the first change; during which Armostes enters.
ARMOSTES. (*Whispers to Calantha.*) The king your father's **dead.**
CALANTHA. To the other change.
ARMOSTES.   Is 't possible?

> (*They dance the second change.*)
> *Enter Bassanes.*

BASSANES. (*Whispers to Calantha.*) O, madam!
    Penthea, poor Penthea's starved.
CALANTHA.   Beshrew thee!
    Lead to the next.
BASSANES.   Amazement dulls **my senses.**

    (*They dance the third change.*)
        Enter Orgilus.

ORGILUS. (*Whispers to Calantha.*) Brave Ithocles
    Js murdered, murdered cruelly.

CALANTHA. How dull this music sounds! Strike up
      more sprightly;
    Our footings are not active like our heart,
    Which treads the nimbler measure . . . .

ORGILUS.   I am thunderstruck.
    (*The last change.*)

CALANTHA. So! let us breathe awhile. (*Music ceases.*)
                Hath not this motion
    Raised fresher colour to our cheeks?

NEARCHUS.   Sweet princess,
    A perfect purity of blood enamels
    The beauty of your white.

CALANTHA.   We all look cheerfully:
    And, cousin, 'tis methinks a rare presumption
    Jn any who prefer our lawful pleasures
    Before their own sour censure, t'interrupt
    The custom of this ceremony bluntly.

NEARCHUS. None dares, lady.

CALANTHA. Yes, yes. Some hollow voice delivered to me
    How that the king was dead.

[*Archer continues*] And so she goes on to take cognisance of the various dismal happenings, and, in her new character of Queen of Sparta, to command the execution of Orgilus. He is bled to death on the open stage; and then Calantha, at the funeral of Ithocles, dies of a broken heart.[4]

The good Elia as excessive "Elizabethaniser" thought of Calantha's dance: "The expression of this transcendent scene almost bears me in imagination to Calvary and the cross; and I seem to perceive some analogy between the scenical suffering I am here contemplating, and the real agonies of that final completion to which I dare no more than hint a reference." Dissenting New Criticism regarded such critical judgment as vulgar error that contributed to the stultification of dramatic development and appreciation. Shaw's own disloyal opposition to the Elizabethans reached incandescence:

    . . . Jonson, Webster, and the whole crew of insufferable bunglers and dullards whose work stands out as

vile even at the beginning of the seventeenth century.
. . . The leaders of [the Renaissance] were dead long before the Elizabethan literary rabble became conscious
that "ideas" were in fashion, and that any author
who could gather a cheap stock of them from murder,
lust, and obscenity, and formulate them in rhetorical
blank verse, might make the stage pestiferous with
plays that have no ray of noble feeling, no touch of
faith, beauty, or even common kindness in them from
beginning to end. . . .[5]

Shakespeare, however, was placed on a lofty pedestal, at
times more out of patriotism or commercial interest than out
of literary discernment. When he was manhandled and
adulterated into bombast, ranting, pageantry at the expense
of insight and finesse, or was made mere vehicle for melo-
dramatic star performance, his influence on the emerging
drama was detrimental. When, however, Shakespeare was
presented with respect and sincerity (even if attended by a
certain amount of error in interpretation and scansion) his
immediate impact on audiences and his general influence on
English drama were sound: hence Shaw accorded the Shakespeare Reading Society and the Elizabethan Stage Society his
finest understanding and most gentlemanly praise as the
preservers and advancers of a worthwhile tradition. The drama
before and during the era of Jones and Pinero could not have
attained its complete identity without the interwoven influence of Elizabethan verse drama.

Shaw first of all held that Shakespeare's plays have to
be appreciated as melody of words and lines, that "in a deaf
nation these plays would have died long ago. . . ." Any
tampering with or misinterpretation of Shakespeare's lines
was picked up by Shaw's acute ear (caressed and harassed
by his years as amateur and professional music critic) and
corrected with a birchmaster's severity. After a performance
of *Hamlet* at the Olympic Theatre, Shaw wrote:

. . . Throwing off the critic, I indulged a silly boyish

affection of mine for the play, which I know nearly by heart, thereby having a distinct advantage over Mr Nutcombe Gould, whose acquaintance with the text is extremely precarious. His aptitude for transposing the adverb "so" in such a way as to spoil the verse, not to mention putting in full stops where there is no stop, and no stop where there is a full stop, is calamitous and appalling. For example:

> For in that sleep of death what dreams may come [*full stop*].
> When we have shuffled off this mortal coil [*full stop*].
> Must give us pause.

And*

> When the grass grows the proverb is somewhat musty.

The effect of changing "'tis" into "it is" was also fully exploited.

Thus—

> Whether it is nobler in the mind to suffer.

Even Mr Foss, otherwise better than most Laerteses, said:

> O Heaven, is it possible a young maid's wits
> Should be as mortal as an old man's life?

Mr Nutcombe Gould gave us all Hamlet's appearance, something of his feeling, and but little of his brains. . . .[6]

It is mistaken, however, to relegate Shaw's criticism of Shakespeare to insight into the mere flow of vowels and consonants. In effect the greatest of the New Dramatists, who was also their best critic, applied the insights of the realism of the age to verse drama that was often, as with Henry

---

*An example of omission of a stop. The Neilson and Hill edition gives the line as: "Ay, but 'While the grass grows,'—the proverb is something musty."

Irving and others, theatrically inflated or distorted: Shaw
held that "the turn of the line . . . lets you into the secret
of its utterer's mood and temperament, not by its commonplace meaning, but by some subtle exaltation, or stultification, or slyness, or delicacy, or hesitancy, or what not [beyond
mere melody] in the sound of it. In short, it is the score and
not the libretto that keeps the work alive and fresh. . . ."

The native drama, it was mentioned above, that led up
to the early days of the New Drama and well into the movement can be divided into the English classics and the
nineteenth-century plays, often rough-and-ready, that helped
make possible the uses of realism. Below is a selected list of
the latter. They show amid all the dross: 1) awareness of
literary craftsmanship and desire and possibilities for improve-
ment; 2) increasing interest in creating verisimilitude; 3) en-
hancement of theatrical effectiveness in everything from the
use of formal verse to excess of purple passage and of sentimentality, farce, melodrama—all three aspects leading to
later dramatic realism of all shadings and degrees, such as
so-called "pure realism" (a chimera), "selective realism,"
"poetic realism," "modified realism," "modern realism," and
others. Present-day readers may take pleasure beyond that of
historical study in finding in these early plays locutions, characters, incidents, and scenes of literary merit:

Virginius (1820) by James Sheridan Knowles; *Black-Ey'd
Susan,* or *All in the Downs* (1829) by Douglas Jerrold;
Richelieu (1839) and *Money* (1840) by Sir Edward Bulwer-
Lytton; *A Blot in the 'Scutcheon* (1843) by Robert Browning;
Masks and Faces, or *Before and Behind the Curtain* (1852)
by Tom Taylor and Charles Reade; *The Colleen Bawn* (1860)
by Dion Boucicault; *The Ticket-of-Leave Man* (1863) by Tom
Taylor; *Lady Audley's Secret* (1863) by C. H. Hazlewood;
Caste (1867) by T. W. Robertson; *Two Roses* (1870) by
James Albery; *The Bells* (1871) by Leopold Lewis; *A Pair of*

Spectacles (1890) by Sydney Grundy; *Becket* (1893) by Alfred Tennyson.

All these plays show minute or substantial modification of prevailing farce, burlesque, melodrama, verse drama, inept adaptation, or general theatrical limitation. They show necessary steps that had to be taken before Jones, Pinero, Wilde, Shaw and others could write plays that presented the realistic statement and the realistic outcome of worthy contemporary problems. (Shaw flatly denied this: he said that no English plays after Shakespeare influenced him. We can regard this as a wayward fillip of the perfect Ibsenite justly confident in his plays of discussion.)

T. W. Robertson (1829-1871) is the best example of a native playwright who in part of his work remained firmly, and happily, within the limitations of the time and in another part took important steps toward the drama to come. Despite unconvincing and rather ungenerous disclaimers, Jones was throughout his life thoroughly aware of Robertson's John Bull contemporaneousness and his often brilliant stage accomplishments. Jones's daughter states in her biography of the playwright: "One day, when he was seventy-six, he started to sing Eccles's song from Mr. Robertson's play *Caste* [1867], and breaking off, he said to me, "Oh, how well I remember how I loved that play the first time I saw it." Pinero once said to his friend, the critic Clayton Hamilton: "If ever you write a history of our modern English drama, be fair to Tom Robertson. If it hadn't been for Robertson, I should never have been able to do what I have done; and that applies also to the other fellows." In his warmly reminiscent comedy *Trelawny of the "Wells"* (1898), Pinero pays homage to Tom Robertson in the character of Tom Wrench, the struggling actor-dramatist. W. S. Gilbert flatly stated (high praise from a notorious martinet of the stage) that Robertson had "invented stage-management. It was an unknown art before his time." And Sir John Hare's recognition of Robertson's plays and management was equally strong.

When Robertson rose beyond the triteness and falsity of the drama of his time it was owing to his awareness of social changes that were taking place in England (those favoring, however remotely, egalitarianism and general dignity and identity of person), to his ability sharply to visualize and to portray specific characters in the social environment, and to his intellectual and theatrical attention to details of setting and of human motivation that broadened into effective dramatic generality and, occasionally, into universality (as in the characters Sam Gerridge, Polly Eccles, and Father Eccles, all in *Caste*).

Robertson is historically important in that by means of his comedies he helped diminish the popularity of burlesque, in that he gave dignity and weight to the institution of the dramatist-director, and in that he wrote English plays that contributed to the diminishing of the foreign influence of Sardou and "Sardoodledom." Robertson is a pleasant and important avenue of approach to the New Drama, as well as an author of occasional intrinsic merit. A production of *Caste* in the clothing, and tone, of the 1860's would be a worthy undertaking.

V

Foreign influences on the emergent English drama consisted of direct translations and close adaptations that retained specific characters and incidents or only slightly modified them; loose adaptations in which Continental and English forces vied for supremacy and presented a mixture that frequently cannot be separated into component parts; the establishment of a tone, aura, or medium that aroused determination on the part of playwrights and stage people toward increased dramatic intensity and tightening of realistic plot, and new expectations of entertainment on the part of theater-goers.

Edward Bulwer-Lytton wrote *The Lady of Lyons* in 1838 and *Richelieu* in 1839. The very settings of the two plays are French. *Richelieu* was patently based on Victor Hugo and the elder Dumas at their worst. Only an actor focusing attention on himself rather than on dramatic substance could, by means of spellbinding utterance, rescue the play from its pseudo-romantic insufficiencies: Macready, Phelps, Irving, and Edwin Booth all played the chief role with varying orotundity. It was revived, in a new version, in New York as late as 1929.

The Lady of Lyons presents a more important admixture of foreign and native forces: Hugo and the elder Dumas, and Lord Byron animate parts of the play. The French romantics' rhapsodic outpouring, their depiction of adventure and of fiery pride and honor, their exotic or at least foreign settings, and their sensationalism intermingle with Byronic gloom and piquancy, restlessness and heroic striving: Bulwer-Lytton writes that one of his character's (the mysterious Morier's) "constant melancholy, the loneliness of his habits, —his daring valor, his brilliant rise in the profession . . . all tend to make him as much the matter of gossip as of admiration," and thus gives a good description of the Byronic hero. (The playwright in his youth was nicknamed "Childe Harold".) Further, the play contains definite elements of English sentimentalism, as in the maxims that adorn the conclusion.

> Ah! the same love that tempts into sin,
> If it be true love, works out its redemption;
> And he who seeks repentance for the Past
> Should woo the Angel Virtue in the Future.

Satiric and mundane elements in the play are, again, both foreign and domestic. The diamond-in-the-rough soldier Damas and the designing and worldly Mme. Deschappelles have touches of international realism. The influence of Shakespeare is seen in the playwright's use of prose in some situations and of verse in others. The chief influence, however, was that of Scribe, who taught the Englishman to use a well-constructed plot of satisfying surprise, suspense, and theatrical variety. (About fifteen years later Scribe was to teach similar dramatic structure to the distant young Norwegian dramatist-manager Ibsen.)

William Archer accounts for the French influence on the ground that the "romantic uprising" of Hugo and the elder Dumas, and the "humble bourgeois movement" of Scribe had "discovered the central secret of modern technique —the infinite ductility or malleability of dramatic material." Bulwer-Lytton was thought of as the first English playwright to embrace this double foreign influence.

By the broad terms "ductility" and "malleability" are meant the general structural features of the well-made play (exposition, suspense, peripeteia, *scene a faire*, dramatic irony, *quiproquo*, startling or satisfying outcome, and so on) and also the dramatic realism that, despite later excessive deprecation of the well-made play as foreign hindrance, very definitely attended the clock-work plots of writers under Scribe's influence. It must be understood that foreign influences were interwoven with native developments in such a way that the resultant pattern was regarded as a finished English product: the enthusiastic audiences were Englishmen attending theaters in their own cities and country.

A mixture of Hugo, Scribe, the younger Dumas, Augier, and Sardou influenced Tom Taylor. His *Ticket-of-Leave Man* (1863) was adapted from the French story (later a drama), *Le Retour de Melun*, by Brisbarre and Nus. His *Fool's*

Revenge (1859) was taken from Hugo's *Le Roi s'Amuse* (the basis of the story of Verdi's *Rigoletto*). Not all adaptations or borrowings held back the progress of English drama toward later significant realism. Taylor's English hackles rose when he was accused of plagiarism, and with a touch of Ibsen's stern self-belief he countered by insisting that he improved on "so much that was defective" in Hugo.

Even the sturdily native plays of T. W. Robertson were, inevitably, under foreign influence:

> . . . little did Robertson realize at the time he wrote his story, "David Garrick", based on Mélesville's three-act play, "Sullivan", that this would be the beginning of his career. Here is a strange indication of the way in which dramas were evolved on the British stage in those days: a novel is shaped out of a French play, and a dramatization of that novel results in the script of "David Garrick", which Robertson sold to Lacy for ten pounds. . . . "David Garrick" afterwards became a steadfast addition to the repertory of the actor, Sir Charles Wyndham. . . . [And Robertson's] *Home* [1869] . . . was taken from Augier's *L'Aventurière*.

> . . . [The drama critic Clement Scott amusingly] emphasizes the dependence of the English people upon French drama, by telling this anecdote: when [Robertson's] "Ours" [1866] was announced for production, the London papers insisted on thinking that the name of the play was "L'Ours", French for "The Bear."[7]

Leopold Lewis's adaptation of *Le Juif Polonais* was entitled *The Bells* (1871), and in this melodrama Henry Irving began his rise to fame and knighthood. But Irving needed no foreign plays for his theatrical bravado and bravura: his handling of Shakespeare and Tennyson was enough to establish his influence, which was probably the most praised and most condemned in the annals of the English-speaking stage.

The French influence was particularly strong on Sydney Grundy, who looked to Gallic plays throughout his career. His *Pair of Spectacles* (1890) was successfully adapted from Labiche and Delacour's *Les Petits Oiseaux*. Here again we have a foreign and domestic blending that advanced English drama, however slightly, toward the realism of the New Drama. Grundy's play points toward a general valid use of the French well-made play by Jones, Pinero, Wilde, and others. Similarly, Bulwer-Lytton's *Money* (1840) helped show the way to social insights in Robertson's *Society* (1865) and Pinero's *The Times* (1891), just as Taylor's *Ticket-of-Leave Man* (1863) foreshadowed significant dramas of social problems. In the long run, native ideas and writing won out: J. T. Grein wrote in 1899 of Pinero's *Gay Lord Quex*:

> When the curtain fell and the joyful house had done homage to the author, Mr. John Hare was called upon to speak. And in the simple words that sprang from his lips, he was the spokesman of us all, for he proclaimed Pinero: A master of his craft.
>
> He is the master builder of our stage. We have often felt and said it, in spite of the jibes of the envious; and now the fact has been proved to the very hilt, for he has given us a play that would shine in the Ville Lumière, which is the fountain-head of modern wit and ingenuity.
>
> This is no jest—no exaggeration. "The Gay Lord Quex" is cleverer than the cleverest comedy Sardou has ever written, it is as brilliant, and as full of observation as the best of Dounay and Lavedan. But it is much deeper; it is more human; it is—though very daring—never vulgar.[8]

As for Ibsen's influence, "the brooding giant of the North" (would that his brooding kept him quiet is partly implied in the phrase) changed the world of drama. Shaw said that "the influence which Ibsen has had on England is almost equal to the influence which three revolutions, six crusades, a couple of foreign invasions and an earthquake would produce." Ibsen's specific characters, themes, and techniques could be resisted: his universal "high seriousness" and fearless revelation of "ideals," "duty," and human self-realization penetrated everywhere.

Yet Jones energetically denied that Ibsen had influenced him, despite early professional contact with the Norwegian's work. Jones's daughter relates in her biography of the play-wright:

> For some little time after the success of *The Silver King* [1882] my father continued to work in collaboration with Herman and Wilson Barrett. He would not have objected to the term "hack-work" as applied to *Breaking a Butterfly*, a free adaptation from Ibsen's *A Doll's House*, which he wrote in collaboration with Herman. It was produced at the Prince's Theatre on 3rd March, 1884, and received some very good notices. H.A.J. always became very indignant when anyone said he had been influenced by Isben. He knew very little of the great dramatist's plays till he was long past middle age, and he resented the imputation that his work had been guided or moulded in any way by Ibsen. In 1928, speaking of Ibsen, he said to me, "Every now and then he flashes out a bit of imagination, which is his only value to me."

> In 1924 he wrote to Mr. James Waldo Fawcett repudiating a suggestion that Ibsen had influenced him when he was writing *Saints and Sinners* [1891]. He said:

> "In reply to yours relating to the question of Ibsen's influence on *Saints and Sinners*:

> "I cannot remember when I first read *Pillars of Society*, and I am not sure whether I saw the play when it was done for a matinee in 1880. I am under the impression that I did see this single performance; but I think I may safely say that I was not indebted to Ibsen's *Pillars of Society* for the drift and bearing of *Saints and Sinners*.

> "The setting in my play was mainly that of my own early life in a small English Dissenting community, and the view that I took of English middle-class life was that of Matthew Arnold. If you read his prose writings, you will note their influence on *Saints and Sinners*.
>
> "I should not in the least mind acknowledging my indebtedness to Ibsen, if I thought I owed anything to him; but, although it has often been supposed that Ibsen influenced me in my work, I think I should have written very much the same plays if he had not existed. At the same time, I own to a great admiration for the imaginative side of Ibsen's work, and for his searching veracity."
>
> In 1891, he made a public protest against "a school of modern realism which founded dramas on disease, ugliness, and vice," a direct reference to Ibsen's influence on the English Theatre.[9]

This assertion by Jones of Ibsen's meager influence on him is not to be taken literally: as an active lecturer and writer on theories of modern drama, Jones had read Ibsen in early translations from the German, and knew well the London productions and the Archer translations. (It is known that Pinero attended the first London production of *Ghosts* at J. T. Grein's Independent Theatre in 1891.) An abyss opens between Jones and Ibsen: 1) the Englishman did not seek an equivalent of Ibsen's loving-savage allegorical and realistic attacks on his countrymen; 2) did not seek to bring about a transvaluation of human character;* 3) did not possess the Norwegian's sense of tragic fulfillment.

Pinero, on the other hand, set out deliberately to study Augier, Scribe, the younger Dumas, and Ibsen. *The Second*

---

*Jones would have regarded as alien and mischievous Ibsen's sentiments expressed to a labor union that honored him with a torch-light procession. ". . . This nobility of character and will which I hope will be granted to our nation will come to us from . . . two groups which have not as yet been harmed by party pressure. It will come to us from our women and from our workingmen."

Mrs. Tanqueray (1893) has significant echoes of *Olympe's Marriage*. In *The Notorious Mrs. Ebbsmith* (1895), Mrs. Thorpe's preoccupation with her child in its grave follows the behavior of Agnes in Ibsen's *Brand*. Mrs. Ebbsmith's donning of the alluring evening gown is patterned (so it seems to the writer of this appraisal) on Nora's use of the tarantella shawl and costume. When Mrs. Ebbsmith casts the Bible into the fire we are reminded of Hedda Gabler's burning of Eilert Lovborg's manuscript. Ibsen's Nora goes out into the cruel masculine world and so does Pinero's Iris. Yet the convictions of superior literary excellence held by the New Drama were again expressed by the devoted Clayton Hamilton, writing in 1917:

> As a practical exponent of modern dramaturgic craftsmanship, Pinero is even more adroit than Ibsen. His traditional, synthetic formula has overcome in practice the analytic, revolutionary pattern that was attempted by the great Norwegian in *Ghosts*. Pinero has also proved himself superior to Ibsen in the conduct of the time-scheme of his plays. He has never capitulated to the sort of error which conquered Ibsen in the final act of *Hedda Gabler,* when the author allowed him to falsify an apparently inevitable outcome, in a vain endeavor to complete the full-compass of the action within a pre-determined temporal limit.[10]

VI

The author of plays in the era of the New Drama was a professional writer speaking as a peer to his contemporaries in their established concerns. He rejected or toned down lyrical intensification, the rhapsodic, the antique, and the formally poetic (of all the Jones plays, only one, *The Tempter* (1893), was written in verse: it failed). It is easy to visualize the New Dramatist going from his club to his bank, visiting his publisher or stage-manager, boarding a train for a luxurious country weekend, addressing a civic group on matters of reform, reading the daily papers, writing a letter to the editor, sending a contribution to a charity. Such an author was deep in the currents and crosscurrents of daily metropolitan life in London, "the man's capital" (in partial contrast to Paris, which Sinclair Lewis later called "that feminine and flirtatious refuge from reality").

London life was above all else formally and solidly bourgeois and aristocratic—except for the teeming poor, who were a reliable source of devoted servants for the characters peopling the New Drama. The drawing-rooms, sitting-rooms, and estates in the emergent drama cannot be conceived without servants. Time for leisurely and dignified exchange of words, time for going from one elegant place to another and from England to the Continent and back,* time for watching, for striving, and for measuring the gradations of society could be had only by means of servants and other drawers of water and hewers of wood. Crichton is a most admirable butler. In *Dandy Dick* (1887) the wonderful Blore not only attends to the needs of the Deanery but takes bold initiative. In *The Second Mrs. Tanqueray* (1893) Morse serves well and unobtrusively. Shaw's *Mrs. Warren's Profession* deals with the most captive of servants—prostitutes.

---

* English travellers and residents abroad were often regarded as arrogant and insensitive. Many English trailed the aura of colonialism to the lesser breeds of the Riviera, Baden-Baden, Venice.

Appalling contrasts of luxury and destitution marked the English milieu of the New Drama—contrasts that disturbed the characters not at all, a little bit, or with the zeal of reform. (Shaw said: "Do not waste your time on [recondite analysis of] Social Questions. What is the matter with the poor is Poverty: what is the matter with the rich is Uselessness.") Yet London possessed a harmony and a discipline unknown in the other great capitals: English society was "not yet upheaved or greatly disturbed by radical reforms and demagogues. Those lines of the hymn

> The rich man in his castle,
> The poor man at his gate,
> God made them, high or lowly,
> And order'd their estate

could still [in 1907 and even later] be sung in village churches, and *were* sung, without acute discomfort in the squire's pew, *con amore* by the new rich aping squiredom, and with no outward signs of irritation or ridicule in the body of the church . . ."[11]

The spirit of God's in his heaven, all's right with London dominated the New Drama. Whatever sympathy the dramatists had for the fallen woman attempting reinstatement, the social climber, the suppressed free spirit, the unrealized striver was contained within a *status quo* held to be essentially the best. Shaw and Ibsen themselves were committed to most of the gradations of a society honoring rank, riches, and the uses of established authority and success. Jones and Pinero must be judged on the total scale of their era.

Despite the fact that the era of the New Drama is close to the present day, such nearness is not helpful to us unless we have detailed awareness (as of course the dramatists did) of the changes and shifts that took place before and during the span of the New Drama, and then in the artistic and social developments and tone that followed. The age of Jones and Pinero needs almost as much new understanding as does the age of Otway or the age of T. W. Robertson. We need critical aid primarily because two great upheavals break our line of vision into the England of *Michael and His Lost Angel* (1896), *The Second Mrs. Tanqueray* (1893) and *Heartbreak House* (written between 1913 and 1919).

The first upheaval is the World War of 1914-1918, which is so murky to the present-day student that Edith Cavell could be a starlet, Roger Casement a Boston ward heeler, Black Tom a hood, Rupert Brooke a clothier, Orlando a pal of DiMaggio. Only scholarship and sound fantasy by means of the arts (preferably aided by loquacious grandparents) permit a backward look through the barrier of a period that started or consolidated Horace Mann and John Dewey; the cover girl and public sex appeal; prohibition and the lost generation (F. Scott Fitzgerald, Hemingway, and other authors will have to give the student the tones and overtones); the crystal set becoming mass-media radio; the destruction of town and village life; André Siegfried's *America Comes of Age* and the Lynds' *Middletown*; the stimulation of internal combustion and the rumble seat; movies day and night and veneration of the star; Ivy Lee; the donning of mortarboards in high schools and even in gradeschools; the managerial revolution; the device of cocktails for the empty and tired stomach; America as creditor nation; jazz; the weakening of bourgeois hierarchies; and so on.

Arrays of facts and factors such as these, and others, go far beyond mere listing: they point out and suggest or are an approximation of the forces and auras, the expanding and contracting daily media in which modern dramatists perform the compression and distillation of their literary form. Jones and Pinero, at work before the First World War, were men of affairs immersed in the sorted and unsorted, the established and changing ideas, emotions, and values of the capital of the busiest nation in the world: their awareness of interplay among solemn social forces must be recognized fully—the age is one of the gravest and most polemic in literary history; hence at its worst it is stolid and ponderous, like a martinet *paterfamilias* lecturing his daughters, or a banker moralizing about the deserving poor, or a commonplace man and woman buoyed by exterior elegance, or a heavy-handed critic playing at Boileau—a different nadir from that of, say, romanticism or expressionism.

The second upheaval, that of today, is one of the three or four truly fundamental ones in human personal and institutional history, and is indubitably the most fundamental in man's obsessions and capacities to alter the detailed and the grand environment: it is comparable in magnitude to glacial movements. The age of today produces human beings (the kind that can be written into dramas—this remains our point) who talk at length about melting the polar cap, diverting the Gulf Stream, or planning human evolution, whether of brain power or color of hair, after further research in amino acids and nucleotides. The present-day reader's gaze must penetrate backward through this second upheaval characterized by population explosion; military domination; vague Freudianism and Comtism; TV as opium of the people; insuperable if concealed necessity to judge the atom bomb; outer space as latest utopia; space-age realities and delusions; drag race, hot rod, and obsessive motion: "not for food and not for love"; the bulldozer; all the world with Music by Musak; angry young men and beats; the anti-novel, the theater of the absurd, and the metatheatre; confusion of orthodoxies; *Webster's Third International Dictionary* and language permissiveness (a point wholly germane to our subject: modern drama is fundamentally involved with the creation and use of language. Ibsen and Shaw were expert linguists watching trends and proposing reforms—they and a dozen dramatists, including assuredly Jones and Pinero, would be unsettled by our mass debasing of the great words "miracle" and "magic"); galloping automation; worship of the young *per se*; pollution and destruction of natural resources; omnipresent and explosive breakdowns of tradition; and so on for all to see, particularly students of drama who may wonder in what way present-day dramatists are treating these daily matters, or in what way Jones, Pinero, Ibsen, Shaw, Galsworthy, and Clyde Fitch (in America) would have treated them.

Jones and Pinero must first of all, then, be viewed as belonging to a previous era, and this by means of penetrating the two upheavals mentioned above.

But upheavals as here used are a figure of speech that may mislead us into thinking that there are no continuously flowing currents from *Mrs. Dane's Defence* (1900) and *Mid-Channel* (1909) up to the moment of our present understanding. The movements of such currents need to be seen clearly, as indeed they are in the writings of Jacques Barzun, whose stress on their free flow starting before the First World War is a major cultural insight: ". . . the former uncritical belief that everything was made new around 1920 has lost ground."[12] Barzun tells us that, before the War, the first pictures he saw were Cubist; the first music was Stravinsky's *Le Sacre du Printemps* (1913); the first poetry and drama were Futurist, Simulantist, and "experimental"; the first new building was the "modernistic" skyscraper apartment created by August Perret;—that Apollinaire told him stories; that Marie Laurencin sketched him; that he saw Duchamp's *Nude Descending a Staircase* (later exhibited in 1913 at the New York Armory Show). Flowing forward with these currents were those of the themes and techniques of the New Drama, so that as late as 1922 William Archer, in some matters the final authority on the New Drama, could say that the movement had not yet fulfilled its potentialities, that in fact the future belonged to it.

Barzun's adducing of specifics, in themselves fascinating, is a necessary critical corrective to hasty interpretations of cultural unfolding. We are, then, obliged to know the currents that flowed through the denser disturbances of the War. And beginning farther back at another point in cultural history, we are obliged to know the currents, English as well as Continental, that flowed up to Jones and Pinero, such as Darwinism; Manchester free trade and laissez faire; political franchise; marriage laws; the white man's burden as source of rank and pride (in *The Liars* (1897) one of the main characters is asked to curb his love for a married woman on the ground that he is needed in Africa to handle the native chiefs); stirrings among the lower classes; the rise of the New Woman; possibilities of profit for authors and stage people; mental and social squirearchy; the dominance of the public schools and of Cambridge and Oxford; Dickens; Marx; Gilbert and Sullivan; Wagner and other musical importations; lurking fears of coming war; Ibsen—these and others in that social, philosophic, and artistic commingling that is as significant as Romanticism or Restoration or Elizabethan: for what we are dealing with is a noble segment, in the English tongue, of the great world movement called Realism.

VII

The aggregate of English energy and productivity named after Queen Victoria favored the uses of realism. In the drama and theater this realism developed by various steps and intershadings until in the 1880's the appearance of Henry Arthur Jones, Arthur Wing Pinero (the two last syllables pronounced as in Nero), Oscar Fingall O'Flahertie Wills Wilde, and George Bernard Shaw gave it such form and tone that a strong sense of literary demarcation arose and spread.

Pinero's *The Squire* (1881, St. James's Theatre) pointed toward the author's later significant social dramas. His rough note of the idea on which this play is based reads as follows: "The notion of a young couple secretly married—the girl about to become a mother—finding that a former wife is still in existence. The heroine amongst those who respect and love her. The fury of a rejected lover who believes her to be a guilty woman. Two men face to face at night-time. Query— Kill the first wife?" The first part of the drama is excellent. But in the words of H. Hamilton Fyfe, who was in the midst of the New Drama:

> Then comes the scene in which the young husband and wife learn that they are not legally married, that between them stands the previous wife, supposed honestly by both of them to be dead. [The great German dramatist and theoretician Hebbel had said: "All characters must be in the right."] In this scene the husband is concealed behind a curtain. He has come in by the window while his rival is telling the story.
>
> This is the moment that brings us to the parting of the ways. Up to now the play has been full of interest, original, sincere. This is the *crux* upon which all the rest turns. When the teller of the sad story has gone, will the husband come out at once from behind the curtain and act as a man would in such circumstances, or will he remain hidden while his wife has a scene all to herself, and then appear and behave like a stage puppet? It is a moment of breathless excitement. Unfortunately, the playwright was not strong enough to follow the bolder course. The solution took the wrong turn, insincerity laid hold upon the play, and the rest of it is mere artifice. . . . The final scenes are really no more than tedious devices to keep the story afloat until, upon the stroke of eleven, the death of the inconvenient first wife can be whispered and the curtain fall upon a fresh prospect of wedding bells.[13]

Now, the explanation given for this lapse of dramatic (and therefore human and ethical) insight is important for the understanding of the New Drama. Critics said that Pinero did not yet have the force of mind to break with the commonplace of the day, that he needed leadership and sustenance, but then hastily and proudly added that "there was no one in 1881 to show the way to better things. . . ." Two points about the New Drama emerge here: first, the plays are often partly superb and partly weak; second, the spirit of pioneer accomplishment appears constantly during the era.

Jones's melodrama *The Silver King* (1882, Princess's Theatre) was almost immediately recognized as the outstanding drama in its category. A friend of Jones, Clayton Hamilton, states:

> . . . it should be remembered that *The Silver King* was written for a type of playhouse that was much larger than the type which is prevalent today and for a kind of acting which was more robust than that which has become habitual in the eavesdropping drama of more recent decades. The "intimate" drama had not yet been conceived, nor could it have been housed in the huge theatres of the time; and it was not yet regarded as a duty for the dramatic writer to ape the under-emphasis of casual conversation.[14]

Jones's *Saints and Sinners* (1884, Vaudeville Theatre) was, as the author himself says, ". . . hooted on the first night and condemned by nearly all the London press. It narrowly escaped failure, and only obtained success through Matthew Arnold's generous advocacy, and because of the discussion caused in religious circles by its presentation of certain phases of English dissenting life."

Matthew Arnold wrote to Jones as to an accomplished author: "I went to see *Saints and Sinners*, and my interest was kept up throughout, as I expected. You have remarkably the art—so valuable in drama—of exciting interest and sustaining it. The piece is full of good and telling things, and one cannot watch the audience without seeing that by strokes of this kind faith in the middle-class fetish is weakened, however slowly, as it could be in no other way. —I must add that I dislike seduction-dramas (even in *Faust* the feeling tells with me), and that the marriage of the heroine with her farmer does not please me as a dénouement. —Your representative middle-class man (Hoggard) was well drawn and excellently acted."[15]

Of utmost importance to the understanding of modern drama is Arnold's classification of the Senior Deacon, Hoggard, a callous and money-grabbing tradesman, as a "representative middle-class man." To understand the way in which the aristocracy, the upper middle class, the general middle class, professional persons, dramatists and other artists, the working classes and servants met and mingled or were in any way held aloof is to get to the heart of the New Drama, which can be defined as one of hierarchical acceptance or rejection, of social and financial hindrance or furtherance, of the workings of the freest or most restrictive of all institutions, namely marriage and family.* Not even the confrontation in Molière of the nobility and the bourgeoisie is more vital and productive. The student has to be aware that the characters in New Drama are not rooted casually or equalitarianally in their environment. Class stratification was still rigid and tone-setting and most formal. It amounted to moral judgment—to a form of fate. Matthew Arnold's definition of a middle-class man can serve as a starting point for subsequent definitions and treatments of the great class in the developing drama. The terms "middle class" and "suburban" as used in connection with modern plays must be probed as accurately as are the terms "wit," "nature," and "sentiment" in an older literature.

---

* The heavy emphasis on one particular marriage irregularity led the critic Gilbert Norwood to quip that "Your pseudo-advanced writer invariably reveals his calibre by this assumption that the 'problem-play' must treat of marital infidelity: there is only one sin—the Decalogue has become a monologue."

Pinero now wrote several successful farces, all presented at the Court Theatre (hence the designation Court farces): *The Magistrate* (1885—it ran more than a year); *The Schoolmistress* (1886); *Dandy Dick* (1887); *The Cabinet Minister* (1889); *The Amazons* (1893). These excellent plays raised Pinero's position to the very top. The critic H. Hamilton Fyfe pointed out in 1902:

> In this delightful series of farces, and in the Savoy operettas, we have the only two original dramatic art forms which England can claim to have evolved during the nineteenth century. . . . When he wrote this series Mr. Pinero recreated the *farce of character*. The farce of intrigue had, in 1885, long held the stage unchallenged. . . . In this kind the author's figures are but puppets who move according as he pulls their strings. The plot has them in an iron grip. They do not build up the story on natural lines as they go along. They are merely dolls used for the convenient presentment of some one comic idea. There are no surprises, no sudden turns of merriment in the farce of intrigue. You see exactly how it will reach its appointed end. . . . In the Court series the characters are astonishingly actual. They live and move and have their being quite apart from the demands of the plot.[16]

It is altogether hasty to underrate these early light pieces of the New Drama: no less a critic than George Jean Nathan, of the trinity of "Mencken, Nathan, and God," said in 1924 that "two of these farces are as good as anything the English-speaking stage has offered." (He probably meant *The Magistrate* and *Dandy Dick*, or one of these and *The Schoolmistress*).

Pinero's *The Profligate* (1889, Garrick Theatre) is a good example of "high seriousness" in the early New Drama. On the playbill appeared the following poem:

> It is good and sooth-fast saw,
> Half-roasted never will be raw;
> No dough is dried once more to meal,

No coach new-shapen by the wheel.
You can't turn curds to milk again,
Nor Now by wishing back to Then;
And, having tasted stolen honey,
You can't buy innocence for money.

H. Hamilton Fyfe praised the moral tone and purpose of the play:

> . . . Mr. Pinero set out . . . to stand on the edge of a precipice and to warn all passers-by to give it a wide berth. He set out to show, in a word, that the man who leads a dissolute life before marriage will pretty certainly have bitter cause to repent afterwards.[17]

Out of respect for the actor-manager John Hare, who was timorous about going against the popular taste of the time that demanded a happy ending in the last act of new plays, Pinero rewrote the closing words. Another critic of the time, Malcolm C. Salaman, wrote in 1892:

> [Mr. Pinero] had ended his play with the suicide of the penitent profligate at the very moment that the wife is coming to him with pity and forgiveness in her heart, resolved to share his life again, to bear with him the burden of his past as well as his future—a grimly ironical trick of fate which the author considered to be the legitimate and logical conclusion of this domestic tragedy.[18]

This was changed into a happy ending (too often thought of by Europeans as an American commodity) that allowed the hero to live on with promise of future happiness. Here follow the original closing as written by the author and the made-to-order happy ending as demanded by the actor-manager, an insight into the early New Drama at work:

DUNSTAN RENSHAW. Fool! fool! Why couldn't you have died in Florence? Why did you drag yourself all these miles—to end it *here?* I should have known better—I should have known better. [*He takes a phial from his pocket and slowly pours some poison into a tumbler.*] When I've proved that I could not live away from her, perhaps she'll pity me. I shall never know it, but perhaps she'll pity me then. [*About to drink.*] Supposing I am blind! Supposing there is some chance of my regaining her. Regaining her! How dull sleeplessness makes me! How much could I regain of what I've lost! Why, *she knows me*—nothing can ever undo that—*she knows me.* Every day would be a dreary, hideous masquerade; every night a wakeful, torturing retrospect. If she smiled, I should whisper to myself —"Yes, yes, that's a very pretty pretence, but—*she knows you!* The slamming of a door would shout it, the creaking of a stair would murmur it—"*she knows you;*" And when she thought herself alone, or while she lay in her sleep, I should be always stealthily spying for that dreadful look upon her face, and I should find it again and again as I see it now—the look which cries out so plainly—"Profligate! You taught one good woman to believe in you, but now *she knows you!*" No, no—no, no! [*He drains the contents of the tumbler.*] The end—the end. [*Pointing towards the clock.*] The hour at which we used to walk together in the garden at Florence—husband and wife— lovers. [*He pulls up the window-blind and looks out.*] The sky—the last time—the sky. [*He rests drowsily against the piano.*] Tired—tired. [*He walks rather unsteadily to the table.*] A line to Murray. [*Writing.*] A line to Murray—telling him—poison—morphine—message— [*The pen falls from his hand and his head drops forward.*] The light is going out. I can't see. Light—I'll finish this when I wake—I'll rest. [*He staggers to the sofa and falls upon it.*] I shall sleep tonight. The voice has gone. Leslie—wife—reconciled—. [LESLIE *enters softly and kneels by his side.*] LESLIE. Dunstan, I am here. [*He partly opens his eyes, raises himself, and stares at her; then his head falls back quietly.* LESLIE's *face averted.*] Dunstan, Dunstan, I have returned to you. We are one and we will make atonement for the past together. I will be your Wife, not your Judge—let us from this moment begin the new life you spoke of. Dunstan! [*She sees the paper which has fallen from his hand, and reads it.*] Dunstan! Dunstan! No, no! Look at me! Ah! [*She catches him in her arms.*] Husband! Husband! Husband!

The about-face of the happy ending regaled and appeased English audiences as follows:

DUNSTAN RENSHAW. [*He is raising the glass to his lips when he recoils with a cry of horror.*] Ah! stop, stop! This is the deepest sin of all my life —blacker than that sin for which I suffer! No, I'll not! I'll not! [*He dashes the glass to the ground.*] God, take my wretched life when You will, but till You lay Your hand upon me, I will live on! Help me! Give me strength to live on! Help me! Oh, help me! [*He falls on his knees, and buries his face in his hands.* LESLIE *enters softly, carrying a lamp which she places on the sideboard; she then goes to* DUNSTAN.]

LESLIE. Dunstan! Dunstan!

DUNSTAN. [*Looking wildly at her.*] You! You!

LESLIE. I have remembered. When we stood together at our prayerless marriage, my heart made promises my lips were not allowed to utter. I will not part from you, Dunstan.

DUNSTAN. Not—part—from me?

LESLIE. No.

DUNSTAN. I don't understand you. You—will—not—relent? You cannot forget what I am!

LESLIE. No. But the burden of the sin you have committed I will bear upon my shoulders, and the little good that is in me shall enter into your heart. We will start life anew—always seeking for the best that we can do, always trying to repair the worst that we have done. [*Stretching out her hand to him.*] Dunstan! [*He approaches her as in a dream.*] Don't fear me! I will be your wife, not your judge. Let us from this moment begin the new life you spoke of.

DUNSTAN. [*He tremblingly touches her hand as she bursts into tears.*] Wife! Ah, God bless you! God bless you, and forgive me! [*He kneels at her side, she bows her head down to his.*]

LESLIE. Oh, my husband.

This play as creation of a dramatist was changed by a "practical" actor-manager dominated by the theater-going public. When the play was printed, the author's values were reinstated for the more discerning reading public. It was the belief of the entire era that the reading of plays in the study fosters the meaning, philosophy, tone, and language necessary for great drama. Playwrights for years cried out to have their plays published as the means of bringing a great art form from bondage to renaissance.

Wilde's *Lady Windermere's Fan* (1892, St. James's Theatre), and his other plays and writings, gave to the New Drama wit, polish, epigrammatical flourish, lofty social elegance, settings in Park Lane, the half-weary gestures of the elite, glamorous paradox, well-heeled audacity, and the mentality of aesthetic Socialism (a mentality possessed, often intensely, by Ruskin, Shaw, Wagner, Morris). Admirers went so far as to hail Wilde as the most exquisite stylist that had written for the stage since Congreve. Detractors, from their high seriousness, grandly concluded that he was mere ornament or that anybody could dash off plays like his in the superior atmosphere of the time; hence Shaw, with countering wit and graciousness, said that "As far as I can ascertain, I am the only person in London who cannot sit down and write an Oscar Wilde play at will."

George Bernard Shaw's *Widowers' Houses* was begun in

the study in 1885 and was presented by the Independent Theatre Society in 1892.   This first play by the only New Dramatist whose genius matches that of Ibsen takes place abroad and at home among the rich.   To be sure, they are the scheming and undeserving rich, but what matters more is that Shaw's setting is not a hovel, a workhouse, a cold-water slum, a shopkeeper's rear apartment.   The New Drama forces the reader to decisions on the class structure of society, particularly concerning the middle classes and the changes they have undergone, and initiated, up to the present moment.

In the turmoil of dramatic forces in England, the plays dealt with above stand as representative of the best of the early New Drama.   None of the four authors had as yet reached his creative heights save Pinero, whose Court farces are his best work in the genre.

VIII

Women of spirit and energy, strength of will, and desire to make decisions and plans concerning their values and their lives have of course always existed and have, in one way or an-other, entered into conflict with dominant males. Antigone, the Wife of Bath, and Joan of Arc, despite major and lesser dif-ferences, are women who refused to yield altogether to con-ventions and authority, and who entered into rivalry with men, whether such rivalry was of nobility and tenacity of concept, superior ethical and practical insight, sheer sensual sway.   We can not, however, speak of the New Woman until the rise of modern vocations, bourgeois society, and commercial ma-terialism.   Only in such a milieu could Shaw broadly advance his famous divisions of the womanly woman, the pursuing woman, the mother woman, and the New Woman.

The New Woman can, like Ibsen's Nora, achieve her selfhood out of desperate resolve and the severing of ties no longer believed in. Or she can arise without meeting serious obstacles, in an environment of ease, stability, and high tone. The distinguishing points are her sense of rivalry with males, her desire to exercise leadership, her hatred of self-sacrifice, her drive toward general independence and equality. The question of whether the New Woman is a happy, contented, or successful human being is so profound that it admits of no firm answer. Hence Shaw partially evades the issue, first by combining in his female characters varying degrees of his four kinds of women, and second by submerging female characters in a great prophetic mission, as in the case of Joan of Arc, or in his philosophy of the Life Force and Creative Evolution, as in the case of dozens of his women. Thus it is often closer to the realities of human character in actual setting to study the status of women in Jones, Pinero, Barrie, and others who presented no organized Shavian polemics to change the world.*

In Pinero's *Iris* (1901) one of the male characters describes his ideal of a woman

> . . . that she should be beautiful to the eye and gentle
> to the ear; that her face should brighten when I en-

---

* To define the New Woman as one "who rides a bicycle and smokes" is mere attempt at epigram. Shaw's mother was the dramatist's prototype of the New Woman who forges her way despite marital, social, and financial difficulties. Shaw's Vivie Warren is the too-masculine New Woman who forges her way in the midst of financial and social ease. Both women are characterized by the assumption of initiative of all sorts and by denial of masculine superiority. The key to understanding the New Woman is not to expect her to be a pure specimen. Vivie was indifferent to Beethoven and Wagner, and thus was shut off from "advanced" aesthetic pleasure. The recent biography of Shaw's wife (another New Woman arising in an environment of financial and social ease and power) sharpens the issue of Shaw's sexuality and sensuality. Do Shaw's Vivie and Pinero's Agnes Ebbsmith sufficiently enjoy the delights of the body, including artistic delights, to be at ease among men of middling sensuality? Max Beerbohm held that the New Woman was an ephemeral dramatic creation.

tered, her hand linger in mine when I departed; that she should never allow me to hear her speak slightingly of any honest man, thereby assuring me she indulged in no contemptuous criticism of me when I was out of her company; that she should be bountiful to the poor, unafraid of the sick and unsightly, fond of dumb animals and strange children, and tearful in the presence of fine pictures and at the sound of rich music.

Clearly a woman of this sort, in a society of leisure, finesse, and gradations, must be able at all times to please men or at least not to counter them. And such abilities to please and to accept rest in large part on personal and sexual charm and on skills in social management. Hence the New Drama deals inevitably with the problems of the double standard and the single standard, with women's satisfactions and dissatisfactions in an essentially masculine environment (all too soon to be rocked by trench warfare),* with expiation as poetic justice of the group, with little lapses magnified by belief in the sacredness of the surrounding class structure and large lapses leading to banishment and struggle for rehabilitation, with deceptions held to be justified by the greater virtue of the formalized milieu, with life as a grand pageant in which it is so satisfactory to move that rebellion is bad taste.

---

* The pervasive masculinity of the New Drama expressed itself militarily at Khartoum and in both Boer Wars. Jingling spurs and mass English "worship of the horse," glitter of regalia, smartness of gesture and utterance, love of firm hierarchy, fixed movement of troops, fervor of colonial mission were representative ingredients of plots unfolding on the larger stage of war. British and Boers had equal bravery and heroism, but the "uniforms" of Boer officers and men, the loose "democracy" of Boer military organization, the spontaneous prayers and hymns, the patriarchal and other Old Testament aura, intense love of soil, non-urban informality—all these were dramatic in a way mostly alien to the characters in the plays of Jones and Pinero, Shaw and Ibsen. The broader setting of the First World War was the last military stage for characters of the New Drama, which in many ways (by no means all) lost its vigor and focus in the 1920's. The Second World War and various alignments and resistance movements were the macrocosmic stage for characters of present-day dramatists, however heightened or veiled by symbolic treatment unknown to the New Drama.

Nevertheless, there are rebellion and challenge in the establishment of Jones and Pinero, but only to the extent that the total scheme is to be obliquely improved. To compromise and temporize are virtues because they touch only lightly or are correctives suited to those who set the tone. Jones would have little to do with assertive or rebellious woman. In a conversation with his daughter about Ibsen's Nora, he said: "She was the first of the tiresome hussies—Candida was another." He avowed further that *"The Doll's House* should have ended with the husband helping himself to a whisky-and-soda and saying, 'Thank God, she's gone'."* This in no way diminishes Jones's insistence that courage, honesty, manliness, and grace must be cultivated to insure the stability and flavor of the times.

Both the New Woman and the non-rebellious woman must be judged on the scale of the entire New Drama, but inevitably they must also be judged on the scale of the present-day reader's accumulated information and insights: the flapper; the bobby-soxer; the hard-working office secretary who takes her vacation in the Caribbean; the devoted and often unsung homemaker; the avid consumer; the woman in her own or in her husband's employment protocol; the club woman; the status seeker; the woman doctor, politician, ambassador and careerist in general; the woman of bold and racy masculine vocabulary; above all, the woman of the social register and its many approximations held with great seriousness throughout our society, even in student social life, which no longer can be thought of as outside the main stream. No other approach to the New Drama is more necessary than the social-economic, even in those scenes, characters, and plays where the New Drama as an art-form has achieved dramatic universality. Such an approach is the most direct in establishing relevant contrasts between the New Drama and the plays of London, New York, Paris, and Berlin today.

IX

In order to make even a preliminary statement of Jones' and Pinero's rank in English drama, we must stress once again that it is not possible to dissect them out from the total London milieu that contained George Bernard Shaw; William Archer (patriarch-translator of the remote Norwegian, and a founding father of the emergent drama);* Henry Irving (the first actor to be knighted—1895) and more important stage people such as Mrs. Patrick Campbell, Charles Wyndham, and Harley Granville Barker; Jack Thomas Grein (founder of the Independent Theatre in 1891, and perhaps "the greatest Dutch import since William of Orange"); the *Yellow Book*; the *Almanach de Gotha*; the Fabians; bardolatry; Ibsen himself.

In this pulsating environment Jones and Pinero were major personages and major dramatists: the totality of praise and blame touching them places them at the pinnacle of recognition and impact. They were on hand as were the Tower of London, Fleet Street, pea soupers, the *noli-me-tangere* of Rotten Row, the polemicists of Hyde Park (called "public-park vermin" in *The Notorious Mrs. Ebbsmith*, 1895). Shaw himself, whose vision went to the heart of almost everything, felt no impulse to classify Jones and Pinero as outside the pale:† he dealt them authentic Shavian lauding and lam-

---

* Not all critics hold Archer in high esteem. Eric Bentley states that Archer "hindered the recognition of legitimate modernity in drama by basing the defense of Ibsenite realism partly on Philistinism." Archer's blind spots, such as his deprecation of Shaw, arose from his generous enthusiasms. The age of the New Drama cannot be conceived without Archer. J. T. Grein asserted that ". . . Archer's name is respected in Paris, in Berlin, in Vienna, as a critic worthy to be named in the same breath with Lessing or Lemaitre . . ." (*Dramatic Criticism* [London: John Long, 1899]), p. 195.

† Shaw sought Pinero's advice on a suitable actor to play the part of the lion in *Androcles and the Lion*. And he asked Jones to recommend an actor to do the role of the poet in *Candida*: Jones recommended Esmond and Granville Barker. The three playwrights were all

basting, always of course with rigorous awareness of his own superiority. In one of the heady rivalries of the time, Shaw championed Jones, and Archer advanced the colors of Pinero. Only as Ibsen, Shaw, Galsworthy, and others established their impact and rank, and as society itself changed, did the idea arise that Jones and Pinero were, in the grand concourse, transitional or minor. But literary criticism knows the caprices of reputation over a span of time, and knows the differences, after the event, between being minor and being not popular. To trace drama from the time when Jones and Pinero were "secure" at the apex to the time when they "inevitably" became less significant is to understand dramatic development and plays *per se*, particularly English and American plays. As long after the flowering of the New Drama as the 1930's, the first Brander Matthews Professor of Dramatic Literature gave Jones and Pinero almost the same attention that Archer and Shaw had given.*

---

at work in the broad London theatrical world. It is misleading to regard Jones and Pinero as wholly "commercial" and thus inferior. When they produced a good play it was accepted as England's best and given as serious attention as if it were written for J. T. Grein or as if it came from Norway or Germany.

* Professor Brander Matthews himself was a staple of the New Drama by virtue of his temperament, his social position, his learning. He knew many of the authors and critics of the movement and thought of himself as the grand academic explicator of all drama old and New. Much of present-day New York and London would strike him as meaningless or hopeless. In 1900 he was appointed Professor of Dramatic Literature at Columbia: he occupied the first chair of that subject in America. George C. D. Odell (author of *Annals of the New York Stage*) was appointed first Brander Matthews Professor in 1929. In 1943 Joseph Wood Krutch became the second to receive the title, which he held until 1953. The present bearer is the distinguished Eric Bentley, whose critical goals and championship of, say, Bertolt Brecht attest the profound changes in drama that arose after the days when Jones dedicated his *Foundations of a National Drama* (1913) to Matthews, and when the latter regretted an unfulfilled obligatory scene in *He Can't Be as Bad as All That* (1910).

X

Karl Baedeker, cicerone to an age that knew what it wanted in culture, tells the visitor in his *London and Its Environs* (1896) that

> The performance at most of the London theatres begins about 7:30 or 8 and lasts till 11 p.m. The ticket-office is usually opened half-an-hour before the performance. Many theatres also give so-called 'morning performances' or 'matinées,' beginning about 2:30 or 3 p.m. For details consult the notices 'under the clock' (i.e. immediately before the summaries and leaders) in the daily papers.
>
> London possesses 50 - 60 theatres and about 500 music halls, which are visited by 325,000 people nightly or nearly 100,000,000 yearly. A visit to the whole of the theatres of London . . . would give the traveler a capital insight into the social life of the people throughout all its gradations. Copies of the play are often sold at the theatres for 6d. or 1s. At some of the better theatres all extra fees have been abolished, but many of them still maintain the objectionable custom of charging for programmes, the care of wraps, etc. Opera glasses may be hired for 1s. or 1s. 6d. . . .
>
> The best seats are the *Stalls*, next to the Orchestra, and the *Dress Circle*. . . .
>
> Evening dress is not now compulsory in any of the London theatres, but is customary in the stalls and dress circle and *de rigueur* in most parts of the opera-houses. . . .[19]

Baedeker lists London theatrical offerings as follows: comedies, Shakespeare's plays, spectacular plays, English opera, pantomime, English comedy, dramas, society plays, operettas, melodramas, farces, opera-bouffes, burlesques, domestic dramas, extravaganzas, nautical dramas. The plays of Jones and Pinero were carefully classified by the authors themselves and by the attending critics of the New Drama. Such zeal to classify is a manifestation of the era's abounding belief in its creativity; at the same time, it has an air of apologia.

Jones began by writing melodramas, Pinero by writing farces and sentimental comedies. After producing about a dozen unimportant plays, Jones produced "the most famous English melodrama of the nineteenth century," *The Silver King* (1882), which brought in enough money to make him independent in purse and mind. In view of the lofty condescension or even contempt displayed today toward melodrama, we need to gain insight into the genre from the New Drama's greatest critic: Shaw says

> As a superior person . . . I hold . . . melodrama in high consideration. A really good . . . melodrama is of first-rate literary importance, because it only needs elaboration to become a masterpiece. Molière's Festin de Pierre and Mozart's Don Juan are elaborations of Punch and Judy, just as Hamlet, Faust, and Peer Gynt are elaborations of popular stories. Unfortunately, a really good . . . melodrama is very hard to get. It should be a simple and sincere drama of action and feeling, kept well within the vast tract of passion and motive which is common to the philosopher and the laborer, relieved by plenty of fun, and depending for variety of human character, not on the high comedy idiosyncracies which individualize people in spite of the closest similarity of age, sex, and circumstances, but on broad contrasts between types of youth and age, sympathy and selfishness, the masculine and the feminine, the serious and the frivolous, the sublime and the ridiculous, and so on. The whole character of the piece must be allegorical, idealistic, full of generalizations and moral lessons; and it must represent conduct as producing swiftly and certainly on the individual the results which in actual life it only produces on the race in the course of many centuries. . . .[20]

Jones's *Saints and Sinners* (1884) is a serious study of contemporary life. The central character is a non-conformist minister whose daughter is seduced; the father tries to hide her downfall from the congregation, but eventually confesses her shame in public—a confession that is the first of such scenes that occur several times in later plays (for example, *Michael and His Lost Angel*).

The Middleman (1889) is a blend of melodrama, sentimentality, and social analysis. "It was the best English play of its time," despite asides, soliloquies, and resounding curtain speeches. It was presented successfully for over twenty years and was seen by millions of play-goers in England and America.

Judah (1890) is almost wholly free of melodrama and comes to grips realistically with a serious social problem.

> It seems to contain half a dozen of [Jones's] abler plays in embryo. It sets forth, for the first time, his favorite type of love story—a study of the love of a lofty-souled, pure-minded hero for a worldly woman who, in one way or another, is unworthy of him,—a love which leads the hero to descend first to the woman's level in order ultimately to lead her up to his own . . . and [the heroine] is the earliest of those "strange women" who, all the more alluring because . . . they are regarded askance by conventional society, exercise their fascination in so many of his plays . . . . we have the usual confession scene in the last act. It is also characteristic of Mr. Jones that the play should be directed against a type of imposter . . . that in all periods has preyed upon society. . . . Mr. Jones used his minor characters for the first time to satirise various fads and foibles of the day.[21]

The Crusaders (1891) is a satirical romance. In Jones's words: "I gave William Morris *carte blanche* for the scenery and furniture, and he advised me on the whole production. I engaged the best possible cast, filling even the small parts with actors of great ability. It was hooted and booed. . . . I lost four thousand pounds, and had to go out and collect the general public around me again." Clayton Hamilton wrote that *The Crusaders*

> . . . seems to have started a fashion in the early eighteen-nineties. It was almost precisely contem-

porary with Pinero's "The Times" (1891), which was
followed by "The Amazons" in 1893; and it antedated
by a year or two Shaw's first play, "Widowers'
Houses" (1892), and his second effort, "The Phi-
landerer" (1893). All these were comedies of social
groups, in which the authors satirised certain intellectual and emotional tendencies. . . .[22]

The Tempter (1893), a tragedy, is Jones's only play written in blank verse: the present-day reader will have to decide for
himself whether Jones's verse convinces or disturbs, whether
blank verse is to begin with the proper medium for modern
drama.

The Masqueraders (1894) is classified as a sentimental
romance or a social comedy. In the same year Jones produced *The Case of Rebellious Susan,* and with it began a
new style: it is "the first of that long line of thoroughly
characteristic comedies on which the fame of Henry Arthur
Jones is mainly founded." It is classified as high comedy,
comedy of character, or comedy of manners. The confrontation of social classes in this instance is that of the author
and his own characters. The ladies and gentlemen of the play
are of the class deeply admired by Jones, the playwright of
humble origin who rose on the financial and social ladder
and then wrote plays about and for the most aristocratic
theater-goers in London—those who attended the Criterion
Theatre. Jones was both removed from the aristocracy and
at one with it, very much as Ibsen, rising from a bankrupt
and harassed youth and early manhood, was both distant
from and close to Rosmer and Rosmersholm. Both Jones
and Ibsen, in different veins, felt that they could see into the
upper classes better than the latter themselves could. In
both the Englishman and the Norwegian the desire to preserve something lofty and tone-setting was strong, despite all
colorings of satire and irony. If we regard the entire New
Drama as revealing a wish on the part of leading playwrights
(including to a large extent even Shaw) to preserve most

of the values informing an England of strong social and financial gradations and firm ideas on the relation of men to women in and out of marriage—if we so regard the New Drama, we can judge it with better perspective in relation to present-day drama and its points of departure in a fluid society in a time termed most often the Age of Anxiety and characterized by varieties of permissiveness previously unknown or untolerated.

The general development of Jones's art was from melodrama to romance and social satire and then to high comedy. This sequence was interrupted by *Michael and His Lost Angel* (1896), which some critics regard as his best play. It is a tragedy with the usual background and tone of the approval and disapproval of entrenched society and its "social problems." Shaw immediately caught the spirit of the play and praised it warmly. Jones wrote that "It was savagely hooted and booed by a first-night audience at the leading London theatre" (the Lyceum), and Shaw held that "The melancholy truth of the matter is that the English stage got a good play, and was completely and ignominiously beaten by it."

The Liars (1897) likewise received solid praise from Shaw, who enjoyed its wealth of comedy and its penetrating picture of Smart Society. Jones again held the mirror up to nature to produce an almost flawless realistic play. The balance of plot, satire, dialogue, and worthy outcome is that of best comedy of manners. The New York première (1898) gave rise to the inevitable comparison with Sheridan. Alan Dale of the *New York Journal* thought that *The Liars* was "A delightful comedy, that almost induces you to say, 'Don't talk to me of *The School for Scandal* any more.' Here's something more modern and better. . . ." Jones's daughter gives an interesting side light of the London drama world: "My father was very much amused that at the time the play was produced it was rumored that it had really been written by Oscar Wilde and that Henry Arthur Jones had put his name to it because of the scandal attaching to Wilde." Max Beerbohm recognized the consummate skill with which Jones had put together a complex plot.

Mrs. Dane's Defence (1900) Jones himself classified as a "drawing-room melodrama"; it is in keeping with the nature of the drama of the time that the play is a mixture of melodrama, drawing-room comedy, and serious social problem.

The Hypocrites (1906) was produced in New York before it was put on in London. Pinero never visited America but Jones crossed the Atlantic several times and felt at home in the United States. He lectured at Yale, Columbia, and Harvard, and from the last-named university received the honorary degree of Master of Arts. *The Hypocrites* is a serious social drama that lashes out at "that organized hypocrisy which so often in England is regarded as respectability."

Mary Goes First (1913) is comic drama that would rank high in the literature of any nation. The mingling of groups of social climbers who rival each other and the influence of the aristocracy looming in the background are highly amusing and revelatory. The story is reduced to the minimum (only a single incident is narrated) so that the effect is achieved by conversation in the microcosm of the drawing-room. The critic Montrose J. Moses judges the play to be "an example of the purest and best High Comedy the modern English drama has produced."

In a letter (1923) to Clayton Hamilton, Jones asserts his belief that ". . . my plays, taken as a whole, will give a truthful picture of English life and character from the year 1885 to 1915. I have drawn more English types in these years than any other English dramatist. . . ." The panorama of Jones's and Pinero's plays is one of the longest and most detailed in dramatic literature.

XI

The New Drama's confidence in itself was never voiced more strongly than in the piece on Recent English Drama in the eleventh edition (1910) of *The Encyclopaedia Britannica*. Since it was written by William Archer it belongs among the articles of faith of the New Criticism. Archer held that

> On the 27th of May 1893 *The Second Mrs. Tanqueray* was produced at the St. James's Theatre. With *The Second Mrs. Tanqueray* the English acted drama ceased to be a merely insular product, and took rank in the literature of Europe. Here was a play which, whatever its faults, was obviously comparable with the plays of Dumas, of Sudermann, of Bjornson, of Echegaray. . . . The fact that such a play could not only be produced, but could brilliantly succeed, on the London stage gave a potent stimulus to progress. It encouraged ambition in authors, enterprise in managers. What *Hernani* was to the romantic movement of the 'thirties, and *La Dame aux Camelias* to the realistic movement of the 'fifties, *The Second Mrs. Tanqueray* was to the movement of the 'nineties towards the serious stage-portraiture of English social life. All the forces which we have been tracing—Robertsonian realism of externals, the leisure for thought and experiment involved in vastly improved financial conditions, the substitution in France of a simpler, subtler technique for the outworn artifices of the Scribe school, and the electric thrill communicated to the whole theatrical life of Europe by contact with the genius of Ibsen—all these slowly converging forces coalesced to produce, in *The Second Mrs. Tanqueray*, an epoch-making play.[23]

Shaw held no such high opinion of the play. Yet his restrictions were not those of a dramatist remote from his fellow authors: he thought Pinero sufficiently worthy to receive a knighthood and strongly urged the government to grant the award, which it did in 1909.

The following Pinero plays led up to the climax repre-
sented by *The Second Mrs. Tanqueray*. *The Squire* (1881)
has been dealt with above. It is mentioned again in this
sequence of Pinero's major plays because the playwright was
accused of having plagiarized Hardy's *Far From the Madding
Crowd* (1874). Pinero asserted publicly that the ideas and
characters of his play were "thoroughly in my head" before
he read the Hardy novel, and there seems no reason to doubt
this. What is important is further evidence that the leading
English dramatists and novelists knew each others' works.
The significant farces that followed *The Squire* have been
dealt with in Section VII.

Beginning with *The Hobby-Horse* (1886), Pinero established himself as a writer of sentimental comedies: *Sweet
Lavender* (1888), *Lady Bountiful* (1891), and later *The
Princess and the Butterfly* (1897) and the famous *Trelawny
of the "Wells"* (1898), which ran for 684 performances.
These plays contain elements of serious social problems,
melodrama, and even farce, but the elements are blended
to a misty sentimentality that not only appealed to Englishmen as something altogether natural and pleasing (like the
pantomime) but was an antidote to Zola and *naturalisme*
and to tendencies to present tawdry and seamy pictures of
English life. Pinero presented scene after scene of touching
pictorial charm to which even hostile critics occasionally
yielded: Shaw spoke of the "dainty workmanship" in *Trelawny of the "Wells"*. The dominant emotions aroused for
English audiences were broad nostalgia, general delight in
English characteristics and their non-controversial ups and
downs, the pleasures of feeling both superior to and detached
from the plays' emotional involvements. Not all literary eras
encourage the flourishing of sentimental comedies: England
at this time produced some of the best.

The farce *The Magistrate* (1885) and the sentimental
comedy *Sweet Lavender* (1888) brought in considerable money

for Pinero, but more importantly his success in the two genres cleared his mind so that he could deal with serious aspects of the English establishment to which he belonged. These serious plays are classified as "society dramas" or as "problem plays," in keeping with the era's proclivity to mark literary boundaries. One scholarly analysis holds that

> The term "society drama" needs definition. Plays which properly fall under this heading are too often carelessly designated "problem plays." The problem play differs from the society drama in this essential respect, that whereas the problem play concerns itself with the examination of some social abuse, the society drama concerns itself with the depiction of dramatically effective situations among the upper classes, and touches upon social problems only obliquely. The natural result of this essential difference was that the problem play reached the very limited audience which, in the late 'eighties and in the 'nineties, was receptive to the highly critical ideas which it presented. The society drama, on the other hand, was designed specifically to please everyone. It combined and refined the best features of the popular melodrama, the problem play, and the Robertsonian cup-and-saucer drawing-room drama. The society drama was always concerned with life among the upper classes and involved either the efforts of the *nouveaux riches* to crash Society, or the efforts of a "woman with a past" to be rehabilitated, or various domestic and erotic complications above stairs. Always the object was to give the appearance of presenting some social problem so that the audience could be convinced that they had indulged in some intellectual exercise while being entertained; but at the end the problem was always neatly sidestepped and the situation resolved in accordance with currently prevailing standards of morality. Thus the audience was sent home not only with the illusion of having indulged in some emancipated thought, but also with the comfortable conviction that their former opinions had stood the test of objective examination and had to come out as strong and valid as ever.[24]

Such distinction is helpful mostly to the extent that it shows that Jones and Pinero had no plans for a changed future as did Ibsen, who wanted everybody to become a noble man (of sorts), or Shaw, whose Life Force is one of the great hopes for a changing world expressed in modern drama, despite the supreme dullness of "life" in his projections in the last part of *Back to Methuselah*. But the distinction is not helpful if one assumes that a society drama is in itself inferior to a problem play. Some of the outstanding plays of Shaw and Ibsen are society dramas or a combination of both types. Jones and Pinero wanted to take their society as it was and make its tone-setters and upper groups as stable, understanding, compassionate, and effective as possible. An Edwardian diary gives part of the tone and purpose of the drama of the era:

> We pillage the pantomimes for our year's humour, we snatch from the "Gaiety" the tunes we shall whistle in our baths and strum on the drawing-room piano for the ensuing twelve months. We wait upon Mr. Graves for our *bon mots*; on Mr. Grossmith for the shape of our collars and the length of our coats; we look to Mr. Shaw for our politics and religion; to Sir Pinero for our morals; to Mr. Barrie for our dinner-table topics. . . .[25]

The Notorious Mrs. Ebbsmith (1895) is one of several plays dealing with the fate of erring women. The heroine, Agnes Ebbsmith, is aided by the spiritual and social force of the Anglican Church and by her own strength of values. The play is a compelling combination of religion, high society, and the New Woman, in which the latter is defeated according to one point of view or validly rehabilitated according to another. Agnes loves a man who turns out to be superficial and ordinary, however solid and elegant his habitual milieu. The unfolding of his true character and Agnes's efforts to change hers in order to hold him reveal a human crisis known to every present-day clergyman, counselor, and intelligent observer. When the advanced New Woman, rationally shining and free, changes into a frantic Circe, Pinero gives us incandescent drama. When the heroine casts the Bible into the fire and then snatches it out again she arouses so many views pro and con that the reader had best make up his own mind. The wonderful Mrs. Patrick Campbell played Agnes to perfection. The conservative critic Clement Scott reported an apex of the New Drama as follows:

> . . . We talk of the nature of Eleanor Duse . . . but she is not always convincing. From the first line to the last of Mrs. Ebbsmith it was impossible to distract the attention from Mrs. Patrick Campbell. . . .
>
> The actress took us to wonderland. . . . Her defiant attitude in connection with her own [i. e. Mrs. Ebbsmith's] bold but mistaken opinions, was no less superb than her contemptuous and supercilious scorn of the Duke, whom she treats with outward courtesy, but with veiled insolence. . . . but the performance was full of beautiful, human and womanly touches —the defeat of Agnosticism and Materialism, and Free-Love jargon, at the mere danger of her Lover's departure; the gradual rebirth of an almost buried affection; the consummate victory of nature over unfaithfulness; the scornful rejection of the Bible, followed by the reaction of penitence; the natural scorn of scorn; the equally natural love of love; and in the end the very martyrdom of ruined hopes and aspirations.[26]

The Gay Lord Quex (1899) can be classified as a comedy of manners. The struggle between Sophy Fullgarney, a working-class girl, and the Marquess of Quex, mirror of fashion and "the wickedest man in London" has dramatic insight and climax that belong to the best comedy of any literature. Clayton Hamilton rose to the pitch of his critical enthusiasm: ". . . the famous third act . . . is the ablest third act in the English language [with the possible exception of the third act of *Othello*]* and one of the most perfectly constructed

---

* Brackets inserted by Hamilton.

single acts in the entire dramaturgy of the world." Brander Matthews, scholar and devotee extraordinary, repeated the old refrain: "We have just witnessed the ablest English comedy since *The School for Scandal*." More to the point in the totality of modern drama is Pinero's unabashed revelation of unpleasant and unworthy persons: we have a superb socio-artistic representation of an important segment of London. The individuals, types, and incidents are universal, and hold for today's affluent and permissive society: clubs, cruise ships, and resorts come to mind.

Iris (1901) is, in effect, a moral judgment against a woman who deserves her fate. Some critics analyze the play as showing the disintegration of a fine woman or at least a moderately good woman who could not face adversity. It better fits the facts, however, to view *Iris* as a study of a social parasite who is amoral rather than immoral. Perhaps better than any other, this play raises the issue of whether Pinero, beneath his acceptance of the social establishment, was not aware that English aristocracy and upper bourgeoisie needed partial reform as national institutions. Sir James Matthew Barrie said in the 1930's that *Iris* was the best play written in his lifetime.

Letty (1903) is a contrast piece to *Iris*: the latter reveals the ruin of a woman used to a life of luxury and high social position; the former reveals the salvation of a woman who begins life in poverty and in low position, and as in *The Gay Lord Quex* we find a personal battle between a working girl and a dominating aristocrat. The upper, middle, and lower classes are brought together in *Letty* to form an outstanding dramatic revelation of society.

The Thunderbolt (1908) has as its subtitle *An Episode in the History of a Provincial Family*. It is often classified as an ironic comedy, or a comedy of bourgeois manners. It belongs in any list of dramas that set forth middle-class family life: Ibsen's *Pillars of Society* is not a superior canvas of family interaction. Archer says: "It is a little exasperating to find critics ignoring or pooh-poohing *The Thunderbolt* while going into raptures over Ben Jonson's *Volpone* because it is old, and Becque's *Les Corbeaux* because it is French. I mention these two plays because they, too, happen to deal with heritage-hunting."[27]

Mid-Channel (1909) and *The Thunderbolt* are often acclaimed the best of Pinero's plays: they rank with the finest of realistic drama. Favoring critics assert that Pinero has caught his characters as definitively as did Hogarth, and that the language of the plays is so authentic that they will serve as "linguistic documents." The heroine's suicide in *Mid-Channel* is prepared with consummate skill and thus takes place with inevitability that necessitates moral explanation—Hedda herself is not better presented in this respect. If we no longer share the beliefs of critics who held that *Mid-Channel* is a greater play than *Hedda Gabler* or *A Doll's House*, we owe it to all good specimens of the English New Drama to judge them on the total scale of their era and with sufficient comparative data.

APPENDIX

The convictions of great creativity and of international scope held by the New Drama are again revealed in Archer's account of the production of one of its plays in America:

> I do not know whether the architecturally dignified and delightful Repertory Theatre in Birmingham has evoked any strictly-speaking local talent; but it enabled Mr. John Drinkwater to develop his remarkable powers, and it witnessed the first production of his *Abraham Lincoln* (1918), an international event of real importance. I have seldom seen anything that moved me more than the performance in New York of this portraiture by an English author of the greatest of Americans. The play had been running for months, yet the theatre was crowded; and it has since, I believe, met with similar success wherever it has gone throughout the length and breadth of America.[28]

American New Dramatists were James A. Herne, Bronson Howard, William Gillette, Clyde Fitch, William C. DeMille, Langdon Mitchell, William Vaughn Moody, Augustus Thomas, Eugene Walter, Percy Mackaye, David Belasco, and others—all at work before Eugene O'Neill established himself.

Two American New Dramas thought worthy of inclusion in an anthology introduced by the eclectic and generous Brander Matthews are William C. DeMille's *Strongheart* (1905, Hudson Theatre, New York) and Langdon Mitchell's *New York Idea* (1906, Lyric Theatre, New York).

"Argument: Strongheart, an Indian student [son of a chief] at Columbia, is in love with the sister of his friend and classmate, the captain of the football team, and is anxious to distinguish himself in his last football game, but a member of the team has given the signals to their opponents. Suspicion of having betrayed Columbia is cast on Strongheart, and the captain not only takes him out of the game, but forbids him, as a member of an inferior race, to pay court to his sister. Will Strongheart be vindicated, and will he win the girl?"[29]   It is hasty to condemn to oblivion this play and many other American dramas before O'Neill: as indigenous literary expression (touched, of course, by the usual European influences) they merit continued study, particularly in relation to the temper and values of audiences and readers of the time.

Mitchell's play is one of the best American high comedies. "Argument: Joe Brooks, attributing his failure of advancement to injustice instead of to his lack of ability, misappropriates funds which he believes he can recoup by gambling. Detected in his wrong-doing and panic-stricken at the imminence of punishment, he asks his wife to intercede with his employer by trading on her charms. What sort of a bargain the young woman will propose, the terms that the employer will exact, and the future relations of Joe with the girl who married him for love remain to be solved."[30]   To judge this play by the scale of Jones and Pinero is valid comparative analysis.

NOTES

1. Arthur Wing Pinero, *The Social Plays*, Edited, with a General Introduction and a Critical Preface to Each Play by Clayton Hamilton (New York: E. P. Dutton and Company, 1917), pp. 3-4.

2. John Alexander Pierce and Brander Matthews, *The Masterpieces of Modern Drama, English and American* (Garden City: Doubleday, Page and Company, 1915), p. xxi.

3. Rupert Brooke, *John Webster and the Elizabethan Drama* (New York: John Lane Company, 1916), p. 93.

4. William Archer, *The Old Drama and the New: An Essay in Revaluation* (Boston: Small, Maynard and Company, [1923]), pp. 63-64.

5. Bernard Shaw, *Dramatic Opinions and Essays* . . . (New York: Brentano's, 1916) Vol. I, p. 112.

6. Shaw, *op. cit.*, Vol. II, p. 264.

7. Montrose J. Moses (ed.), *Representative British Dramas, Victorian and Modern* (Boston: Little, Brown, and Company, 1922), pp. 272-273, 275.

8. J. T. Grein, *Dramatic Criticism* (London: John Long, 1899), p. 264.

9. Doris Arthur Jones, *Taking the Curtain Call: The Life and Letters of Henry Arthur Jones* (New York: The Macmillan Company, 1930), pp. 61-62.

10. Pinero, *op. cit.*, Vol. I, pp. 25-26.

11. John Gore, *Edwardian Scrapbook* (London: Evans Brothers Limited, 1951), p. 12.

12. Jacques Barzun, *The Energies of Art* (New York: Vintage Books, [1962]), p. 6.

13. H. Hamilton Fyfe, *Arthur Wing Pinero, Playwright: A Study* (London: Greening and Company Limited, 1902), pp. 21-23.

14. Henry Arthur Jones, *Representative Plays*, Edited, with Historical Biographical, and Critical Introductions, by Clayton Hamilton (Boston: Little, Brown, and Company, 1925), Vol. I, p. xxxii.

15. Quoted by Hamilton, *op. cit.*, p. xl.

16. Fyfe, *op, cit.*, pp. 27-28.

17. Fyfe, *op, cit.*, p. 132.

59

18. Arthur Wing Pinero, *The Profligate* ["Introductory Note" by Malcolm C. Salaman] (Boston: Walter H. Baker and Company, [1892]), p. vi.

19. Karl Baedeker, *London and Its Environs* (Leipsic: Karl Baedeker, Publisher, 1896), p. 62.

20. Shaw, *op. cit.*, Vol. 1, pp. 72-73.

21. Henry Arthur Jones, *op. cit.*, Vol. I, pp. xliv-xlv.

22. Henry Arthur Jones, *op. cit.*, Vol. II, p. viii.

23. William Archer, "Recent English Drama," *Encyclopaedia Britannica,* 11th ed., VIII, 536.

24. George E. Wellwarth, "A Critical Study of the Reputation of Sir Arthur Wing Pinero in London and New York" (unpublished Ph.D. dissertation, Department of English, University of Chicago), p. 100.

25. Gore, *op. cit.*, pp. 84-85.

26. Clement Scott, *The Drama of Yesterday and To-day* (London: Macmillan and Company, Limited, 1899), Vol. II, pp. 339-340.

27. William Archer, *The Old Drama and the New: An Essay in Revaluation* (Boston: Small, Maynard and Company, [1923], p. 320.

28. Archer, *op. cit.*, p. 376.

29. Pierce and Matthews, *op. cit.*, p. 117.

30. Pierce and Matthews, *op. cit.*, p. 223.

THE LIARS

AN ORIGINAL COMEDY IN FOUR ACTS
by
HENRY ARTHUR JONES

SYNOPSIS OF SCENES

Time: The Present

The Liars was originally produced at the Criterion Theatre, London, October 6, 1897.

Original Cast

Colonel Sir Christopher Deering	Sir Charles Wyndham
Edward Falkner	Mr. T. B. Thalberg
Gilbert Nepean, Lady Jessica's husband....	Mr. Herbert Standing
George Nepean, Gilbert's brother	Mr. Leslie Kenyon
Freddie Tatton, Lady Rosamund's husband	Mr. A. Vane Tempest
Archibald Coke, Dolly's husband	Mr. Alfred Bishop
Waiter at "The Star and Garter"	Mr. Paul Berton
Gadsby, Footman at Freddie Tatton's	Mr. C. Terric
Taplin, Sir Christopher's servant	Mr. R. Lambart
Footman at Cadogan Gardens	Mr. A. Eliot
Lady Jessica Nepean ......⎫ sisters ⎧	Miss Mary Moore
Lady Rosamund Tatton ...⎭ ⎩	Miss Irene Vanbrugh
Dolly Coke, their cousin	Miss Sarah Brooke
Beatrice Ebernoe	Miss Cynthia Brook
Mrs. Crespin	Miss Janette Steer
Ferris, Lady Jessica's maid	Miss M. Barton

"Above all things, tell no untruth;
no, not in trifles; the custom of it is
naughty." — Sir Henry Sidney's letter to
his son Philip Sidney.

THE LIARS

ACT I

SCENE. *Interior of a large tent on the lawn of Freddie Tatton's house in the Thames valley. The roof of the tent slopes up from the back of the stage. An opening at back discovers the lawn, a night scene of a secluded part of the Thames, and the opposite bank beyond. Small opening, left. The tent is of Eastern material, splendidly embroidered in rich Eastern colours. The floor is planked and some rugs are laid down. The place is comfortably furnished for summer tea- and smoking-room. Several little tables, chairs and lounges, most of them of basket-work. On the table spirit-decanters, soda-water bottles, cigars, cigarettes, empty coffee-cups, match-box, etc. Some plants in the corners. Lamps and candles lighted. Time, after dinner on a summer evening.*

Discover Archibald Coke and Freddie Tatton. Coke, a tall, pompous, precise man, about fifty, is seated at side table, smoking. Freddie, a nervous, weedy little creature about thirty, with no whiskers, and nearly bald, with a very squeaky voice, is walking about.

FREDDIE (*very excited, very voluble, very squeaky*). It's all very well for folks to say, "Give a woman her head: don't ride her on the curb." But I tell you this, Coke, when a fellow has got a wife like mine, or Jess, it's confoundedly difficult to get her to go at all without a spill, eh?

COKE. It is perplexing to know precisely how to handle a wife—(*drinks, sighs*) — very perplexing!

FREDDIE. Perplexing? It's a d———d silly riddle without any answer! You know I didn't want to have this house-party for the Regatta — (*Coke looks at him.*) — I beg your pardon. Of course I wanted to have you and Dolly, and I didn't mind Gilbert and Jess. But I didn't want to have Falkner here. He's paying a great deal too much attention to Jess, and Jess doesn't choke him off as she should. Well, I thoroughly made up my mind if Jess came Falkner shouldn't.

COKE. Yes?

FREDDIE. Well, Rosamund said he should. So I stuck out, and she stuck out, in fact we both stuck out for a week. I was determined he shouldn't come.

COKE. Then why did you give in?

FREDDIE. I didn't.

COKE. But he's here!

FREDDIE. Yes; but only for a few days. Rosamund invited him, unknown to me, and then — well — you see, I was obliged to be civil to the fellow. (*Very confidential*) I say, Coke — we're tiled in, aren't we? Candidly, what would you do if you had a wife like Rosamund?

COKE (*sententiously*). Ah! Just so!

[*Drinks.*

FREDDIE. You're the lucky man of us three, Coke.

COKE. I must own my wife has some good points —

FREDDIE. Dolly got good points! I should think she has!

65

COKE. But she's terribly thoughtless and frivolous.

FREDDIE. So much the better. Give me a woman that lets a man call his soul his own. That's all I want, Coke, to call my soul my own. And (*resolutely*) some of these days (*very resolutely*) I will, that's all! [*Enter Mrs. Crespin, a sharp, good-looking woman between thirty and thirty-five.*

MRS. CRESPIN. Is Mr. Gilbert Nepean leaving for Devonshire to-night?

FREDDIE. Yes. He takes the eleven-thirty-four slow, and waits for the down fast at Reading.

MRS. CRESPIN. To-night?

FREDDIE. Yes. His steward, Crampton, has been robbing him for years, and now the fellow has bolted with a heap of money and a farmer's wife.

MRS. CRESPIN. Mr. Nepean must go to-night?

FREDDIE. Yes. Why?

MRS. CRESPIN. Lady Jessica and Mr. Falkner have gone for a little moonlight row. I thought Mr. Nepean might like to stay and steer.

FREDDIE. Oh, Lady Jessica knows the river well.

MRS. CRESPIN. Ah, then Mr. Nepean can look after the steward. After all, no husband need emphasise the natural absurdity of his position by playing cox to another man's stroke, need he?

[*Enter Colonel Sir Christopher Deering, a genial, handsome Englishman about thirty-eight, and George Nepean, a dark, heavy-looking man about the same age.*

SIR CHRISTOPHER. Oh, nonsense, Nepean; you're mistaken!

GEORGE. You'd better say a word to Falkner —

SIR CHRISTOPHER (*with a warning look*). Sh!

GEORGE. If you don't, I shall drop a very strong hint to my brother.

SIR CHRISTOPHER (*more peremptorily*). Sh, sh!

FREDDIE. What's the matter?

SIR CHRISTOPHER. Nothing, Freddie, nothing! Our friend here (*trying to link his arm in George's — George stands off*) is a little old-fashioned. He doesn't understand that in all really innocent flirtations ladies allow themselves a very large latitude indeed. In fact, from my very modest experience with the sex — take it for what it's worth — I should say the more innocent the flirtation, the larger the latitude the lady allows herself, eh, Mrs. Crespin?

MRS. CRESPIN. Oh, we are all latitudinarians at heart.

SIR CHRISTOPHER. Yes; but a lady who practises extensively as a latitudinarian rarely becomes a—a—a longitudinarian, eh?

MRS. CRESPIN. Oh, I wouldn't answer for her! It's a horrid, wicked world; and if once a woman allows one of you wretches to teach her the moral geography of it, it's ten to one she gets her latitude and longitude mixed before she has had time to look at the map.

FREDDIE (*to Sir Christopher*). I say, I'm awfully sorry about this. You know I told Rosamund how it would be if we had Falkner here—

SIR CHRISTOPHER (*draws Freddie aside*). Sh! Tell Lady Rosamund to caution Lady Jessica —

FREDDIE. I will. But Rosamund generally does just the opposite of what I tell her. Don't be surprised, old fellow, if you hear some of these days that I've — well, don't be surprised.

SIR CHRISTOPHER. At what?

FREDDIE. Well, I shall — now, candidly, old fellow — we're tiled in, quite between ourselves — if you found yourself landed as I am, what would you do?

SIR CHRISTOPHER. You mean if I found myself married?

FREDDIE. Yes.

SIR CHRISTOPHER. I should make the best of it.

GEORGE (to Sir Christopher). Then it's understood that you'll give Falkner a hint?

SIR CHRISTOPHER. My dear fellow, surely your brother is the best judge—

GEORGE. Of what he doesn't see?

SIR CHRISTOPHER. He's here.

GEORGE. He's leaving for Devonshire to-night — unless I stop him. Will that be necessary?

SIR CHRISTOPHER. No. Falkner is my friend. I introduced him to Lady Jessica. If you insist, I'll speak to him. But I'm sure you're wrong. He's the very soul of honour. I didn't live with him out there those three awful years without knowing him.

GEORGE. I don't see what your living three years in Africa with him has got to do with it, eh, Mrs. Crespin?

MRS. CRESPIN. Let's see how it works out. Falkner behaves most gallantly in Africa. Falkner rescues Mrs. Ebernoe. Falkner splendidly avenges Colonel Ebernoe's death, and strikes terror into every slave-dealer's heart. Falkner returns to England covered with glory. A grateful nation goes into a panic of admiration, and makes itself slightly ridiculous over Falkner. Falkner is the lion of the season. Therefore we may be quite sure that Falkner won't make love to any pretty woman who comes in his way. It doesn't seem to work out right.

SIR CHRISTOPHER. But Falkner is not an ordinary man, not even an ordinary hero.

MRS. CRESPIN. My dear Sir Christopher, the one cruel fact about heroes is that they are made of flesh and blood! Oh, if only they were made of waxwork, of Crown Derby ware, or Britannia metal; but, alas and alas! they're always made of flesh and blood.

COKE. Where did Falkner come from? What were his people?

SIR CHRISTOPHER. His grandfather was what Nonconformists call an eminent divine; his father was a rich city merchant; his mother was a farmer's daughter. Falkner himself is a — well, he's a Puritan Don Quixote, mounted on Pegasus.

MRS. CRESPIN. Put a Puritan Don Quixote on horseback, and he'll ride to the — Lady Jessica, eh?

SIR CHRISTOPHER. Hush! He'll love and he'll ride away.

MRS. CRESPIN (significantly). I sincerely hope so.

COKE. I must say that Falkner is less objectionable than Dissenters generally are. I have an unconquerable aversion to Dissenters.

SIR CHRISTOPHER. Oh, I hate 'em. But they saved England, hang 'em! And I'm not sure whether they're not the soundest part of the nation to-day.

MRS. CRESPIN. Oh, pray don't tell them so, just as they're getting harmless and sensible — and a little artistic. (*A piano is played very softly and beautifully at a distance of some twenty yards. They all listen.*) Is that Mrs. Ebernoe?

SIR CHRISTOPHER. Yes.

MRS. CRESPIN. What a beautiful touch she has!

SIR CHRISTOPHER. She has a beautiful nature.

MRS. CRESPIN. Indeed! I thought she was a little stiff and unsociable. But perhaps we are too frivolous.

SIR CHRISTOPHER. Perhaps. And she hasn't quite recovered from poor Ebernoe's death.

[*Enter Lady Rosamund and Dolly Coke in evening dress. Dolly is without any wrap on her shoulders.*

MRS. CRESPIN. But that's nearly two years ago. Is it possible we still have women amongst us who can mourn two years for a man? It gives me hopes again for my sex.

FREDDIE (*his back to Lady Rosamund*). I know jolly well Rosamund won't mourn two years for me.

LADY ROSAMUND (*a clear-cut, bright, pretty woman*). You're quite right, Freddie, I shan't. But if you behave very prettily meantime, I promise you a decent six weeks. So be satisfied, and don't make a disturbance down there (*with a little gesture pointing down*) and create the impression that I wasn't a model wife.

COKE (*in a very querulous, pedantic tone, to Dolly*). No wrap again! Really, my dear, I do wish you would take more precautions against the night air. If you should take influenza again—

DOLLY (*pretty, empty-headed little woman*). Oh, my dear Archie, if I do, it is I who will have to cough and sneeze!

COKE. Yes; but it is I who will be compelled to listen to you. I do wish you would remember how very inconvenient it is for me when you have influenza.

DOLLY. Oh, my dear, you don't expect me to remember *all* the things that are inconvenient to you. Besides, other people don't wrap up. Jessica is out on the river with absolutely nothing on her shoulders.

MRS. CRESPIN. Is it not a physiological fact that, when our hearts reach a certain temperature, our shoulders may be, and often are, safely left bare?

[*George Nepean has been listening. He comes some steps towards them as if about to speak, stops, then turns and exit with great determination.*

SIR CHRISTOPHER. Mrs. Crespin, you saw that?

MRS. CRESPIN. Yes. Where has he gone?

SIR CHRISTOPHER. I suppose to tell his brother his suspicions. I'm sure you meant nothing just now, but—(*glancing round*)—we are all friends of Lady Jessica's, aren't we?

MRS. CRESPIN. Oh, certainly. But don't you think you ought to get Mr. Falkner away?

SIR CHRISTOPHER. He'll be leaving England soon. These fresh outbreaks amongst the slave-traders will give us no end of trouble, and the Government will have to send Falkner out. Meantime—

MRS. CRESPIN. Meantime, doesn't Mrs. Ebernoe play divinely?

SIR CHRISTOPHER (*politely interrupting her*). Meantime it's understood that nothing more is to be said of this?

MRS. CRESPIN. Oh, my dear Sir Christopher, what more can be said?

[*Exit Mrs. Crespin.*

SIR CHRISTOPHER (*holds the curtains aside for her to pass out; looks after her, shakes his head, perplexed, then turns to Coke*). Coke, what do you say, a hundred up?

COKE. I'm agreeable! Dolly! Dolly!

[*Lady Rosamund, Dolly, and Freddie are chattering very vigorously together.*

DOLLY (*does not turn round to him*). Well?

[*Goes on chattering to Lady Rosamund and Freddie.*

COKE. You had a tiresome hacking cough, dear, during the greater portion of last night.

DOLLY. Did I?

[*Same business.*

COKE. It would be wise to keep away from the river.

DOLLY. Oh, very well, dear. I'll try and remember.

[*Same business.*

COKE (*turns, annoyed, to Sir Christopher*). I'm a painfully light sleeper. The least thing disturbs me, and— (*Looks anxiously at Dolly, who is still chattering, then turns to Sir Christopher.*) Do you sleep well?

SIR CHRISTOPHER (*links his arm in Coke's*). Like a top. Never missed a night's rest in my life.

[*Takes Coke off at opening.*

FREDDIE (*has been talking angrily to Lady Rosamund*). Very well then, what am I to do?

DOLLY. Oh, do go and get a whisky and soda, there's a dear Freddie!

FREDDIE. That's all very well; but if Jessica goes and makes a fool of herself in my house, people will say it was my fault.

LADY ROSAMUND. What—example, or influence, or sheer desperate imitation?

FREDDIE (*pulls himself up, looks very satirical; evidently tries to think of some crushing reply, without success*). I must say, Rosamund, that your continued chaff of me and everything that I do is in execrable taste! For a woman to chaff her husband on all occasions is—well, it's in very bad taste, that's all I can say about it!

[*Exit Freddie.*

DOLLY. Freddie's getting a dreadful fidget. He's nearly as bad as Archie.

LADY ROSAMUND. Oh, my dear, he's ten times worse. One can't help feeling some small respect for Archie.

DOLLY. Oh, do you think so? Well, yes, I suppose Archie is honourable and all that.

LADY ROSAMUND. Oh, all men are honourable. They get kicked out if they aren't. My Freddie's honourable in his poor little way.

DOLLY. Oh, don't run Freddie down. I rather like Freddie.

LADY ROSAMUND. Oh, if you had to live with him—

DOLLY. Well, he always lets you have your own way.

LADY ROSAMUND. I wish he wouldn't. I really believe I should love and respect him a little more if he were to take me and give me a good shaking, or do something to make me feel that he's my master. But (sighs) he never will! He'll only go on asking everybody's advice how to manage me—and never find out. As if it weren't the easiest thing in the world to manage a woman—if men only knew.

DOLLY. Oh, do you think so? I wonder if poor old Archie knows how to manage me!

LADY ROSAMUND. Archie's rather trying at times.

DOLLY. Oh, he is! He's so frumpish and particular, and he's getting worse.

LADY ROSAMUND. Oh, my dear, they do as they grow older.

DOLLY. Still, after all, Freddie and Archie aren't quite so awful as Gilbert.

LADY ROSAMUND. Oh, Gilbert's a terror. I hope Jessica won't do anything foolish—

[A very merry peal of laughter heard off, followed by Lady Jessica's voice.

LADY JESSICA (heard off). Oh, no, no, no, no, no! Please keep away from my dress! Oh, I'm so sorry! (Laughing a little.) But you are —so—so—

[Another peal of laughter.

FALKNER (heard off—a deep, rich, sincere, manly tone). So ridiculous? I don't mind that!

LADY JESSICA (heard off). But you'll take cold. Do go and change!

FALKNER (heard off). Change? That's not possible!

[Lady Jessica appears at opening at back, looking off, smothering her laughter. She is a very bright, pretty woman about twenty-seven, very dainty and charming. Piano ceases.

LADY JESSICA. Oh, the poor dear, foolish fellow! Look!

LADY ROSAMUND. What is it?

LADY JESSICA. My ten-and-sixpenny brooch! He kept on begging for some little souvenir, so I took this off. That quite unhinged him. I saw he was going to be demonstrative, so I dropped the brooch in the river and made a terrible fuss. He jumped in, poor dear, and fished it up. It was so muddy at the bottom! He came up looking like a fin-de-siècle Neptune—or a forsaken merman—or the draggled figure-head of a penny Thames steamboat.

LADY ROSAMUND (very seriously). Jess, the men are talking about you.

LADY JESSICA (very carelessly). Oh, are they? Who is?

LADY ROSAMUND. My Freddie says that you—

LADY JESSICA (interrupting on "says"). My dear Rosy, I don't mind what your Freddie says any more than you do.

LADY ROSAMUND. But George has been fizzing up all the evening.

LADY JESSICA. Oh, let him fizz down again.

LADY ROSAMUND. But I believe he has gone to give Gilbert a hint—

LADY JESSICA (*showing annoyance*). Ah, that's mean of George! How vexing! Perhaps Gilbert will stay now.

LADY ROSAMUND. Perhaps it's as well that Gilbert should stay.

LADY JESSICA. What? My dear Rosy, you know I'm the very best of wives, but it does get a little monotonous to spend all one's time in the company of a man who doesn't understand a joke—not even when it's explained to him!

LADY ROSAMUND. Jess, you really must pull up.

DOLLY. Yes, Jess. Mrs. Crespin was making some very cattish remarks about you and Mr. Falkner.

LADY JESSICA. Was she? Rosy, why do you have that woman here?

LADY ROSAMUND. I don't know. One must have somebody. I thought you and she were very goods friends.

LADY JESSICA. Oh, we're the best of friends, only we hate each other like poison.

LADY ROSAMUND. I don't like her. But she says such stinging things about my Freddy, and makes him so wild.

LADY JESSICA. Does she? I'll ask her down for the shooting. Oh! I've got a splendid idea!

LADY ROSAMUND. What is it?

LADY JESSICA. A new career for poor gentlewomen. You found a school and carefully train them in all the best traditions of the gentle art of husband-baiting. Then you invite one of them to your house, pay her, of course, a handsome salary, and she assists you in "the daily round, the common task" of making your husband's life a perfect misery to him. After a month or so she is played out and retires to another sphere, and you call in a new—lady-help!

LADY ROSAMUND. Oh, I don't think I should care to have my Freddie systematically henpecked by another woman.

LADY JESSICA. No; especially as you do it so well yourself. Besides, your Freddie is such a poor little pocket-edition of a man—I hope you don't mind my saying so—

LADY ROSAMUND. Oh, not at all. He's your own brother-in-law.

LADY JESSICA. Yes; and you may say what you like about Gilbert.

DOLLY. Oh, we do, don't we, Rosy?

LADY JESSICA. Do you? Well, what do you say?

DOLLY. Oh, it wouldn't be fair to tell, would it, Rosy? But Mrs. Crespin said yesterday—

[*Lady Rosamund glances at Dolly and stops her.*

LADY JESSICA. About Gilbert?

DOLLY. Yes.

LADY JESSICA. Well, what did she say?

[*Dolly glances at Lady Rosamund inquiringly.*

LADY ROSAMUND. No. Dolly, no!

LADY JESSICA. Yes, Dolly! Do tell me.

LADY ROSAMUND. No, no!

LADY JESSICA. I don't care what she said, so long as she didn't say he could understand a joke. That would be shamefully untrue. I've lived with him for five years, and I'm sure he can't. But what did Mrs. Crespin say, Rosy?

LADY ROSAMUND. No, it really was a little too bad.

DOLLY. Yes. I don't much mind what anybody says about Archie, but if Mrs. Crespin had said about him what she said about Gilbert—

LADY JESSICA. But what did she say? Rosy, if you don't tell me, I won't tell you all the dreadful things I hear about your Freddie. Oh, do tell me! There's a dear!

LADY ROSAMUND. Well, she said—

[*Begins laughing. Dolly begins laughing.*

LADY JESSICA. Oh, go on! go on! go on!

LADY ROSAMUND. She said—No, I'll whisper!

[*Lady Jessica inclines her ear; Lady Rosamund whispers; Dolly laughs.*

LADY JESSICA. About Gilbert?

[*Beginning to laugh.*

LADY ROSAMUND. Yes.

[*Laughing.*

[*They all join in a burst of laughter which grows louder and louder. At its height enter Gilbert Nepean. He is a man rather over forty, much the same build as his brother George: rather stout, heavy figure, dark complexion; strong, immobile, uninteresting features; large, coarse hands; a habit of biting his nails. He is dressed in tweeds, long light ulster and travelling cap, which he does not remove. As he enters, the laughter, which has been very boisterous, suddenly ceases. He goes up to table without taking any notice of the ladies; very deliberately takes out cigar from case, strikes a match which does not ignite, throws it down with an angry gesture and exclamation; strikes another, which also does not ignite; throws it down with a still angrier gesture and exclamation. The third match ignites, and he deliberately lights his cigar. Meantime, as soon as he has reached table, Lady Jessica, who stands behind him, exchanges glances with Dolly and Lady Rosamund, and makes a little face behind his back. Lady Rosamund winks at Lady Jessica who responds by pulling a mocking long face. Lady Rosamund steals off. Dolly shrugs her shoulders at Lady Jessica, who pulls her face still longer. Dolly steals quietly off after Lady Rosamund. Gilbert is still busy with his cigar. Lady Jessica does a little expressive pantomime behind his back.*

GILBERT. What's all this tomfoolery with Falkner?

LADY JESSICA. Tomfoolery?

GILBERT. George says you are carrying on some tomfoolery with Falkner.

LADY JESSICA. Ah! that's very sweet and elegant of George. But I never carry on any tomfoolery with any one—because I'm not a tomfool, therefore I can't.

GILBERT. I wish for once in your life you'd give me a plain answer to a plain question.

LADY JESSICA. Oh, I did once. You shouldn't remind me of that. But I never bear malice. Ask me another, such as—if a herring and a half cost three ha'pence, how long will it take one's husband to learn politeness enough to remove his cap in his wife's presence?

GILBERT (*instinctively takes off his cap; then, glancing at her attitude, which is one of amused defiance, he puts the cap on again*). There's a draught here.

LADY JESSICA. The lamp doesn't show it. But perhaps you are right to guard a sensitive spot.

GILBERT. I say there's a confounded draught.

LADY JESSICA. Oh, don't tell fibs, dear. Because if you do, you'll go —where you *may* meet me; and then we should have to spend such a very long time together.

GILBERT. (*nonplussed, a moment or two; takes out his watch*). I've no time to waste. I must be down in Devonshire, to-morrow, to go into this business of Crampton's. But before I go, I mean to know the truth of this nonsense between you and Falkner.

LADY JESSICA. Ah!

GILBERT. Shall I get it from you—or from him?

LADY JESSICA. Wouldn't it be better to get it from me? Because he mightn't tell you *all*.

GILBERT. *All?* Then there is something to know?

LADY JESSICA. Heaps. And if you'll have the ordinary politeness to take off that very ugly cap I'll be very sweet and obedient and tell you *all*.

GILBERT. Go on!

LADY JESSICA. Not while the cap sits there!

GILBERT. I tell you I feel the draught.

[*Lady Jessica rises, goes to the tent openings, carefully draws the curtains. He watches her, sulkily.*

LADY JESSICA. There! now you may safely venture to uncover the sensitive spot.

GILBERT (*firmly*). No.

LADY JESSICA (*serenely, seated*). Very well, my dear. Then I shan't open my lips.

GILBERT. You won't?

LADY JESSICA. No; and I'm sure it's far more important for you to know what is going on between Mr. Falkner and me than to have that horrid thing sticking on your head.

GILBERT (*takes a turn or two; bites his nails; at length sulkily flings the cap on the chair*). Now!

LADY JESSICA. Mr. Falkner is very deeply attached to me, I believe.

GILBERT. He has told you so?

LADY JESSICA. No.

GILBERT. No?

LADY JESSICA. No; that's only because I keep on stopping him.

GILBERT. You keep on stopping him?

LADY JESSICA. Yes; it's so much pleasanter to have him dangling for a little while, and *then*—

GILBERT. Then what?

LADY JESSICA. Well, it is pleasant to be admired.

GILBERT. And you accept his admiration?

LADY JESSICA. Of course I do. Why shouldn't I? If Mr. Falkner admires me, isn't that the greatest compliment he can pay to your taste? And if he spares you the drudgery of being polite to me, flattering me, complimenting me, and paying me the hundred delicate little attentions that win a woman's heart, I'm sure you ought to be very much obliged to him for taking all that trouble off your hands.

GILBERT (*looks furious*). Now understand me. This nonsense has gone far enough. I forbid you to have anything further to say to the man.

LADY JESSICA. Ah, you forbid me!

GILBERT. I forbid you. And, understand, if you do—

LADY JESSICA. Ah, take care! Don't threaten me!

GILBERT. Do you mean to respect my wishes?

LADY JESSICA. Of course I shall respect your wishes. I may not obey them, but I will respect them.

GILBERT (*enraged, comes up to her very angrily*). Now, Jessica, once for all—
[*Enter George; Gilbert stops suddenly.*

GEORGE. The dog-cart's ready, Gilbert. What's the matter?

GILBERT. Nothing. (*To Lady Jessica.*) You'll please to come on to me at Teignwick to-morrow.

LADY JESSICA. Can't. I've promised to go to Barbara, and I must keep my promise, even though it parts me from you.
[*Enter Servant.*

SERVANT. You've only just time to catch the train, sir.

GILBERT. I'm not going.

SERVANT. Not going, sir?

GILBERT. No.
[*Exit Servant.*

LADY JESSICA (*appeals to George*). Isn't it dear of him to stay here on my account when he knows he ought to be in Devon? Isn't it sweet to think that after five long years one has still that magnetic attraction for one's husband?

GILBERT. No. I'm hanged if I stay on your account. (*Goes up to opening, calls out.*) Hi! Gadsby! I'm coming! Understand, I expect you at Teignwick to-morrow.

LADY JESSICA. Dearest, I shan't come.

GILBERT. I say you shall!

LADY JESSICA. "Shall" is not a pretty word for a husband to use.
[*Takes up the cap he has thrown down and stands twiddling the tassel.*

GILBERT (*after a furious dig at his nails*). George, I expect this business of Crampton's will keep me for a week, but I can't tell. Look after everything while I'm away. (*To Lady Jessica.*) You won't come to Teignwick?

LADY JESSICA. I've promised Barbara. Here's your cap.

GILBERT. Good-bye, George!

[*Looks at Lady Jessica, and is then going off at back.*

LADY JESSICA. Ta, ta, dearest!

GILBERT (*turns, comes a step or two to Lady Jessica, livid with anger; speaks in her ear*). You'll go just one step too far some day, madam, and if you do, look out for yourself, for, by God! I won't spare you!

[*Exit Gilbert. Lady Jessica stands a little frightened, goes up to opening at back, as if to call him back, comes down. George stands watching her, smoking.*

LADY JESSICA (*after a little pause*). George, that was very silly of you to tell Gilbert about Mr. Falkner and me.

GEORGE. I thought you had gone far enough.

LADY JESSICA. Oh, no, my dear friend. You must allow me to be the best judge of how far—

GEORGE. How far you can skate over thin ice?

LADY JESSICA. The thinner the ice, the more delicious the fun, don't you think? Ah, you're like Gilbert. You don't skate—or joke.

GEORGE. You heard what Gilbert said?

LADY JESSICA. Yes; that was a hint to you. Won't it be rather a tiresome task for you?

GEORGE. What?

LADY JESSICA. To keep an eye on me, watch that I don't go that one step too far. And not quite a nice thing to do, eh?

GEORGE. Oh, I've no intention of watching you— (*Enter Falkner. Looking at the two.*) Not the least intention, I assure you.

[*Exit George.*

LADY JESSICA. So to-morrow will break up our pleasant party.

FALKNER (*about forty; strong, fine, clearly-cut features, earnest expression, hair turning grey, complexion pale and almost grey with continued work, anxiety, and abstinence*). And after to-morrow?

LADY JESSICA. Ah, after to-morrow!

FALKNER. When shall we meet again?

LADY JESSICA. Shall we meet again? Yes, I suppose. Extremes do meet, don't they?

FALKNER. Are we extremes?

LADY JESSICA. Aren't we? I suppose I'm the vainest, emptiest, most irresponsible creature in the world—

FALKNER. You're not! you're not! You slander yourself! You can be sincere, you can be earnest, you can be serious—

LADY JESSICA. Can I? Oh, do tell me what fun there is in being serious! I can't see the use of it. There you are, for instance, mounted on that high horse of seriousness, spending the best years of your life in fighting African slave-traders and other windmills of that sort. Oh, do leave the windmills alone! They'll all tumble by themselves by-and-bye.

FALKNER. I'm not going to spend the best years of my life in fighting slave-traders. I'm going to spend them—in loving you.

[*Approaching her very closely.*

LADY JESSICA. Oh, that will be worse than the windmills—and quite as useless. (*He is very near to her.*) If you please—you remember we promised to discuss all love-matters at a distance of three feet, so as to allow for the personal equation. Your three feet, please.

FALKNER. When shall we meet again?

LADY JESSICA. Ah, when? Where do you go to-morrow night, when you leave here?

FALKNER. I don't know. Where do you?

LADY JESSICA. To my cousin Barbara's.

FALKNER. Where is that?

LADY JESSICA. Oh, a little way along the river, towards town; not far from Staines.

FALKNER. In what direction?

LADY JESSICA. About two miles to the nor'-nor'-sou'-west. I never was good at geography.

FALKNER. Is there a good inn near?

LADY JESSICA. There's a delightful little riverside hotel, the Star and Garter, at Shepperford. They make a specialty of French cooking.

FALKNER. I shall go there when I leave here to-morrow. May I call at your cousin's?

LADY JESSICA. It wouldn't be wise. And I'm only staying till Monday.

FALKNER. And then?

LADY JESSICA. On Monday evening I go back to town.

FALKNER. Alone?

LADY JESSICA. No; with Ferris, my maid. Unless I send her on first.

FALKNER. And you will?

LADY JESSICA. No; I don't think so. But a curious thing happened to me the last time I stayed at Barbara's. I sent Ferris on with the luggage in the early afternoon, and I walked to the station for the sake of the walk. Well, there are two turnings, and I must have taken the wrong one.

FALKNER. What happened?

LADY JESSICA. I wandered about for miles, and at half-past seven I found myself, very hot, very tired, very hungry, and in a very bad temper, at the Star and Garter at Shepperford. That was on a Monday, too.

FALKNER. That was on a Monday?

LADY JESSICA. Yes—hark! (*Goes suddenly to back, looks off.*) Oh, it's you, Ferris! What are you doing there?

[*Ferris, a perfectly trained lady's maid, about thirty, dark, quiet, reserved, a little sinister-looking, appears at opening at back with wrap in hand.*

FERRIS. I beg pardon, my lady, but I thought you might be getting chilly, so I've brought you this.

LADY JESSICA. Put it on the chair.

FERRIS. Yes, my lady.

[*Exit Ferris.*

LADY JESSICA (*yawns*). Heigho! Shall we go into the billiard room?

[*Going.*

FALKNER. No. How long do you mean to play with me?

LADY JESSICA. Am I playing with you?

FALKNER. What else have you done the last three months? My heart is yours to its last beat. My life is yours to its last moment. What are you going to do with me?

LADY JESSICA. Ah, that's it! I'm sure I don't know. (*Smiling at him.*) What shall I do with you?

FALKNER. Love me! love me! love me!

LADY JESSICA. You are very foolish!

FALKNER. Foolish to love you?

LADY JESSICA. No; not foolish to love me. I like you for that. But foolish to love me so foolishly. Foolish to be always wanting to play Romeo, when I only want to play Juliet sometimes.

FALKNER. Sometimes? When?

LADY JESSICA. When I am foolish too—on a Monday evening.

FALKNER. Ah! will you drive me mad? Shall I tear you to pieces to find out if there is a heart somewhere within you?

[*Is about to clasp her.*

LADY JESSICA (*struggling*). Hush! some one coming.

[*Falkner releases her.*

[*Sir Christopher saunters in at back, smoking. Exit Lady Jessica.*

SIR CHRISTOPHER. Drop it, Ned; Drop it, my dear old boy! You're going too far.

FALKNER. We won't discuss the matter, Kit.

SIR CHRISTOPHER. Yes we will, Ned. George Nepean has been making a row, and I—well, I stroked him down. I said you were the soul of honour—

FALKNER. You were right. I am the soul of honour.

SIR CHRISTOPHER. And that you didn't mean anything by your attentions to Lady Jessica.

FALKNER. You were wrong. I do mean something.

SIR CHRISTOPHER. Well, what?

FALKNER. That's my business—and Lady Jessica's.

SIR CHRISTOPHER. You forget—I introduced you here.

FALKNER. Thank you. You were very kind.

[*Going off.*

SIR CHRISTOPHER (*stopping him*). No, Ned; we'll have this out, here and now, please.

FALKNER (*angrily*). Very well, let's have it out, here and now!

SIR CHRISTOPHER (*with great friendliness*). Come, old boy, there's no need for us to take this tone. Let's talk it over calmly, as old friends and men of the world.

FALKNER. Men of the world! If there is one beast in all the loathsome fauna of civilization that I hate and despise, it is a man of the world! Good heaven, what men! what a world!

SIR CHRISTOPHER. Quite so, old fellow. It is a beastly bad world—a lying, selfish, treacherous world! A rascally bad world every way. But bad as it is, this old world hasn't lived all these thousands of years without getting a little common sense into its wicked old noddle—especially with regard to its love affairs. And, speaking as an average bad citizen of this blackguardly old world, I want to ask you, Ned Falkner, what the devil you mean by making love to a married woman, and what good or happiness you expect to get for yourself or her? Where does it lead? What's to be the end of it?

FALKNER. I don't know—I don't care! I love her!

SIR CHRISTOPHER. But, my good Ned, she's another man's wife.

FALKNER. She's married to a man who doesn't value her, doesn't understand her, is utterly unworthy of her.

SIR CHRISTOPHER. All women are married to men who are utterly unworthy of them—bless 'em! All women are undervalued by their husbands— bless 'em; All women are misunderstood—bless 'em again!

FALKNER. Oh, don't laugh it off like that. Look at that thick clown of a husband. They haven't a single idea, or thought, or taste in common.

SIR CHRISTOPHER. That's her lookout before she married him.

FALKNER. But suppose she didn't know, didn't understand. Suppose experience comes too late!

SIR CHRISTOPHER. It generally does—in other things besides marriage!

FALKNER. But doesn't it make your blood boil to see a woman sacrificed for life?

SIR CHRISTOPHER. It does—my blood boils a hundred times a day. But marriages are made in heaven, and if once we set to work to repair celestial mistakes and indiscretions, we shall have our hands full. Come down to brass tacks. What's going to be the end of this?

FALKNER. I don't know—I don't care! I love her!

SIR CHRISTOPHER. You don't know? I'll tell you. Let's go over all the possibilities of the case. (*Ticking them off on his fingers.*) Possibility number one—you leave off loving her—

FALKNER. That's impossible.

SIR CHRISTOPHER. Possibility number two—you can, one or the other, or both of you, die by natural means; but you're both confoundedly healthy, so I'm afraid there's no chance of that. Possibility number three—you can die together, by poison, or steel, or cold Thames water. I would'nt trust *you* not to do a fool's trick of that sort; but thank God, she's got too much sense. By the way, Ned, I don't think she cares very much for you—

FALKNER. She will.

SIR CHRISTOPHER. Well, well, we shall see. Possibility number four — you can keep on dangling at her heels, and being made a fool of, without getting any — "forrader."

FALKNER. Mine is not a physical passion.

SIR CHRISTOPHER (*looks at him for a moment*). Oh, that be hanged!

FALKNER. I tell you it is not.

SIR CHRISTOPHER. Well then, it ought to be.

FALKNER (*very angrily*). Well then, it is! And say no more about it. What business is it of yours?

SIR CHRISTOPHER (*nonplussed*). Possibility number five — a liaison with her husband's connivance. Gilbert Nepean won't make a *mari complaisant*. Dismiss that possibility.

FALKNER. Dismiss them all.

SIR CHRISTOPHER. Don't you wish you could? But you'll have to face one of them, Ned. Possibility number six — a secret liaison. That's nearly impossible in society. And do you know what it means? It means in the end every inconvenience and disadvantage of marriage without any of its conveniences and advantages. It means endless discomfort, worry, and alarm. It means constant sneaking and subterfuges of the paltriest, pettiest kind. What do you say to that, my soul of honour?

FALKNER. I love her. I shall not try to hide my love.

SIR CHRISTOPHER. Oh, then you want a scandal! You'll get it! Have you thought what sort of a scandal it will be? Remember you've stuck yourself on a pedestal, and put a moral toga on. That's awkward. It wants such a lot of living up to. Gilbert Nepean is a nasty cuss and he'll make a nasty fuss. Possibility number seven — tableau one: Edward Falkner on his moral pedestal in a toga-esque attitude, honoured and idolized by the British public. (*Striking a heroic attitude.*) Tableau two: a horrible scandal, a field day for Mrs. Grundy; Edward Falkner is dragged from his pedestal, his toga is torn to pieces, his splendid reputation is blown to the winds, and he is rolled in the mud under the feet of the British public who, six months ago, crowned him with garlands and shouted themselves hoarse in his praise. Are you prepared for that, my soul of honour?

FALKNER. If it comes.

SIR CHRISTOPHER (*shakes his head, makes a wry face, then proceeds*). Possibility number eight. Last remaining possibility, only possible possibility—pull yourself together, pack up your traps, start to-morrow morning for Africa or Kamschatka, Jericho or Hong-Kong. I'll go with you. What do you say?

FALKNER. No.

SIR CHRISTOPHER. No?

FALKNER. I wonder at you, Deering—I wonder at you coming to lecture me on love and morality.

SIR CHRISTOPHER. Ah, why?

FALKNER (*with growing indignation*). I love a woman with the deepest love of my heart, with the purest worship of my soul. If that isn't moral, if that isn't sacred, if that isn't righteous, tell me, in heaven's name, what is? And you come to lecture me with your cut-and-dried worldly-wise philosophy, your mean little maxims, you come to lecture me on love and morality—you!

SIR CHRISTOPHER. Yes, I do! I may have had my attachments, I may have done this, that, and the other. I'm not a hero, not on a pedestal, I never put on a moral toga. But I owe no woman a sigh or a sixpence. I've never wronged any man's sister, or daughter, or wife. And I tell you this, Ned Falkner, you're a fool if you think that anything can come of this passion of yours for Lady Jessica, except misery and ruin for her, embarrassment and disgrace for you, and kicking out of decent society for both of you.

FALKNER (*very firmly*). Very well. And will you please be the first to cut me. Or shall I cut you?

SIR CHRISTOPHER. You mean that, Ned?

FALKNER. Yes; if I'm a fool, leave me to my folly. (*Very strongly.*) Don't meddle with me.

SIR CHRISTOPHER. You do mean that, Ned? Our friendship is to end?

FALKNER. Yes.

SIR CHRISTOPHER. Very well. You'll understand some day, Ned, that I couldn't see an old comrade, a man who stood shoulder to shoulder with me all these years—you'll understand I couldn't see him fling away honour, happiness, reputation, future, everything, without saying one word and trying to pull him up. Good-bye, old chap.
[*Going off.*
[*Falkner springs up generously, goes to him warmly, holding out both hands.*

FALKNER (*cries out*). Kit!

SIR CHRISTOPHER. Ned!

[*The two men stand with hands clasped for some time; then Falkner speaks in a soft, low, broken voice.*

FALKNER. I love her, Kit—you don't know how much. When I see her, that turn of her head, that little toss of her curls, the little roguish face she makes—God couldn't make her like that and then blame a man for loving her! If He did—well, right or wrong, I'd rather miss heaven than one smile, one nod, one touch of her finger-tips!

SIR CHRISTOPHER. Oh, my poor dear old fellow, if you're as far gone as that, what the deuce am I to do with you?

[*Enter Beatrice Ebernoe, a tall, dark woman, about thirty, very beautiful and spirituelle.*

BEATRICE. Ned, here's a messenger from the Colonial Office with a very urgent letter for you.

FALKNER. For me?

[*Enter Servant bringing letter to Falkner.*

SERVANT. Important, sir. The messenger is waiting in the hall for your answer.

FALKNER (*taking letter*). Very well, I'll come to him.

(*Exit Servant.*)

(*Reading letter.*) More trouble out there. They want me to go out at once and negotiate. They think I could win over the chiefs and save a lot of bloodshed.

SIR CHRISTOPHER. You'll go, Ned?

FALKNER. I don't know.

SIR CHRISTOPHER (*to Beatrice*). Help me to persuade him.

BEATRICE. Can I? Have I any influence? Ned, for the sake of old days—

FALKNER. Ah, no—let me be—I must think this over.

[*Exit with distracted manner.*

BEATRICE. Have you spoken to him?

SIR CHRISTOPHER. Yes; I gave him a thorough good slanging. Not a bit of use. When one of you holds us by a single hair, not all the king's horses and all the king's men can drag us back to that beggarly, dusty old towpath of duty.

BEATRICE. I won't believe men are so weak.

SIR CHRISTOPHER. Aren't we? There never was so sensible a man as I am in the management of other men's love affairs. You should have heard me lecture Ned. But once put me near you, and I'm every bit as bad as that poor fool I've been basting!

[*Indicating Falkner by inclination of the head towards the direction in which he has gone.*

BEATRICE. Oh, no, Kit, I won't have you say that.

SIR CHRISTOPHER. But I am. How beautifully you played just now.

BEATRICE. Did I?

SIR CHRISTOPHER. Don't do it again.

BEATRICE. Why not?

SIR CHRISTOPHER. It's taking an unfair advantage of me. You oughtn't to rouse those divine feelings in a man's heart. You oughtn't to make me feel like a martyr, or a king, or a saint in a cathedral window, with all heaven's sunlight streaming through me! You oughtn't to do it! Because devil a ha'porth of a king, or a martyr, or a saint is there in me—and after you've been playing to me and lifted me into that seventh heaven of yours, I feel so mean and shabby when I drop down to earth again, and find myself a hard, selfish man of the world.

BEATRICE. Oh, I think there's a great deal of the martyr and saint and king in you.

SIR CHRISTOPHER. Do you? I believe there is! I know there would be if you'd only screw me up to it—and keep me screwed up. Beatrice, there's nothing I couldn't do if you would only—

BEATRICE (*going away from him*). Kit, you mustn't speak of this again. I can't quite forget.

SIR CHRISTOPHER. There's no need. While he was alive I never had one disloyal thought towards him. Now he's dead, who could be so fitted to take care of his dearest treasure as his oldest friend?

BEATRICE (*going away*). I can't quite forget.

SIR CHRISTOPHER. But you're young. What do you mean to do with your life?

BEATRICE. I'd some thoughts of entering a sisterhood.

SIR CHRISTOPHER. Ah, no! Surely there are plenty of dear good ugly women in the world who can do that.

BEATRICE. But I must enjoy the luxury of self-sacrifice. Tell me how I can drink the deepest of that cup.

SIR CHRISTOPHER. Marry me. I'll give you the most splendid opportunities. Now, if you and I were to join our forces, and take our poor Ned in hand, and—

BEATRICE. Hush!

[*Falkner re-enters, evidently very much distracted.*

SIR CHRISTOPHER (*after a little pause, goes up to him*). Well, Ned, what are you going to do?

FALKNER (*in an agony of indecision*). I don't know! I don't know!

SIR CHRISTOPHER. You'll go, Ned? I'll go with you!

[*Enter Lady Jessica at back.*

BEATRICE. You'll go, Ned?

LADY JESSICA. Go? Where?

FALKNER. Nowhere. I shan't go, Kit. The man's waiting. I must give him my answer.

[*Exit Falkner. Lady Jessica looks after him. Sir Christopher shrugs his shoulders at Beatrice.*

SIR CHRISTOPHER. Not all the king's horses, nor all the king's men!

CURTAIN

ACT II

SCENE. *Private sitting-room in the Star and Garter, Shepperford-on-Thames; a room in a small high-class riverside hotel, furnished in the usual incongruous hotel fashion. Large French windows both right and left take up a good part of the back of the stage, and open upon a veranda which runs along outside. The pillars and roof of the veranda are smothered with trails of flowers and creeping plants. Beyond the veranda and very near to it is the Thames, with opposite bank. Door down stage, right. A sofa down stage, right. A sideboard, left. On the sideboard, plates, knives, forks, etc., dishes of fine peaches, grapes and strawberries, and a bottle each of hock, claret, and champagne, as described in the text. A small table with writing materials at back between windows. A small table with white cloth laid, down stage, a little to the left of centre. A fireplace down stage, left.*

Discover Falkner in evening dress and French Waiter.

FALKNER. Crème à la Reine. We might have some trifle before the soup.

WAITER. Anchovy salad? Caviare?

FALKNER. Caviare.

WAITER. Bien, m'sieu. At what hour will m'sieu dine?

FALKNER. I don't know; I'm not sure that my friend will come at all. But tell the cook to have everything prepared, so that we can have dinner very soon after my friend arrives.

WAITER. Bien, m'sieu.

FALKNER (*reading menu*). Caviare. Crème à la Reine. Rouget à l' Italienne. Whitebait. Petites Timbales à la Lucullus. Mousse de Foie Gras en Belle Vue. Is your cook equal to those entrées?

WAITER. Oh, sir, he is equal to anything. Trust to me, sir. The cook shall be magnifique. The dinner shall be magnifique.

FALKNER (*continuing*). Poulardes poêlées, sauce Arcadienne. Selle de Mouton. Ortolans. Salade, Asperges en branches. Pouding Mousseline, sauce Eglantine. Soufflé Glacé à l'Ananas. Dessert? (*Waiter points to the dessert on the sideboard.*) And the wines?

WAITER (*pointing to the wines on the sideboard*). Ayala, seventy-five. Johannesburg, sixty-eight. Château Haut-Brion, seventy-five. I have brought them from London myself. We have not these vintages here.

FALKNER. Good.

WAITER. It is but one friend that m'sieu expect?

FALKNER. Only one friend.

WAITER. Bien, m'sieu.

(*Exit Waiter.*)

(*Falkner, alone, walks restlessly about the room for a few seconds; comes down; is arrested by something he hears outside the door; shows great delight.*)

(*Re-enter Waiter.*)

A lady; she say will Mr. Falkner please to see her? She have lost (*coughing*) her way.

FALKNER. Show her in.

[*Falkner, alone, walks eagerly about room for a few seconds; his manner very eager and impatient and quite different from what it had been before.*

[*Re-enter Waiter, showing in Lady Jessica most charmingly and coquettishly dressed in summer outdoor clothes. She comes in rather tempestuously, speaking as she enters, and going up to Falkner.*

LADY JESSICA (*all in a breath*). Oh, my dear Mr. Falkner, I've been staying with my cousin, and I was walking to the station, and by some unlucky chance I must have taken the wrong turning, for, instead of finding myself at the station, I found myself here; and as I'm very hungry, would you think it very dreadful if I asked you to give me just a mere mouthful of dinner?

FALKNER (*intensely calm low voice*). I'm delighted. (*To Waiter.*) Will you let us have dinner as soon as it is ready?

WAITER. In half an hour, sir. And the friend, sir?

FALKNER. The friend?

WAITER. The friend that m'sieu expect—the friend of the dinner?

FALKNER. Oh, yes—if he comes, show him in.

LADY JESSICA (*alarmed*). You don't expect—

FALKNER (*glancing at Waiter*). Hush!

WAITER (*absolutely impassive face*). Bien, m'sieu!

[*Exit Waiter.*

FALKNER. I'm so glad you've come. Look. (*Holding out his hand.*) I'm trembling with delight. I knew you would be here.

LADY JESSICA. I'm sure you didn't, for I didn't know myself two hours ago. It was only by chance that I happened to take the wrong turning.

FALKNER. No; the right turning. And not by chance. It was not chance that brought you to me.

LADY JESSICA. Oh, please, not that strain. I can't play up to it. Sit down and let us discuss something mundane—say dinner.

FALKNER (*giving her the menu*). I hope you'll like what I've ordered. I sent the waiter up to London for some of the dishes and the wines.

LADY JESSICA (*takes menu, looks at it, shows symptons of great mock terror*). What? You surely don't expect my poor little appetite to stand up to this dinner. Oh, let me be a warning to all, never to take the wrong turning when it may lead to a menu like this.

FALKNER. That's for your choice. You don't suppose I'd offer you anything but the very best.

LADY JESSICA. Yes, but a little of the very best is all I want; not all of it.

FALKNER. Take all of it that I can set before you.

LADY JESSICA. Oh, but think—there may be other deserving ladies in the world.

FALKNER. There is but you.

LADY JESSICA (*looks at him, very much amused*). And I came here to cure you of this folly. Ah, me! (*Reading the menu.*) Mousse de Foie Gras. Poulardes poêlées, sauce Arcadienne—What is sauce Arcadienne?

FALKNER. I don't know. Love is the sauce of life. Perhaps it's that.

LADY JESSICA. Yes, but don't dish it up too often or too strong. It's sure to be wasted.

FALKNER. My love for you is not wasted.

LADY JESSICA. No?

FALKNER. You'll return it. You'll love me at last.

LADY JESSICA. Shall I? Crème à la Reine. Rouget à l'Italienne. And if I did, what then?

FALKNER. Join your life to mine. Come to Africa with me.

LADY JESSICA (*shakes her head*). Impossible! We should only shock the British public. They wouldn't understand us. Ortolans. Salade. Asperges en branches. Besides, what would everybody say?

FALKNER. We shouldn't hear them.

LADY JESSICA. No; but they'd be talking all the same. Ha, ha! They'd call us the eloping philanthropists.

FALKNER. Would that matter?

LADY JESSICA. Oh, yes. A philanthropist may not elope. A tenor may. Doesn't it show the terrible irony there is in the heart of things, that the best-meaning philanthropist in the world may not elope with his neighbour's wife? Pouding Mousseline, sauce Eglantine. What makes you so eager to go hunting slave-traders in Africa?

FALKNER. My father spent half his fortune putting slavery down. My grandfather spent half his life and died a pauper for the same cause.

LADY JESSICA. Well, then, you should send a subscription to the Aborigines' Protection Society. That is how I keep up our family traditions.

FALKNER. How?

LADY JESSICA. My father had a shocking reputation, and my grandfather, Beau Lillywhite—Oh! (*Shrug.*) So I follow in their footsteps —at a respectful distance. I flirt with you. Soufflé Glacé à l'Ananas. There's no flirting in Central Africa, I suppose?

FALKNER. No flirting. Only heat and hunger and thirst, and helpless misery prolonged to a horrible death.

LADY JESSICA (*genuinely moved*). Oh, I'm so sorry! Don't think me heartless about *that*. Perhaps if I had lived amongst it as you have—

FALKNER. Ah, if you had! you'd do as I ask you. You'd give all your heart to me, you'd give all your woman's care and tenderness to them, and you'd never hear one whisper of what people said of you.

LADY JESSICA (*looking at him with real admiration*). How earnest you are! How devoted!

(*Enter Waiter with knives and forks; he goes to table and begins laying it. To Waiter.*)

What is sauce Arcadienne?

WAITER. Pardon! The cook is splendid. He is magnifique—but he has— (*gesture*)—renversée the sauce Arcadienne all over the shop.

FALKNER. It doesn't matter.

LADY JESSICA. Oh, I had set my heart on sauce Arcadienne.

FALKNER. The cook must make some more sauce Arcadienne.

WAITER. Ah, that is impossible till the middle of the night.

LADY JESSICA. Ah, what a pity! It is the one thing I long for, sauce Arcadienne.

FALKNER. Why?

LADY JESSICA. Because I don't know what it is.

WAITER. He will give you some sauce Marguerite.

LADY JESSICA. What is sauce Marguerite?

WAITER (*all the while laying table*). Ah, it is délicieuse. It is the very best sauce that is in all the world.

LADY JESSICA. Va pour la sauce Marguerite! Oh, this dinner!

WAITER. Ah, there is the beast of the organ man.

LADY JESSICA. No, let him be. I like music—and monkeys. (*To Falkner.*) Tell them to make haste.

FALKNER. Hurry the dinner.

WAITER. Bien!

[*Exit Waiter.*

LADY JESSICA (*taking out watch*). Half-past seven; I've not an hour to stay.

FALKNER. Yes, your life if you will.

LADY JESSICA. Ah, no! You must be sensible. Think! what could come of it if I did love you? I should only break your heart or—what would be far worse—break my own.

FALKNER. Break it then—or let me break it. It's better to feel, it's better to suffer, than to be meanly happy. I love you, but I'd rather smother you in tears and blood than you should go on living this poor little heartless, withered life, choked up with all this dry society dust. Oh, can't I make you feel? Can't I make you live? Can't I make you love me?

LADY JESSICA (*after a moment's pause, looking at him with great admiration*). Perhaps I do in my heart of hearts!

FALKNER. Ah!

[*Springs to seize her; she struggles with him.*

LADY JESSICA. Mr. Falkner! Mr. Falkner! If you please. Do you hear? Mr. Falkner! (*Tears herself free.*) Will you please go and stop that horrid organ? Will you, please?

(*Falkner bows, and exit at door. Lady Jessica, panting, flurried, out of breath, goes up to the window fanning herself with handkerchief, passes on to veranda; stays there for a few moments fanning herself; suddenly starts back alarmed, comes into room, and stands frightened, listening. George Nepean appears on veranda, comes up to window, looks in. Lady Jessica tries to appear indifferent.*)

Ah, George!

GEORGE. I thought I caught sight of you. May I come in?

LADY JESSICA. Certainly.

GEORGE (*entering*). I'm not intruding?

LADY JESSICA. Intruding? Oh, no. Have you heard from Gilbert?

GEORGE. Yes, I had a letter this morning. He may be back in two or three days.

LADY JESSICA (*embarrassed*). Yes?

[*A pause. The organ outside stops in the middle of a bar.*

GEORGE (*glancing at table*). You're dining here?

LADY JESSICA. Yes; just a small party. What brings you here?

GEORGE. I was going on to some friends at Hersham. I was waiting for the ferry when I caught sight of you. (*Glancing at table and sideboard.*) You're giving your friends rather a good dinner.

LADY JESSICA. H'm, rather. I've heard the cooking's very good here. (*A little pause.*) There's a nest of cygnets outside. Have you seen them?

GEORGE. No.

LADY JESSICA. Do come and look at them; they are so pretty.

[*Going off at window, followed by George, when Falkner enters at door. The two men look at each other. Lady Jessica shows very great confusion and embarrassment. A long awkward pause. George looks very significantly at the sideboard and table.*

GEORGE (*to Lady Jessica*). Gilbert must know of this. You understand?

[*Bows. Exit by window and veranda.*

LADY JESSICA (*who has stood very frightened and confused*). Did you hear? What can I do? What can I do?

FALKNER (*calm, almost triumphant*). You must join your life to mine now.

LADY JESSICA. No, no! If you wish me ever to have one kind thought of you, get me out of this! Do something, find somebody to dine with us. Understand me, I know myself: if this leads to a scandal, I shall hate you in a week. Oh, do something! do something!

FALKNER. Be calm. Be sure I'll do all I can to save you from a scandal. If that is impossible, be sure I'll do all I can to protect you from it.

LADY JESSICA. Ah, no! Save me from it. I can't face it. I can't give up my world, my friends. Oh, what can I do? I'll go back to town—

FALKNER. What good will that do? You had far better stay now. Sit down, be calm. Trust to me.

LADY JESSICA. Oh, you are good, and I'm such a coward.

FALKNER. Let us think what is the best thing to do.

LADY JESSICA. Can't we get somebody to dine with us?

LADY ROSAMUND (*heard outside*). Oh, can't you wait, Freddie?

LADY JESSICA (*looking off*). Hark! Rosy!

[*Goes up to window.*

FREDDIE (*heard off*). What! Row two more miles without a drink?

LADY JESSICA. She's there in a boat with Freddie and another man. The men are landing. If we could only get them to stay and dine with us! Go and find George Nepean and bring him back here. Make haste. When you come back, I'll have Rosy here.

FALKNER. In any case rely on me. I'm as firm as the earth beneath you.

[*Exit Falkner.*

LADY JESSICA (*goes up to window*). Rosy! Rosy! Come here! Yes, through there. Sh!

[*Lady Rosamund appears in the veranda.*

LADY ROSAMUND. Jess! What's the matter?

[*Entering room.*

LADY JESSICA. Everything. You and Freddie must stay and dine here.

LADY ROSAMUND. We can't, we're going on to dine with Mrs. Crespin at her new place, and we've got Jack Symons with us.

LADY JESSICA. Va pour Jack Symons, whoever he may be! He must stay and dine too!

LADY ROSAMUND. Impossible. Mrs. Crespin has asked some people to meet us. As her place is on the river, Jack proposed we should row down and dress there. What are you doing here? I thought you were at Barbara's.

LADY JESSICA. I was going back to town to-night. I thought I'd walk to the station—it's so delightful across the fields. Well, you know the path; I went on all right till I came to those two turnings, and then—I must have taken the wrong one, for, instead of finding myself at the station, I found myself here.

LADY ROSAMUND. Well?

LADY JESSICA. I'd been wandering about for over an hour; I was very hungry; I remembered Mr. Falkner was staying here; so I came in and asked him to give me some dinner.

LADY ROSAMUND. It was very foolish of you!

LADY JESSICA. Yes, especially as George Nepean was waiting for the ferry and caught sight of me on the veranda.

LADY ROSAMUND. George Nepean!

LADY JESSICA. He came in, saw Mr. Falkner, put a totally wrong construction on it all, and threatened to let Gilbert know.

LADY ROSAMUND. How could you be so imprudent, Jess? You must have known that—

LADY JESSICA. Oh, don't stand there rowing me. Help me out of this and I promise you I won't get into another.

LADY ROSAMUND. Why didn't you explain to George how it happened?

LADY JESSICA. So I would. Only when he came in, I was alone. I felt sure he would put a wrong construction on it, so I told him I was dining here with a little party—then Mr. Falkner came in, and I was too confused to say anything. Besides, I couldn't very well tell him the truth, because—

LADY ROSAMUND. Because what?

LADY JESSICA. Well, it's very curious, but the last time I was staying with Barbara the very same thing happened.

LADY ROSAMUND. What?

LADY JESSICA. I was walking to the station, and I must have taken the wrong turning, for instead of finding myself at the station, I found myself here.

LADY ROSAMUND. What, twice?

LADY JESSICA. Yes.

LADY ROSAMUND. Oh, impossible!

LADY JESSICA. No, it isn't; for it actually happened.

LADY ROSAMUND. Do you mean to tell me that you—

LADY JESSICA (*taking up on the "tell"*). Yes, I do. The sign-post is most deceptive.

LADY ROSAMUND. It must be.

LADY JESSICA. But the other time it was really a mistake, and I dined here all alone.

LADY ROSAMUND. Honour?

LADY JESSICA. Really, really honour!

LADY ROSAMUND. I cannot imagine how you, a woman of the world—

LADY JESSICA. Oh, do not nag me. Mr. Falkner has gone for George. You must stay here and tell George you are dining with me.

LADY ROSAMUND. What about Freddie and Jack? See if they've come back to the boat.

LADY JESSICA (*looking off at window*). Not yet. Here's Mr. Falkner—alone. (*Re-enter Falkner at window.*) Well, where is he?

FALKNER (*to Lady Rosamund*). How d'ye do? (*To Lady Jessica.*) He took a fly that was waiting outside and drove to the post-office. I went there and made inquiries. He stopped, sent off a telegram—

LADY JESSICA. That must have been to Gilbert.

FALKNER. Then he drove off towards Staines. Shall I follow him?

LADY JESSICA. Yes. No. What's the use? He may be anywhere by this.

LADY ROSAMUND. Besides we can't stay to dinner.

LADY JESSICA. You must—you must! I must be able to tell Gilbert that somebody dined with me.

LADY ROSAMUND. Jess, I'll write to George when I get back to-night, and tell him that I dined with you here.

LADY JESSICA. Oh, you good creature! No! Write now, on the hotel paper. Then he'll see you were actually here.

LADY ROSAMUND. Pens, ink, and paper.

FALKNER (*at table up stage*). Here!

LADY JESSICA. Rosy, I've got a better plan than that.

LADY ROSAMUND. What?

LADY JESSICA. Could you be in town to-morrow morning?

LADY ROSAMUND. Yes—why?

LADY JESSICA. Write to George to call on you there. I'll drop in a little before he comes. Then we can see what frame of mind he is in, and explain things accordingly. We can manage him so much better between us.

LADY ROSAMUND. Very well, make haste. Mr. Falkner, will you go into the bar, run up against my husband and his friend, and keep them busy there till I get back into the boat?

FALKNER. Very well.

[*Exit Falkner.*

LADY ROSAMUND. Now, what shall I say?

LADY JESSICA (*dictating*). "My dear George"—

LADY ROSAMUND (*writing*). "My dear George"—Oh, this pen!

[*Throws away the pen, takes up another, tries it.*

LADY JESSICA. We must make it very short and casual, as if you didn't attach much importance to it.

LADY ROSAMUND (*throws away second pen*). That's as bad!

LADY JESSICA (*taking out a gold stylograph, giving it to Lady Rosamund*). Here's my stylograph. Take care of it. It was a birthday present.

LADY ROSAMUND. "Monday evening. My dear George"—

LADY JESSICA (*dictating*). "Jess has told me that you have just been here and that you were surprised at her presence. She fears you may have put a wrong construction on what you saw. She was too flurried at the moment to explain. But if you will call on me to-morrow morning, at Cadogan Gardens at"—what time will suit you?

LADY ROSAMUND. Twelve?

LADY JESSICA. Yes, and I'll be there a few minutes before.

LADY ROSAMUND (*writing*). "Twelve."

LADY JESSICA (*dictating*). "I will give you a full explanation. You will then see how very simple the whole affair was, and how little cause you had for your suspicions of her." That will do, won't it?

LADY ROSAMUND. Yes, I think. "Yours sincerely"—no, "Yours affectionately, Rosy."

LADY JESSICA. "P.S. You had perhaps better say nothing about this to Gilbert until after we have met. When you see how trifling the matter is, you can tell Gilbert or not, as you please."

LADY ROSAMUND (*writing*). "As you please. George Nepean, Esquire." What's his number?

LADY JESSICA. Two-twenty.

LADY ROSAMUND (*writing*). "Two-twenty, Sloane Street."

LADY JESSICA. What about Freddie? Shall we tell him?

LADY ROSAMUND. Oh, no! I wouldn't trust my Freddie in a matter of this kind. He'd put a wrong construction on it—men always do.

[*Puts letter in envelope, seals it.*

LADY JESSICA. But if George asks him?

LADY ROSAMUND. Freddie won't come up to town to-morrow. We'll see how George takes it, and we'll keep Freddie out of it, if we can. (*She has risen, leaving stylograph on writing-table, where it remains. She seals letter.*) Stamp?

LADY JESSICA. I've got one in my purse.

LADY ROSAMUND (*has caught sight of the menu, and taken it up*). Jess, you'll go straight to the station now?

LADY JESSICA. Yes, I'm awfully hungry—

LADY ROSAMUND. Yes, but I don't think this dinner would agree with you.

[*Puts the menu down significantly.*

LADY JESSICA. Very well. But I am hungry.

LADY ROSAMUND. And, Jess, if I get you out of this—you won't take the wrong turning again?

LADY JESSICA. No! no!

LADY ROSAMUND. Honour?

LADY JESSICA. Honour! Really honour! Rosy, you know this is only a silly freak—nothing more.

LADY ROSAMUND. I may be sure of that, Jess? Honour?

LADY JESSICA. Honour! Really, really honour!

LADY ROSAMUND (kisses her). I must be going. To-morrow!

LADY JESSICA. To-morrow at Cadogan Gardens, ten minutes to twelve.

LADY ROSAMUND (at window). Those men are in the boat. My Freddie is looking for me. What shall I tell him?

[Exit at window. Enter Waiter.

LADY JESSICA (giving letter). Please get that posted at once.

WAITER (taking letter). Bien, madame.

[Exit Waiter with letter.

[Re-enter Falkner at window.

LADY JESSICA. They've gone?

FALKNER. Yes. What have you done?

LADY JESSICA. Rosy has written to George to come and see her to-morrow morning at Cadogan Gardens. You had better come too.

FALKNER. At what time?

LADY JESSICA. Say a quarter to one. George will have gone by then and we can tell you if he accepts our explanation.

FALKNER. What is the explanation to be?

LADY JESSICA. That Rosy and I were dining together here; that she hadn't arrived; that you happened to come into the room, and that George saw you and put a wrong construction on it. That will be all right, won't it?

FALKNER. Yes—I daresay. I wish it had been possible to tell the truth.

LADY JESSICA. The truth? What truth? Rosy was actually here, and she might have stayed and dined with me—only she didn't—and—well, if it isn't the truth, it's only a little one.

FALKNER. I think those things are all the same size.

LADY JESSICA. Oh, please don't be disagreeable, just at our last moment too.

FALKNER. Our last moment! Ah, no, no, no!

[Approaching her.

LADY JESSICA. Ah, yes, yes, yes! I promised Rosy I'd go straight to the station—

FALKNER. There's no train till eight-fifty. What harm can there be in your staying to dinner now?

LADY JESSICA. I promised Rosy I wouldn't. I'm fearfully hungry—

[Enter Waiter with letter on salver.

WAITER (advancing with letter on salver to Lady Jessica). Pardon, is this letter for madame?

LADY JESSICA (*takes letter, shows fright*), Yes. Excuse me. Who brought it?

[*Opens letter, takes out telegram.*

WAITER. She is here in the passage.

LADY JESSICA (*opens telegram; shows great alarm. Calls*). Ferris.

FERRIS (*coming to door*). Yes, my lady.

LADY JESSICA. Come in.

WAITER. Bien, madame.

[*Exit Waiter.*

LADY JESSICA. When did this telegram come?

FERRIS. This afternoon, my lady. The moment I got in, Mr. Rawlins said to me, "Mr. Nepean is coming back to-night; I've just had a telegram from him to get his room ready. And I expect this telegram is for her ladyship," he said, and he gave me that telegram, and I said, "I expect it is." "What time will her ladyship be back to-night?" he said. "I don't know," I said. "Where is her ladyship now?" he said. "I don't know," I said.

LADY JESSICA. You didn't know?

FERRIS. No, my lady.

LADY JESSICA. Then why did you come here?

FERRIS (*confused*). The other night when I was bringing your ladyship's shawl to the tent, I happened to hear you mention this hotel. I didn't think anything of it, your ladyship, and I didn't in the least expect to find you here, I assure your ladyship. But I thought your ladyship would like to be apprised that Mr. Nepean was coming home to-night, and so I came, as I may say by pure chance, my lady; just as you might have come yourself, my lady.

LADY JESSICA. Quite right, Ferris. (*To Falkner.*) Mr. Nepean is coming home to-night. He reaches Paddington at ten.

FERRIS. I've got a cab outside, my lady, and I've looked out the trains. If we make haste, we can drive over to Walton and just catch a train there. But we haven't a moment to spare.

LADY JESSICA. Come then.

FERRIS. I hope I've done right, my lady?

LADY JESSICA. Quite right, Ferris. (*To Falkner.*) No. Please don't trouble to come out, I'd rather you didn't. Rosy and I will dine with you some other night. (*Exit Ferris.*) Good-night.

FALKNER. And to-morrow?

LADY JESSICA. To-morrow? (*Grimace.*) Petits rows conjugals, sauce tartare.

[*Exit at door.*

[*Enter Waiter with two little morsels of caviare.*

FALKNER. What's that?

WAITER. Caviare on toast, sir.

FALKNER. Hang the caviare. Bring in the soup.

WAITER. Ah, it is not yet ready—two, three minutes. I am very sorry, but the cook say the sauce Marguerite—

FALKNER. What about it?

WAITER. It will not be made.

FALKNER. Very well.

WAITER. And the salade?

FALKNER. What about the salad?

WAITER. Will m'sieu mix it?

FALKNER. No; mix it yourself.

WAITER. Bien, m'sieu.

FALKNER. Waiter!

WAITER. Sir!

FALKNER (*pointing to the cover laid for Lady Jessica*). Take those confounded things away.

WAITER. Sir!

FALKNER. Take those confounded things away; I'm going to dine alone.

WAITER. Bien, m'sieu.
[*Takes up the things, the second cover, and the one plate of caviare, leaving the other on the table in Falkner's place. Is going off with them.*

FALKNER. Bring in the soup.

WAITER. Bien, m'sieu.
[*Exit with things. Sir Christopher's voice heard outside.*

SIR CHRISTOPHER. Mr. Falkner?

WAITER. Yes, sir. In number ten, sir.

SIR CHRISTOPHER. Has he dined?

WAITER. Not yet, sir. What name, sir?

SIR CHRISTOPHER. Oh, never mind my name. Show me in.

WAITER (*at door, announcing*). The friend of the dinner.
[*Enter Sir Christopher in morning dress.*
[*Exit Waiter.*

SIR CHRISTOPHER (*very cordially*). Ah, dear old boy, here you are. (*Shaking hands cordially.*) All alone?

FALKNER (*very sulky*). Yes.

SIR CHRISTOPHER (*looking at table*). You haven't dined?

FALKNER. No.

SIR CHRISTOPHER. That's all right. I'll join you. What's the matter?

FALKNER. Nothing.

SIR CHRISTOPHER. Nothing?

FALKNER (*very sulky throughout*). No. What should be?

SIR CHRISTOPHER. You look upset.

FALKNER. Not at all.

SIR CHRISTOPHER. That's all right. (*Going up to table very ravenously.*) I say, old chap, dinner won't be long, eh?

FALKNER. No, why?

SIR CHRISTOPHER. I'm famished. I was over at Hounslow; I had no end of work to get through, so I stuck to it. I've had nothing but a biscuit and a glass of sherry since breakfast. I was going up to town for dinner, then I remembered you wrote to me from here; so I thought I'd run over on the chance of finding you. And here you are. (*Cordially.*) Well, how are you?

FALKNER. I'm very well.

SIR CHRISTOPHER. That's all right. And, and—old fellow—about the lady?

FALKNER. What about her?

SIR CHRISTOPHER. You're going to behave like a good true fellow and give her up, eh?

FALKNER. Yes, I suppose.

SIR CHRISTOHER. That's all right. Love 'em, worship 'em, make the most of 'em! Go down on your knees every day and thank God for having sent them into this dreary world for our good and comfort. But, don't break your heart over 'em! Don't ruin your career for 'em! Don't lose a night's rest for 'em! (*Very softly.*) They're not worth it—except one!

FALKNER (*same sulky mood*). You're full of good advice.

SIR CHRISTOPHER. It's the only thing I am full of. I say, old fellow, could you hurry them up with the dinner? (*Falkner goes and rings bell. Casually taking up the menu.*) No, Ned, they're not worth it, bless their hearts. And the man who— (*Suddenly stops, his face illuminated with delighted surprise.*) Ned!

FALKNER. What?

SIR CHRISTOPHER (*pointing to menu*). This isn't the menu for to-night?

FALKNER. Yes.

SIR CHRISTOPHER (*incredulously*). No! Dear old fellow! (*Looking at him with great admiration.*) Dear old fellow! I say, Ned, you do yourself very well when you're all alone.

FALKNER. Why shouldn't I?

SIR CHRISTOPHER. Why shouldn't you? Why shouldn't you?

[*Perusing menu.*

FALKNER. Why shouldn't I? Excuse me a moment.

[*Exit at door. Sir Christopher, left alone, reads over the menu, showing great satisfaction; then goes up to sideboard, takes up the bottles of wine, looks at them, shows great satisfaction, rubs his hands, brings down champagne, places it right of table; brings down hock, places it left of table; brings down claret, looks at brand, hugs it delightedly; sits on table up centre, puts claret down, picks up stylograph pen, reads inscription; comes down, then goes to window, looks off, gives a sigh, puts pen in waistcoat pocket. Enter Waiter.*

WAITER (*putting soup on table*). Mr. Falkner say will you please excuse him? He has gone to London just now, this minute.

SIR CHRISTOPHER. Gone to London!

WAITER. On very important business. He say will you please make yourself at home with the dinner?

SIR CHRISTOPHER (*puzzled*). Gone to London! What on earth—

(*Resolutely and instantly takes seat at head of table.*) Serve up the dinner! Sharp!

WAITER. Caviare on toast?

SIR CHRISTOPHER. Oh, damn the caviare! Open the champagne!

(*Takes the morsel of caviare and throws it down his throat; helps himself to soup, peppers it vigorously; meantime Waiter opens champagne and pours out a glass.*)
The fish! Quick! And the entrées; bring them both up at the same time—bring up the whole bag of tricks!!

[*Sir Christopher throws spoonful after spoonful of soup down his throat. The organ outside strikes up in the middle of the bar at which it left off, a very rowdy street tune.*

CURTAIN

ACT III

SCENE. *Lady Rosamund's drawing-room, Cadogan Gardens; a very elegant modern apartment, furnished in good taste. Door at back. Door right. Large bow-window forming an alcove up stage right. Fireplace left.*

Lady Rosamund discovered in out-door morning dress. Footman showing in Lady Jessica at back.

FOOTMAN (*announces*). Lady Jessica Nepean.

[*Exit Footman.*

LADY ROSAMUND. Well, dear?

LADY JESSICA (*kisses Lady Rosamund very affectionately*). Oh, Rosy—

LADY ROSAMUND. What's the matter?

LADY JESSICA. Directly you had gone, Ferris came in with a telegram from Gilbert, saying he was coming home last night. Of course I flew back to town. When I got there, I found a later telegram saying he hadn't been able to finish his business, and that he would come back to-day.

LADY ROSAMUND (*taking letter from pocket*). He reaches Paddington at twelve.

LADY JESSICA. How do you know?

LADY ROSAMUND (*giving letter*). Read that.

LADY JESSICA (*looking at handwriting*). From George Nepean.

LADY ROSAMUND. Yes. He came here an hour ago to see me, and left that note. I'm afraid George means to be very horrid.

LADY JESSICA (*reading*). "Dear Lady Rosamund, I shall, of course, be quite ready to listen to any explanation you may have to offer. I will come to Cadogan Gardens on my return from Paddington. I am now on my way there to meet Gilbert, who arrives from Devon at twelve. It is only fair to tell you that on leaving Lady Jessica last evening I telegraphed him I had a most serious communication to make to him, and that on his arrival I shall tell him exactly what I saw." George does mean to be horrid.

[*Retaining letter.*

LADY ROSAMUND. I cannot imagine how you—

LADY JESSICA. Oh, do not preach. I tell you it was the sign-post. It is most deceptive.

LADY ROSAMUND. It must be. The next time you come to that sign-post—

LADY JESSICA. I shall know which turning to take! You needn't fear.

LADY ROSAMUND. My Freddie's in a small fever.

LADY JESSICA. What about?

LADY ROSAMUND. My coming up to town this morning.

LADY JESSICA. You're sure he'll stay down there? He won't come up and—interfere?

LADY ROSAMUND. Oh no, poor old dear! I snubbed him thoroughly and left him grizzling in his tent, like Achilles. He'll stay there all day, fuming and trying to screw up his courage to have a tremendous row with me when I get back to dinner this evening. I know my Freddie so well!

(*Freddie saunters in at back, half-timid half-defiant. Looking at him with amused surprise.*)

Hillo, my friend! Hillo!

FREDDIE (*very severe and dignified, takes no notice of her*). How do, Jess?

[*Lady Jessica alternately reads George's letter and looks at Freddie.*

LADY ROSAMUND. What has brought you to town?

FREDDIE. I came up with a purpose.

LADY ROSAMUND. Oh, don't say that. People are always so horrid who do things with a purpose.

FREDDIE. I came up with Mrs. Crespin. She has lost the address of the cook that you gave her last evening. I told her you were in town. She will call here for it.

LADY ROSAMUND (*sweetly*). Very well.

FREDDIE. Do you intend to stay in or go out this morning?

LADY ROSAMUND. That depends. I may stay in—or I may go out. What are you going to do?

FREDDIE. That depends. I may stay in—or—I may go out.

LADY ROSAMUND. Very well, dear, do as you please. I'll take the alternative. (*To Lady Jessica.*) Come and take your things off in my room.

LADY JESSICA (*glancing at Freddie*). But don't you think—

FREDDIE (*with great dignity*). I have come up to town this morning, because for the future I intend to place everything in this house on a new basis, an entirely opposite basis from that on which it now stands.

LADY ROSAMUND. You're going to turn all the furniture upside down! Oh, I wouldn't!

FREDDIE. Hitherto I have been content to be a cipher in this establishment. I will be a cipher no longer.

LADY ROSAMUND. No, I wouldn't. Come along, Jess!

LADY JESSICA. But—

LADY ROSAMUND. We'll talk it over upstairs. Run away to your club, Freddie, and think over what figure you would like to be. I daresay we can arrange it.

[*Exit Lady Rosamund, taking off Lady Jessica, and closing the door rather sharply behind her.*

FREDDIE (*left alone, marches up to the door, calls out in a forcible-feeble scream*). I will not be a cipher! I will not be a cipher! (*Comes to centre of stage, gesticulates, his lips moving, sits down very resolutely, and then says in a tone of solemn conviction*) I will *not* be a cipher!

[*Enter Footman, announcing.*

FOOTMAN. Sir Christopher Deering!

[*Enter Sir Christopher. Exit Footman.*

SIR CHRISTOPHER (*shaking hands*). I've just come on from Lady Jessica's. They told me I should find her here.

FREDDIE. She's upstairs with my wife.

SIR CHRISTOPHER. Can I see her for a few minutes?

FREDDIE. I don't know. Deering, old fellow, we're tiled in, aren't we? If I ask your advice—

SIR CHRISTOPHER. Certainly, Freddie. What is it?

FREDDIE. I've been married for seven years—

SIR CHRISTOPHER. Seven years, is it? It doesn't seem so long.

FREDDIE. Oh, doesn't it? Yes, it does. Rosy and I have never quite hit it off from the first.

SIR CHRISTOPHER. No? How's that?

FREDDIE. I don't know. When I want to do anything, she doesn't. When I want to go anywhere, she won't. When I like anybody, she hates them. And when I hate anybody, she likes them. And—well—there it is in a nutshell.

SIR CHRISTOPHER. Hum! I should humour her a little, Freddie—let her have her own way. Try kindness.

FREDDIE. Kindness? I tell you this, Deering, kindness is a grand mistake. And I made that grand mistake at starting. I began with riding her on the snaffle. I ought to have started on the curb, eh?

SIR CHRISTOPHER. Well, there's something to be said for that method in some cases. Kindness won't do, you say? Why not try firmness?

FREDDIE. I have.

SIR CHRISTOPHER. Well?

FREDDIE. Well, firmness is all very well, but there's one great objection to firmness.

SIR CHRISTOPHER. What's that?

FREDDIE. It leads to such awful rows, and chronic rowing does upset me so. After about two days of it, I feel so seedy and shaky and nervous, I don't know what to do. (*Has a sudden wrathful outburst.*) And she comes up as smiling as ever!

SIR CHRISTOPHER. Poor old fellow!

FREDDIE. I say, Deering, what would you advise me to do?

SIR CHRISTOPHER. Well, it requires some consideration—

FREDDIE (*with deep conviction*). You know, Deering, there must be some way of managing them.

SIR CHRISTOPHER. One would think so. There must be some way of managing them!

FREDDIE (*has another wrathful outburst*). And I used to go and wait outside her window, night after night, for hours! What do you think of that?

SIR CHRISTOPHER. I should say it was time very badly laid out.

FREDDIE (*pursuing his reminiscences*). Yes, and caught a chill on my liver and was laid up for six weeks.

SIR CHRISTOPHER. Poor old fellow!

FREDDIE. I say, Deering, what would you do?

SIR CHRISTOPHER. Well—well—it requires some consideration.

FREDDIE (*walking about*). You know, Deering, I may be an ass—

SIR CHRISTOPHER. Oh!

FREDDIE (*firmly*). Yes. I may be an ass, but I'm not a *silly* ass. I may be a fool, but I'm not a d——d fool! Now there's something going on this morning between Rosamund and Jess. They're hobnobbing and whispering, and when two of 'em get together—

SIR CHRISTOPHER. Oh, my dear fellow, when two women get together, do you think it can ever be worth a man's while to ask what nonsense or mischief they're chattering? By the way, did you say that I could see Lady Jessica?

FREDDIE. She's upstairs with Rosy. I'll send her to you. Deering, if you were married, would you be a cipher in your own house?

SIR CHRISTOPHER. Not if I could help it.

FREDDIE (*very determinedly*). Neither will I.

[*Exit Freddie. Sir Christopher, left alone, takes out the stylograph and looks at it carefully. In a few seconds enter Lady Jessica. As she enters he drops his left hand, which holds the stylograph.*

SIR CHRISTOPHER. How d' ye do?

LADY JESSICA. How d' ye do? You wish to see me?

[*Sir Christopher presents the stylograph; Lady Jessica shows alarm.*

SIR CHRISTOPHER. I see from the inscription that this belongs to you.

LADY JESSICA (*taking stylograph*). Where did you find it?

SIR CHRISTOPHER. In a private sitting-room at the Star and Garter at Shepperford.

LADY JESSICA. I must have left it there some time ago. I could not imagine where I had lost it. Thank you so much.

SIR CHRISTOPHER. Pray don't mention it. (*An awkward pause.*) Good-morning.

LADY JESSICA. Good-morning. (*Sir Christopher has got to door at back.*) Sir Christopher— (*Sir Christopher stops.*) You were at Shepperford—

SIR CHRISTOPHER. Last evening.

LADY JESSICA. Pretty little spot.

SIR CHRISTOPHER. Charming.

LADY JESSICA. And a very good hotel?

SIR CHRISTOPHER. First class. Such splendid cooking!

LADY JESSICA. The cooking's good, is it? — Oh, yes, I dined there once, some time ago.

SIR CHRISTOPHER. I dined there last night.

LADY JESSICA. Did you? At the table d'hôte?

SIR CHRISTOPHER. No, in a private sitting-room. Number ten.

LADY JESSICA. With a friend, I suppose?

SIR CHRISTOPHER. No. All alone.

LADY JESSICA. All alone? In number ten?

SIR CHRISTOPHER. All alone. In number ten.

LADY JESSICA. I suppose you — I suppose —

SIR CHRISTOPHER. Suppose nothing except that I had a remarkably good dinner, that I picked up that stylograph and brought it up to town with me last night. And there is an end of the whole matter, I assure you. Good-morning.

LADY JESSICA. Good-morning. Sir Christopher — you — (*Sir Christopher is again arrested at door*) you — a— I may trust you?

SIR CHRISTOPHER. If I can help you — yes.

LADY JESSICA. Nothing — nothing is known about my being there?

SIR CHRISTOPHER. Your being there?

LADY JESSICA (*after a pause—embarrassed*). I was to have dined in number ten.

SIR CHRISTOPHER. All alone?

LADY JESSICA (*same embarrassed manner.*) No — with Mr. Falkner. I was coming up to town from my cousin's. I started to walk to the station. I must have taken the wrong turning, for instead of finding myself at the station, I found myself at the Star and Garter. I was very hungry and I asked Mr. Falkner to give me a mere mouthful of dinner.

SIR CHRISTOPHER. A mere mouthful.

LADY JESSICA. And then George Nepean caught sight of me, came in, saw Mr. Falkner, and telegraphed my husband that I — Of course, Gilbert will believe the worst, and I — oh, I don't know what to do!

SIR CHRISTOPHER. Can I be of any service?

LADY JESSICA. How would you advise me to — to get out of it?

SIR CHRISTOPHER. Let us go over the various possibilities of the case. There are only two.

LADY JESSICA. What are they?

SIR CHRISTOPHER. Possibility number one — get out of it by telling fibs. Possibility number two — get out of it by telling the truth. Why not possibility number two?

LADY JESSICA. Oh, I couldn't!

SIR CHRISTOPHER. Couldn't what?

LADY JESSICA. Tell my husband that I was going to dine with Mr. Falkner.

SIR CHRISTOPHER. But it was quite by accident?

LADY JESSICA. Oh, quite!

SIR CHRISTOPHER. Eh?

LADY JESSICA. Quite!

SIR CHRISTOPHER. Well —?

LADY JESSICA. But if Gilbert made inquiries —

SIR CHRISTOPHER. Well?

LADY JESSICA. It was such a very good dinner that Mr. Falkner ordered.

SIR CHRISTOPHER. It was! But, if he didn't expect you, why did he order that very excellent dinner?

LADY JESSICA. I'm sure you ought to be the last person to ask that, for it seems you ate it.

SIR CHRISTOPHER. I did.

LADY JESSICA. It's an ill wind that blows nobody good!

SIR CHRISTOPHER. I'm not grumbling at the wind, or at the dinner, but if I'm to help you out of this, you had better tell me all the truth. Especially as I'm not your husband. Now frankly, is this a mere indiscretion or —

LADY JESSICA. A mere indiscretion, nothing more. Honour—really, really honour.

SIR CHRISTOPHER. A mere indiscretion that will never be repeated.

LADY JESSICA. A mere indiscretion that will never be repeated. You believe me.

SIR CHRISTOPHER (*looking at her*). Yes, I believe you, and I'll help you.

LADY JESSICA. Thank you! Thank you!

SIR CHRISTOPHER. Now, did Falkner expect you?

LADY JESSICA. He ought not.

SIR CHRISTOPHER. He ought not. But he did.

LADY JESSICA. I told him I shouldn't come.

SIR CHRISTOPHER. Which was exactly the same as telling him you would.

LADY JESSICA. Have you seen Mr. Falkner?

SIR CHRISTOPHER. Only for a minute just before dinner. He came up to town.

LADY JESSICA. Without any dinner?

SIR CHRISTOPHER. Without any dinner. To come back to these two possibilities.

LADY JESSICA. Yes, Rosy and I have decided on — on —

SIR CHRISTOPHER. On possibility number one, tell a fib. I put that possibility first out of natural deference and chivalry towards ladies. The only objection I have to telling fibs is that you get found out.

LADY JESSICA. Oh, not always.

SIR CHRISTOPHER. Eh!

LADY JESSICA. I mean, if you arrange things, not perhaps exactly as they were, but as they ought to have been.

SIR CHRISTOPHER. I see. In that way a lie becomes a sort of idealized and essential truth —

LADY JESSICA. Yes. Yes —

SIR CHRISTOPHER. I'm not a good hand at — idealizing.

LADY JESSICA. Ah, but then you're a man! No, I can't tell the truth. Gilbert would never believe me. Would you — after that dinner?

SIR CHRISTOPHER. The dinner would be some tax on my digestion.

[*Lady Rosamund enters, followed by Freddie with a self-important and self-assertive air.*

LADY ROSAMUND. Good-morning, Sir Christopher.

SIR CHRISTOPHER (*shaking hands*). Good-morning, Lady Rosamund.

LADY ROSAMUND. Jess, I've had to tell Freddie.

LADY JESSICA. And I've had to tell Sir Christopher. He was at Shepperford last evening, and he has promised to help us.

FREDDIE. I must say, Jess, that I think you have behaved — well — in a — confounded silly way.

LADY JESSICA. That is perfectly understood.

FREDDIE (*solemnly*). When a woman once forgets what is due —

LADY JESSICA. Oh, don't moralise! Rosy, Sir Christopher, do ask him not to improve the occasion.

SIR CHRISTOPHER. The question is, Freddie, whether you will help us in getting Lady Jessica out of this little difficulty.

FREDDIE. Well, I suppose I must join in.

LADY JESSICA. Now, Rosy, do you fully understand —

SIR CHRISTOPHER. I don't think I do. What is the exact shape which possibility number one has taken — or is going to take?

LADY ROSAMUND. Jess and I had arranged to have a little *tête-à-tête* dinner at Shepperford. Jess got there first. I hadn't arrived. George saw Jess at the window, and came in. At that moment Mr. Falkner happened to come into the room, and Jess, knowing that appearances were against her, was confused, and couldn't on the spur of the moment give the right explanation.

SIR CHRISTOPHER. I suppose the waiter will confirm that right explanation?

LADY JESSICA. The waiter? I hadn't thought of that. Waiters will confirm anything, won't they? Couldn't you settle with the waiter?

SIR CHRISTOPHER. Well, I —

LADY JESSICA. You did have the dinner, you know!

SIR CHRISTOPHER. Very well. I'll settle with the waiter.

[*Enter Footman.*

FOOTMAN (*announcing*). Mrs. Crespin!

[*Enter Mrs. Crespin. Exit Footman.*

MRS. CRESPIN (*shows a little surprise at seeing them all, then goes very affectionately to Lady Rosamund*). Good-morning, dear. Good-morning, Sir Christopher.

(*Sir Christopher bows. To Freddie.*) I've seen you. (*Goes to Lady Jessica.*) Good-morning, dearest.

[*Kisses her.*

LADY JESSICA. Good-morning, dearest.

[*Kisses her.*

MRS. CRESPIN (*to Lady Jessica; looking anxiously at her*). You're looking pale and worried.

LADY JESSICA. Me? Oh, no, I'm sure I don't, do I?

SIR CHRISTOPHER. Not to masculine eyes.

MRS. CRESPIN (*to Lady Rosamund*). Dear, I've lost the address of that cook. Would you mind writing it out again?

LADY ROSAMUND. Certainly.

[*Goes to writing-table and writes.*

MRS. CRESPIN (*to Lady Jessica*). What's the matter with our dear friend George Nepean?

LADY JESSICA. Matter?

MRS. CRESPIN. I ran against him in a post-office on my way from Paddington just now.

LADY JESSICA. Yes?

MRS. CRESPIN. Your husband is quite well, I hope?

LADY JESSICA. My husband? Oh, quite! He always is quite well. Why?

MRS. CRESPIN. George Nepean seemed so strange.

LADY JESSICA. How?

MRS. CRESPIN. He said he was going to Paddington to meet your husband — and he made so much of it.

LADY JESSICA. Ah! You see, my husband is a big man, so naturally George would make much of it.

MRS. CRESPIN. I always used to go to the station to meet my husband — when I had one.

LADY JESSICA (*a little triumphantly*). Ah, Rosy and I know better than to kill our husbands with too much kindness.

MRS. CRESPIN. Still, I think husbands need a little pampering —

SIR CHRISTOPHER. Not at all. The brutes are so easily spoilt. A little overdose of sweetness, a little extra attention from a wife to her husband, and life is never the same again!

FREDDIE (*who has been waiting eagerly to get a word in*). I suppose you didn't mention anything to George Nepean about our dining with you last evening?

MRS. CRESPIN (*alert*). Did I? Let me see! Yes! Yes! I did mention that you were over. Why?

[*They all look at each other.*

FREDDIE. Oh, nothing, nothing!

MRS. CRESPIN. I'm so sorry. Does it matter much?

LADY JESSICA. Not in the least.

LADY ROSAMUND. Oh, not in the least.

FREDDIE. Not in the least.

SIR CHRISTOPHER. Not at all.

MRS. CRESPIN. I'm afraid I made a mistake.

LADY ROSAMUND. How?

MRS. CRESPIN. Your husband—

LADY ROSAMUND. Oh, my dear, what does it matter what my Freddie says or does or thinks, eh, Freddie? (*Frowning angrily aside at Freddie.*) There's the address of the cook.

[*Giving the paper on which she has been writing.*

MRS. CRESPIN. Thank you so much. Good-morning, dearest.

[*Kiss.*

LADY ROSAMUND. Good-morning, dearest.

[*Kiss.*

MRS. CRESPIN (*going to Lady Jessica*). Good-bye dearest.

[*Kiss.*

LADY JESSICA. Good-bye, dearest.

[*Kiss.*

MRS. CRESPIN (*very sweetly, shaking hands*). Good-bye, Sir Christopher.

SIR CHRISTOPHER. Good-bye.

MRS. CRESPIN. You are quite sure that I didn't make a mistake in telling George Nepean that Lady Rosy and Mr. Tatton dined with me last evening?

SIR CHRISTOPHER. It was the truth, wasn't it?

MRS. CRESPIN. Of course it was.

SIR CHRISTOPHER. One never makes a mistake in speaking the truth.

MRS. CRESPIN. Really? That's a very sweeping assertion to make.

SIR CHRISTOPHER. I base it on my constant experience — and practice.

MRS. CRESPIN. You find it always answers to tell the truth?

SIR CHRISTOPHER. Invariably.

MRS. CRESPIN. I hope it will in this case. Good-bye! Good-bye! Good-bye!

[*Exit Mrs. Crespin. They all stand looking at each other, nonplussed, Sir Christopher slightly touching his head, with perplexed gesture.*

SIR CHRISTOPHER. Our fib won't do.

LADY ROSAMUND. Freddie, you incomparable nincompoop!

FREDDIE. I like that! If I hadn't asked her, what would have happened? George Nepean would have come in, you'd have plumped down on him with your lie, and what then? Don't you think it's jolly lucky I said what I did?

SIR CHRISTOPHER. It's lucky in this instance. But if I am to embark any further in these imaginative enterprises, I must ask you, Freddie, to keep a silent tongue.

FREDDIE. What for?

SIR CHRISTOPHER. Well, old fellow, it may be an unpalatable truth to you, but you'll never make a good liar.

FREDDIE. Very likely not. But if this sort of thing is going on in my house, I think I ought to.

LADY ROSAMUND. Oh, do subside, Freddie, do subside!

LADY JESSICA. Yes, George—and perhaps Gilbert—will be here directly. Oh, will somebody tell me what to do?

SIR CHRISTOPHER. We have tried possibility number one. It has signally failed. Why not possibility number two?

LADY JESSICA. Tell the truth? My husband would never believe it! Besides, he threatened that he wouldn't spare me. And he won't. No! No! No! Somebody dined with me last night, or was going to dine with me, and that somebody was a woman.

[*Enter Footman.*

FOOTMAN (*announcing*). Mrs. Coke!

[*Enter Dolly.*

DOLLY (*going to Lady Rosamund*). Ah, my dear Lady Rosamund —

[*Exit Footman.*

LADY JESSICA (*goes affectionately and a little hysterically to her*). Dolly! How good of you!

[*Kissing her.*

DOLLY. What's the matter?

LADY JESSICA. Dolly, you dined with me, or were going to dine with me at the Star and Garter at Shepperford last evening. Don't say you can't, and didn't, for you must and did!

DOLLY. Of course I'll say anything that's — necessary.

LADY JESSICA. Oh, you treasure!

DOLLY. But I don't understand —

[*Lady Jessica takes her aside and whispers eagerly.*

SIR CHRISTOPHER (*glancing at Lady Jessica and Dolly*). Possibility number one—with variations. I'm not required any further.

LADY ROSAMUND. Oh, Sir Christopher, you won't desert us?

SIR CHRISTOPHER. Certainly not, if I can be of any use. But if this is to be a going concern, don't you think the fewer partners the better?

LADY ROSAMUND. Oh, don't go. You can help us so much.

SIR CHRISTOPHER. How?

LADY ROSAMUND. Your mere presence will be an immense moral support to us.

SIR CHRISTOPHER (*uncomfortable*). Thank you! Thank you!

LADY ROSAMUND. You can come to our assistance whenever we are in the lurch, corroborate us whenever we need corroboration — and —

SIR CHRISTOPHER. Bolster up generally.

LADY ROSAMUND. Yes. Besides, everybody knows you are such an honourable man. I feel they won't suspect you.

SIR CHRISTOPHER (*uncomfortable*). Thank you! Thank you!

DOLLY. (*to Lady Jessica*). Very well, dear, I quite understand. After George went away, you were so upset at his suspicions that you came back to town without any dinner. Did I stay and have the dinner?

SIR CHRISTOPHER. No, no. I wouldn't go so far as that.

DOLLY. But what did I do? I must have dined somewhere, didn't I? Not that I mind if I didn't dine anywhere. But won't it seem funny if I didn't dine somewhere?

LADY JESSICA. I suppose it will.

DOLLY. Very well then, where did I dine? Do tell me. I know I shall get into an awful muddle if I don't know. Where did I dine?

[*Enter Footman.*

FOOTMAN (*announcing*). Mr. George Nepean.

[*Enter George Nepean. Exit Footman.*

GEORGE (*enters very frigidly, bows very coldly. Very stiffly*). Good-morning, Lady Rosamund! (*To the others, bowing.*) Good-morning.

LADY ROSAMUND (*very cordially*). My dear George, don't take that tragic tone. (*Insists on shaking hands.*) Any one would suppose there was something dreadful the matter. I've just explained to Sir Christopher your mistake of last night.

GEORGE. My mistake?

LADY JESSICA. You shouldn't have left so hurriedly, George. I sent Mr. Falkner after you to explain. Dolly, tell him.

DOLLY. Jess and I had arranged to have a little dinner all by our two selves —

GEORGE. Indeed!

DOLLY. There's nothing strange in that, Sir Christopher?

SIR CHRISTOPHER. Not at all. I am sure any person of either sex would only be too delighted to dine *tête-à-tête* with you.

DOLLY. And when I got there, I found poor Jess in an awful state. She said you had come into the room and had made the morst horrid accusations against her, poor thing!

GEORGE. I made no accusation.

LADY JESSICA. What did you mean by saying that Gilbert must know?

GEORGE. Merely that I should tell him what I saw.

LADY JESSICA. And you have told him?

GEORGE. Yes, on his arrival an hour ago.

LADY JESSICA. Where is he?

GEORGE. Round at Sloane Street waiting till I have heard Lady Rosamund's explanation.

LADY ROSAMUND. Well, you have heard it. Or, rather, it's Dolly explanation. The whole thing is so ridiculously simple. I think you ought to beg Jess's pardon.

GEORGE. I will when I am sure that I have wronged her.

FREDDIE. Oh, come, I say, George! you don't refuse to take a lady's word —

LADY ROSAMUND. Freddie, subside!

DOLLY (*to George*). Poor Jess was so much upset by what you said that she couldn't eat any dinner, she nearly had hysterics, and when she got a little better, she came straight up to town, poor thing!

GEORGE. What was Mr. Falkner doing there?

LADY JESSICA. IIc was staying in the hotel and happened to came into the room at that moment.

[*A little pause.*

LADY ROSAMUND. Is there anything else you would like to ask?

GEORGE. No.

LADY ROSAMUND. And you're quite satisfied?

GEORGE. The question is not whether I'm satisfied, but whether Gilbert will be. I'll go and fetch him. Will you excuse me?

SIR CHRISTOPHER (*stops him*). Nepean, I'm sure you don't wish to embitter your brother and Lady Jessica's whole future life by sowing jealousy and suspicion between them. Come, now, like a good fellow, you'll smooth things over as much as you can.

GEORGE. I shall not influence my brother one way or the other. He must judge for himself.

[*Exit. Sir Christopher shrugs his shoulders.*

DOLLY (*to Lady Jessica*). I got through very well, didn't I?

LADY JESSICA. Yes, dear. Thank you so much. But George didn't seem to believe it, eh?

FREDDIE. It's so jolly thin. A couple of women dining together! What should a couple of women want to dine together for? Oh, it's too thin, you know!

LADY JESSICA. And you don't think Gilbert will believe it? He must! he must! Oh, I begin to wish that we had tried —

SIR CHRISTOPHER. Possibility number two. I'm afraid it's too late now.

LADY JESSICA. Oh, what shall I do? Do you think Gilbert will believe Dolly?

LADY ROSAMUND. He must if Dolly only sticks to it.

DOLLY. Oh, I'll stick to it. Only I should like to know where I dined. Where did I dine?

[*Enter Footman.*

FOOTMAN (*to Dolly*). If you please, ma'am, Mr. Coke is waiting for you below.

DOLLY (*with a scream*). Oh, dear! Oh, dear! I'd quite forgotten!

LADY ROSAMUND. What?

DOLLY. I arranged to meet Archie here and take him on to the dentist's. (*To Footman.*) Tell Mr. Coke I'll come in a moment.

(*Exit Footman.*)

(*To Lady Jessica.*) Dear, I must go —

LADY JESSICA. You can't! You must stay now and tell Gilbert — mustn't she, Sir Christopher?

SIR CHRISTOPHER. I'm afraid you must, Mrs. Coke. You are our sheet-anchor.

DOLLY. But what can I tell Archie?

LADY ROSAMUND. Can't you put him off, send him away?

DOLLY. What excuse can I make? He is so fidgety and inquisitive. He'll insist on knowing everything. No, I must go.

LADY JESSICA (*desperate*). You can't! You can't! You must stay! Couldn't we tell Archie and ask him to help us?

SIR CHRISTOPHER (*impatiently to Lady Rosamund*). Oh!

DOLLY. Oh, I wouldn't tell Archie for the world. He wouldn't understand.

[*Enter Archibald, in very correct frock-coat, very prim and starchy.*

COKE. Good-morning, Rosy! Freddie! Sir Christopher! (*Nodding all round.*) Now, Dolly, are you ready?

DOLLY. I — I —

LADY JESSICA. She can't go, Archie.

COKE. Can't go?

LADY JESSICA. She — she isn't well.

COKE. Not well? (*Alarmed.*) Not influenza again?

DOLLY. No, not influenza. But I'd rather not go.

COKE. Oh, nonsense! I cannot take the gas alone. (*To Sir Christopher.*) I've a terrible dread of the gas. I'm sure they'll give me too much some day. Now, Dolly.

LADY ROSAMUND (*to Sir Christopher*). Gilbert will be here directly. Can't you get him away?

SIR CHRISTOPHER. Coke, your wife isn't just the thing, as you can see. I'll go to the dentist's with you. Come along! I'll see they give you the right dose.

COKE (*resisting*). No. My wife is the proper person to go to the dentist with me, and see that the gas is rightly administered. Come, Dolly!

LADY JESSICA (*comes desperately to Coke*). Dolly can't go!

COKE. Why not?

LADY JESSICA. She must stay here and tell Gilbert that she dined with me last evening.

COKE. Tell Gilbert that she dined with you last evening! What for?

SIR CHRISTOPHER (*aside to Lady Rosamund*). We're taking too many partners into this concern.

COKE. She dined with me. Why should she tell Gilbert she dined with you?

LADY JESSICA. If you must know, I was coming to the station from Barbara's, and I must have taken the wrong turning —

COKE (*very suspicious*). The wrong turning —

LADY JESSICA. Yes, for instead of finding myself at the station, I found myself at the Star and Garter.

COKE. The Star and Garter!

LADY JESSICA. And as I was frightfully hungry, I asked Mr. Falkner to give me a little dinner.

COKE. A little dinner.

LADY JESSICA. George Nepean happened to come in, and seeing the dinner things laid, actually suspected me of dining with Mr. Falkner! And he has told Gilbert, and don't you see — if Dolly will only say that it was she who was dining with me — don't you see?

COKE. No, I don't. I cannot lend myself to anything of the sort. And I expressly forbid Dolly to say that she dined with you.

LADY JESSICA. But she has said so. She has just told George Nepean.

COKE. Told George Nepean!

DOLLY. I couldn't leave poor Jess in a scrape. And now I have said so, I must stick to it, musn't I? You wouldn't have me tell another one now?

COKE. Well, I'm surprised! Really, I consider it quite disgraceful.

FREDDIE. Look here, Coke, we can't let Gilbert think that Jess was dining with Falkner, can we? He'd only make a howling scandal, and drag us all into it. We've got to say something. I know it's jolly thin, but can you think of a better one?

COKE. No, and I decline to have anything to do with this! I should have thought my character was too well known for me to be asked to a — a — It is too disgraceful! I will not lend my countenance to anything of the kind!

LADY ROSAMUND. Very well then, will you please take yourself off and leave us to manage the affair ourselves?

COKE. No, I will not forfeit my self-respect, I will not permit my wife to forfeit her self-respect by taking part in these proceedings. Really, it is — it is — it is too disgraceful.

[*Lady Jessica suddenly bursts into tears, sobs violently.*

SIR CHRISTOPHER (*comes up to him, very calm, touches him on the shoulder*). Coke, I assure you that theoretically I have as great an objection to lying as you or any man living. But Lady Jessica has acted a little foolishly. No more. Of that I am sure. If you consent to hold your tongue, I think Gilbert Nepean will accept your wife's explanation and the affair will blow over. If, however, you insist on the truth coming out, what will happen? You will very likely bring about a rupture between them, you may possibly place Lady Jessica in a position where she will have no alternative but to take a fatal plunge, and you will drag yourself and your wife into a very unpleasant family scandal. That's the situation.

COKE. But it places me in a very awkward position. No, really, I cannot consent — I'm an honourable man.

SIR CHRISTOPHER. So are we all, all honourable men. The curious thing is that ever since the days of the Garden of Eden, women have had a knack of impaling us honourable men on dilemmas of this kind, where the only alternative is to be false to the truth or false to them. In this instance I think we may very well keep our mouths shut without suffering any violent pangs of conscience about the matter. Come now!

COKE (*overwhelmed*). Well, understand me — if I consent to keep my mouth shut, I must not be supposed to countenance what is going on. That is quite understood?

SIR CHRISTOPHER. Oh, quite! Quite! We'll consider you as strictly neutral.

COKE (*rising up, violently*). No! On second thoughts, I really cannot. I cannot!

LADY ROSAMUND. Very well! Then will you go away and leave us to manage it as we can?

COKE. And I had arranged to take the gas so comfortably this morning. It's most unfair to place me in a position of this kind. I must protest — I really —

[*Enter Footman.*

FOOTMAN (*announcing*). Mr. Gilbert Nepean. Mr. George Nepean.

COKE. Oh!

[*Enter Gilbert and George Nepean. Exit Footman.*

LADY ROSAMUND (*advances very cordially to Gilbert, who does not respond*). Good-morning, Gilbert.

GILBERT. Good-morning. Good-morning, Coke.

COKE (*very uncomfortable*). Good-morning.

GILBERT (*nodding*). Freddie! Deering! (*Looks at Lady Jessica, who looks at him. They do not speak. Pause, looking round.*) I thought I was coming here for a private explanation.

[*Sir Christopher starts to leave the room. Lady Rosamund catches him by his coat-tails and brings him back.*

LADY ROSAMUND. No, Sir Christopher. If Gilbert is determined to carry this any further, we shall need the unbiased testimony of an impartial friend, so that everybody may know exactly what did occur. Please stay.

SIR CHRISTOPHER (*puts down hat. To himself*). Whew!

LADY ROSAMUND. Gilbert, don't be foolish. Everybody here knows all about the stupid affair of last evening.

GILBERT. Everybody here knows? Well, I don't. I shall be glad to be informed.

[*Looks round.*

[*Coke shows symptoms of great discomfort.*

SIR CHRISTOPHER. Nepean, I'm sure you don't wish to make any more than is necessary of Lady Jessica's trifling indiscretion —

GILBERT. I wish to make no more of it than the truth, and I'll take care that nobody makes less of it. Now — (*to Lady Jessica, very furiously*) — you were dining with this fellow Falkner last evening?

LADY JESSICA. No.

GILBERT. No? Then whom did you dine with?

LADY JESSICA. If you speak like that, I shan't answer you.

GILBERT. Will you tell me what I ask?

LADY JESSICA. No!

GILBERT. No, you won't? Perhaps, as you all know, somebody else will oblige me. Coke —

COKE (*most uncomfortably*). Really, I — I don't know all the particulars, and I would prefer not to be mixed up in your private affairs.

GILBERT. Deering — you?

SIR CHRISTOPHER. My dear fellow, I only know what I've heard, and hearsay evidence is proverbially untrustworthy. Now, if I may offer you a little advice, if I were you, I should gently take Lady Jessica by the hand, I should gently lead her home, I should gently use all those endearing little arts of persuasion and entreaty which a husband may legitimately use to his wife, and I should gently beguile her into telling me the whole truth, I should believe everything she told me, I shouldn't listen to what anybody else said, and I should never mention the matter again. Now, do as I tell you, and you'll be a happy man to-morrow, and for the rest of your life.

[*Pause.*

GILBERT (*looks at Lady Jessica*). No. (*Sir Christopher shrugs his shoulders.*) I came here for an explanation, and I won't go till I've got it.

LADY ROSAMUND. My dear Gilbert, we're patiently waiting to give you an explanation, if you'll only listen to it. Dolly, do tell him how it all happened, and let him see what a donkey he is making of himself.

DOLLY. Yes, Gilbert, I wish you wouldn't get in these awful tempers. You frighten us so that in a very little while we shan't know whether we're speaking the truth or whether we're not.

GILBERT. Go on!

DOLLY. Jess and I had arranged to have a little *tête-à-tête* dinner at Shepperford and talk over old times, all by our two selves (*Coke gets very uncomfortable*) — hadn't we, Jess? Rosy, you heard us arranging it all?

LADY ROSAMUND. Yes, on the last night you were at our place.

DOLLY. Yes. Well, Jess got there first, and then Mr. Falkner happened to come into the room, and then George happened to come in and wouldn't wait to listen to Jess's explanation, would he, Jess? Well, when I got there, I found Jess in strong hysterics, poor old dear! I couldn't get her round for ever so long. And as soon as she was better she came straight up to town. And that's all.

[*Pause.*

GILBERT. And what did you do?

DOLLY (*very nervous*). I came up to town too.

GILBERT. Without any dinner?

DOLLY. No — I —

GILBERT. Where did you dine?

DOLLY. I didn't really dine anywhere — not to say dine. I had some cold chicken and a little tongue when I got home — (*pause*) — and a tomato salad.

COKE (*very much shocked at Dolly*). Oh, of all the —
[*Sir Christopher nudges him to be quiet.*

GILBERT. Coke, what do you know of this?

COKE. Well — I know what Dolly has just told you.

GILBERT. You allow your wife to dine out alone?

COKE. Yes — yes — on certain occasions.

GILBERT. And you knew of this arrangement?

COKE. Yes—at least, no—not before she told me of it. But after she told me, I did know.

GEORGE. But Jessica said that she expected a small party.

DOLLY. I was the small party.

GILBERT (*to Coke*). What time did Dolly get home last evening?

COKE. Eh? Well, about —

DOLLY. A little before nine.

GEORGE. Impossible! I was at Shepperford after half-past seven. If Lady Jessica had hysterics, and you stayed with her, you could scarcely have reached Kensington before nine.

DOLLY. Well, perhaps it was ten. Yes, it was ten.

GILBERT. Coke, were you at home last evening when your wife got back?

COKE. I? No — yes, yes — no — not precisely.

GILBERT (*growing indignant*). Surely you must know whether you were at home or not when your wife returned?

COKE. No, I don't. And I very much object to being cross-questioned in this manner. I've told you all I know, and — I — I withdraw from the whole business. Now, Dolly, are you ready?

GILBERT. No, stop! I want to get at the bottom of this and I will. (*Coming furiously to Lady Jessica.*) Once more, will you give me your version of this cock-and-bull story?
[*Enter Footman.*

FOOTMAN (*announcing*). Mr. Falkner!

GILBERT. Ah!

SIR CHRISTOPHER. Nepean! Nepean! Control yourself!
[*Enter Falkner. Exit Footman.*

GILBERT. Let me be, Deering. (*Going to Falkner.*) You were at Shepperford last evening. My wife was there with you?

FALKNER. I was at Shepperford last evening. Lady Jessica was there. She was dining with Lady Rosamund—

LADY ROSAMUND. No! No!

GILBERT. Lady Jessica was dining with Lady Rosamund?

FALKNER. I understood her to say so, did I not, Lady Rosamund?

LADY ROSAMUND. No! No! It was Mrs. Coke who was dining with Lady Jessica.

FALKNER. Then I misunderstood you. Does it matter?

GILBERT. Yes. I want to know what the devil you were doing there?

SIR CHRISTOPHER. Nepean! Nepean!

GILBERT. Do you hear? What the devil were you doing there? Will you tell me, or —

[*Tries to get at Falkner. Sir Christopher holds him back.*

LADY JESSICA (*rises very quietly*). Mr. Falkner, tell my husband the truth.

FALKNER. But, Lady Jessica —

LADY JESSICA. Yes, if you please — the truth, the whole truth, and nothing but the truth. Tell him all. I wish it.

GILBERT. You hear what she says. Now then, the truth — and be damned to you!

FALKNER (*looks around, then after a pause, with great triumph*). I love Lady Jessica with all my heart and soul! I asked her to come to me at Shepperford last evening. She came. Your brother saw us and left us. The next moment Lady Rosamond came, and she had scarcely gone when the maid came with your telegram and took Lady Jessica back to town. If you think there was anything more on your wife's side than a passing folly and amusement at my expense, you will wrong her. If you think there is anything less on my side than the deepest, deepest, deepest love and worship, you will wrong me. Understand this: she is guiltless. Be sure of that. And now you've got the truth, and be damned to you. (*Goes to door at back — turns.*) If you want me, you know where to find me. (*To Lady Jessica.*) Lady Jessica, I am at your service — always!

[*Exit Falkner at back. They all look at each other.*

SIR CHRISTOPHER (*very softly to himself*). Possibility number two — with a vengeance!

CURTAIN

ACT IV

SCENE. *Drawing-room in Sir Christopher's flat in Victoria Street. Left, at back, a large recess, taking up half the stage. The right half is taken up by an inner room furnished as library and smoking room. Curtains dividing library from drawing-room. Door up stage, left. A table down stage, right. The room is in great confusion, with portmanteau open, clothes, etc., scattered over the floor; articles which an officer going to Central Africa might want are lying about. Time: night, about half-past nine o'clock.*

Sir Christopher and Taplin are busy packing.
Ring at door.

SIR CHRISTOPHER. See who it is, Taplin; and come back and finish packing the moment I am disengaged.

[*Exit Taplin. He re-enters in a few moments, showing in Beatrice in evening dress. Sir Christopher goes to her, and shakes hands cordially. Exit Taplin.*

BEATRICE. I was out dining when you called. But I got your message and I came on at once.

SIR CHRISTOPHER. I couldn't wait. I had to come back and pack. (*Going on with his packing.*) I haven't one half-moment to spare.

BEATRICE. When do you start?

SIR CHRISTOPHER. To-morrow morning. It's very urgent. I've been at the War Office all the afternoon. You'll excuse my going on with this. I've three most important duties to fulfil to-night.

BEATRICE. What are they?

SIR CHRISTOPHER (*packing*). I've got to pack. I've got to persuade Ned to come out there with me — if I can. And I've got (*looking straight at her*) to make you promise to be my wife when I come home again.

BEATRICE. Oh, Kit, you know what I've told you so often!

SIR CHRISTOPHER (*packing always*). Yes, and you're telling it me again, and wasting my time when every moment is gold. Ah, dear, forgive me; you know I think you're worth the wooing. And you know I'm the man to woo you. And you know I'm ready to spend three, five, seven, fourteen, or twenty-one years in winning you. But if you'd only say "Yes" this minute, and let me pack and see Ned, you'd save me such a lot of trouble. And I'll do all the love-making when I get back.

BEATRICE. Where is Ned?

SIR CHRISTOPHER. Playing the fool for Lady Jessica. There never was but one woman in this world that was worth playing the fool for, and I'm playing the fool for her. I've sent for Ned to come here. That's a digression. Come back to brass-tacks. You'll be my wife when I come home?

BEATRICE. Let me think it over, Kit.

SIR CHRISTOPHER. No. You've had plenty of time for that. I can't allow you to think it over any longer.

BEATRICE. But it means so much to me. Let me write to you out there?

SIR CHRISTOPHER (*very determinedly*). No. (*Leaves his packing, takes out his watch.*) It's a little too bad of you when I'm so pressed. Now, I can only give you five minutes, and it must absolutely be fixed up in that time. (*With great tenderness and passion.*) Come, my dear, dear chum, what makes you hesitate to give yourself to me? You want me to come well out of this, don't you?

BEATRICE. You know I do!

SIR CHRISTOPHER. Then you don't love your country if you won't have me. Once give me your promise, and it will give me the pluck of fifty men! Don't you know that if I'm sure of you I shall carry everything before me?

BEATRICE. Will you? Will you? But if you were to die —

SIR CHRISTOPHER. I won't die if you're waiting to be my wife when I come home. And you will? You will? I won't hear anything but "Yes." You shan't move one inch till you've said "Yes." Now! say it! Say "Yes!" Say "Yes" — do you hear?

BEATRICE (*throwing herself into his arms*). Yes! Yes! Yes! Take me! Take me!

SIR CHRISTOPHER (*kissing her very reverently*). My wife when I come home again.

[*A pause.*

BEATRICE. You know, Kit, I can love very deeply.

SIR CHRISTOPHER. And so you shall, when I come home again. And so will I when I come home again. (*Looking at his watch.*) A minute and a quarter! I must get on with my packing.

BEATRICE. Kit, there will be some nursing and other woman's work out there?

SIR CHRISTOPHER. Yes, I suppose —

BEATRICE. I'll come with you.

SIR CHRISTOPHER. Very well. How long will it take you to pack?

BEATRICE. Half an hour.

SIR CHRISTOPHER. All right! I must wait here for Ned. Come back and have some supper by-and-bye.

BEATRICE. Yes — in half an hour.

SIR CHRISTOPHER. We might be married at Cairo — on our way out?

BEATRICE. Just as you please.

SIR CHRISTOPHER. Or before we start to-morrow morning.

BEATRICE. Will there be time?

SIR CHRISTOPHER. Oh, I'll make time.

[*Enter Taplin.*

TAPLIN. Mr. Gilbert Nepean is below, Sir Christopher.

SIR CRISTOPHER (*glancing at his packing*). Show him up, Taplin.

(*Exit Taplin.*)

(*Holding Beatrice's hand*). To-morrow morning, then?

BEATRICE. Yes, I've given you some trouble to win me, Kit?

SIR CHRISTOPHER. No more than you're worth.

BEATRICE. I'll give you none now you have won me.

[*Enter Taplin.*

TAPLIN (*announcing*). Mr. Gilbert Nepean.

[*Enter Gilbert Nepean. Exit Taplin.*

BEATRICE. How d'ye do?

GILBERT. How d'ye do?

[*Shaking hands.*

BEATRICE. And good-bye. (*To Sir Christopher.*) No, I won't have you come down all those stairs, indeed I won't. Au revoir.

[*Exit Beatrice.*

GILBERT. Excuse my coming at this hour.

SIR CHRISTOPHER. I'm rather pressed. What can I do for you?

GILBERT. I have been down to Shepperford this afternoon. It seems you dined there last evening.

SIR CHRISTOPHER. I did.

GILBERT. I want to get all the evidence.

SIR CHRISTOPHER. What for?

GILBERT. To guide me in my future action. Deering, I trust you. Can I take that fellow's words that my wife is guiltless?

SIR CHRISTOPHER. I'm sure you can.

GILBERT. How do you know?

SIR CHRISTOPHER. Because he'd give his head to tell you that she is not.

GILBERT. Why?

SIR CHRISTOPHER. It would give him the chance he is waiting for—to take her off your hands.

GILBERT. Take her off my hands—he's waiting for that?

SIR CHRISTOPHER. Don't you see he is? And don't you see that you're doing your best to make him successful?

GILBERT. How?

SIR CHRISTOPHER. Don't think, when you've married a woman, that you can sit down and neglect her. You can't. You've married one of the most charming women in London, and when a man has married a charming woman, if he doesn't continue to make love to her, some other man will. Such are the sad ways of humankind! How have you treated Lady Jessica?

GILBERT. But do you suppose I will allow my wife to go out dining with other men?

SIR CHRISTOPHER. The best way to avoid that is to take her out to dinner yourself—and to give her a good one. Have you dined to-night?

GILBERT. Dined? No! I can't dine till I know what to believe.

SIR CHRISTOPHER. The question is, what do you want to believe? If you want to believe her innocent, take the facts as they stand. If you want to believe her guilty, continue to treat her as you are doing, and you'll very soon have plenty of proof. And let me tell you, nobody will pity you. Do you want to believe her innocent?

GILBERT. Of course I do.

SIR CHRISTOPHER. Where is she?

GILBERT. I don't know—at home, I suppose.

SIR CHRISTOPHER. Go home to her—don't say one word about what has happened, and invite her out to the very best dinner that London can provide.

GILBERT. But after she has acted as she has done?

SIR CHRISTOPHER. My dear fellow, she's only a woman. I never met but one woman that was worth taking seriously. What are they? A kind of children, you know. Humour them, play with them, buy them the toys they cry for, but don't get angry with them. They're not worth it, except one! Now I must get on with my packing.

[*Sir Christopher sets to work packing. Gilbert walks up and down the room, biting his nails, deliberating; after a moment or two, he speaks.*

GILBERT. Perhaps you're right, Deering.

SIR CHRISTOPHER. Oh, I know I am!

GILBERT. I'll go to her.

SIR CHRISTOPHER (*busy packing*). Make haste, or you may be too late.

[*Gilbert goes to door. At that moment enter Taplin.*

TAPLIN (*announcing*). Mr. Falkner.

[*Enter Falkner. Exit Taplin.*

[*Gilbert and Falkner stand for a moment looking at each other. Exit Gilbert; Falkner looks after him.*

SIR CHRISTOPHER. Well?

FALKNER. (*very elated*). You want to see me?

SIR CHRISTOPHER. Yes. You seem excited.

FALKNER. I've had some goods news.

SIR CHRISTOPHER. What?

FALKNER. The best. She loves me.

SIR CHRISTOPHER. You've seen her?

FALKNER. No.

SIR CHRISTOPHER. Written to her?

FALKNER. Yes. I've just had this answer.

[*Taking out letter.*

SIR CHRISTOPHER. Where is she?

FALKNER. Still at her sister's. (*Reading.*) "I shall never forget the words you spoke this morning. You were right in saying that your love would not be wasted. I have learned at last what it is worth. You said you would be at my service always. Do not write again. Wait till you hear from me, and the moment I send for you, come to me." I knew I should win her at last, and I shall!

SIR CHRISTOPHER. Après?

FALKNER. What does it matter? If I can persuade her, I shall take her out to Africa with me.

SIR CHRISTOPHER. Africa? Nonsense! There's only one woman in the world that's any use in that part of the globe, and I'm taking her out myself.

FALKNER. Beatrice.

SIR CHRISTOPHER. We are to be married to-morrow morning.

FALKNER. I congratulate you—with all my heart.
[Shaking hands warmly.

SIR CHRISTOPHER. Thank you. (Pause.) You'll come with us, Ned?

FALKNER. If she will come too.

SIR CHRISTOPHER. Oh, we can't have her.

FALKNER. Why not?

SIR CHRISTOPHER. In the first place, she'd be very much in the way. In the second place—it's best to be frank—Lady Deering will not recognize Lady Jessica.

FALKNER. Very well. (Turns on heel. Very curtly.) Good-night, Kit!

SIR CHRISTOPHER. No. Ned, you're still up that everlasting cul-de-sac— playing the lover to a married woman, and I've got to drag you out of it.

FALKNER. It's no use, Kit. My mind is made up. Let me go.

SIR CHRISTOPHER. To the devil with Lady Jessica? No, I'm going to stop you.

FALKNER. Ah, you'll stop me! How?

SIR CHRISTOPHER. There was a time when one whisper would have done it. (Whispers.) Duty. You know that you're the only man who can treat peaceably with the chiefs. You know that your going out may save hundreds, perhaps thousands of lives.

FALKNER. I'm not sure of that.

SIR CHRISTOPHER. You're not sure? Well, then, try it—put it to the test. But you know there's every chance. You know the whole country is waiting for you to declare yourself. You know that you have a splendid chance of putting the crown on your life's work, and you know that if you don't seize it, it will be because you stay here skulking after her!

FALKNER. Skulking!

SIR CHRISTOPHER. What do you call it? What will everybody call it? Ned, you've faced the most horrible death day after day for months. You've done some of the bravest things out there that have been done by any Englishman in this generation; but if you turn tail now, there's only one word will fit you to the end of your days, and that word is "Coward!"

FALKNER. Coward!

SIR CHRISTOPHER. Coward! And there's only one epitaph to be written on you by-and-bye—"Sold his honour, his fame, his country, his duty, his conscience, his all, for a petticoat!"

FALKNER. Very well, then, when I die, write that over me. I tell you this, Kit, if I can only win her—and I shall, I shall, I feel it—she'll leave that man and come to me; and then!—I don't care one snap of the fingers if Africa is swept bare of humanity from Cairo to Cape Town, and from Teneriffe to Zanzibar! Now argue with me after that!

SIR CHRISTOPHER. Argue with you? Not I! But I wish there was some way of kidnapping fools into sense and reason and locking them up there for the rest of their lives.
[Enter Taplin.

TAPLIN (announcing). Lady Jessica Nepean, Lady Rosamund Tatton.
[Enter Lady Jessica and Lady Rosamund. Exit Taplin.

[*Lady Jessica shows delighted surprise at seeing Falkner, goes to him cordially. Lady Rosamund tries to stop Lady Jessica from going to Falkner.*

LADY JESSICA (*to Falkner*). I didn't expect to find you here.

FALKNER. I am waiting for you.

LADY ROSAMUND (*interposing*). No, Jess, no. Sir Christopher! (*Aside to him.*) Help me to get her away from him.

[*Lady Jessica and Falkner are talking vigorously together.*

SIR CHRISTOPHER. One moment. Perhaps we may as well get this little matter fixed up here and now. (*Takes out watch, looking ruefully at his packing.*) Lady Jessica, may I ask what has happened since I left you this morning?

LADY JESSICA. Nothing. My husband went away in a rage. I've stayed with Rosy all day.

LADY ROSAMUND. We've been talking it all over.

LADY JESSICA. Oh, we've been talking it all over—(*gestures*)—and over and over, till I'm thoroughly—*seasick* of it!

LADY ROSAMUND. And so I persuaded her to come and talk it over with you.

SIR CHRISTOPHER (*glancing at his packing, to Lady Jessica*). You can't arrive at a decision?

LADY JESSICA. Oh, yes, I can! only Rosy won't let me act on it.

LADY ROSAMUND. I should think not.

SIR CHRISTOPHER. What is your decision?

LADY JESSICA. I don't mind for myself. I feel that everything is in a glorious muddle, and I don't care how I get out of it, or whether I get out of it at all.

SIR CHRISTOPHER. But on the whole the best way of getting out of it is to run away with Mr. Falkner?

LADY JESSICA. Mr. Falkner has behaved splendidly to me.

SIR CHRISTOPHER. He has! He's a brick! And I'm quite sure that in proposing to ruin your reputation, and make you miserable for life, he is actuated by the very best intentions.

LADY JESSICA. I don't care whether I'm happy or miserable for the rest of my life.

SIR CHRISTOPHER. You don't care now, but you will to-morrow, and next week, and next year, and all the years after.

LADY JESSICA. No, I shan't! I won't!

FALKNER. I'll take care, Lady Jessica, that you never regret this step. Your mind is quite made up?

LADY JESSICA. Yes, quite.

FALKNER. Then no more need be said.

[*Offers arm. Gesture of despair from Lady Rosamund. Sir Christopher soothes her.*

SIR CHRISTOPHER. One moment, Ned! (*Takes out his watch, looks ruefully at his packing, half aside.*) Good Lord! when shall I get on with my packing? (*Puts watch in pocket; faces Falkner and Lady Jessica very resolutely.*) Now! I've nothing to say in the abstract against running

away with another man's wife! There may be planets where it is not
only the highest ideal morality, but where it has the further advantage
of being a practical way of carrying on society. But it has this one
fatal defect in our country—it won't work! You know what we English
are, Ned. We're not a bit better than our neighbours, but, thank God!
we do pretend we are, and we do make it hot for anybody who disturbs
that holy pretence. And take my word for it, my dear Lady Jessica,
my dear Ned, it won't work. You know it's not an original experiment
you're making. It has been tried before. Have you ever known it to be
successful? Lady Jessica, think of the brave pioneers who have gone
before you in this enterprise. They've all perished, and their bones whiten
the anti-matrimonial shore. Think of them! Charley Gray and Lady
Rideout—flitting shabbily about the Continent at cheap *table d'hôtes*
and gambling clubs, rubbing shoulders with all the blackguards and
demi-mondaines of Europe. Poor old Fitz and his beauty—moping down
at Farnhurst, cut by the county, with no single occupation except to
nag and rag each other to pieces from morning to night. Billy Dover
and Polly Atchison—

LADY JESSICA (*indignant*). Well!

SIR CHRISTOPHER—cut in for fresh partners in three weeks. That old
idiot, Sir Bonham Dancer—paid five thousand pounds damages for being
saddled with the professional strong man's wife. George Nuneham and
Mrs. Sandys—George is conducting a tramcar in New York, and Mrs.
Sandys—Lady Jessica, you knew Mrs. Sandys, a delicate, sweet little
creature. I've met her at your house—she drank herself to death, and
died in a hospital. Not encouraging, is it? Marriage may be disagreeable,
it may be unprofitable, it may be ridiculous; but it isn't as bad as that!
And do you think the experiment is going to be successful in *your case*?
Not a bit of it! No. Ned, hear me out. (*Turns to Lady Jessica.*) First
of all, there will be the shabby scandal and dirty business of the divorce
court. You won't like that. It isn't nice! You won't like it. After the
divorce court, what is Ned to do with you? Take you to Africa? I do
implore you, if you hope for any happiness in that state to which it is
pleasing Falkner and Providence to call you, I do implore you, don't go
out to Africa with him. You'd never stand the climate and the hard-
ships, and you'd bore each other to death in a week. But if you don't
go out to Africa, what are you to do? Stay in England, in society?
Everybody will cut you. Take a place in the country? Think of poor
old Fitz down at Farnhurst! Go abroad! Think of Charley Gray and
Lady Rideout. Take any of the other dozen alternatives, and find yourself stranded in some shady hole or corner, with the one solitary hope
and ambition of somehow wriggling back into respectability. That's your
side of it, Lady Jessica. As for Ned here, what is to become of him?
(*Angry gesture from Falkner.*) Yes, Ned, I know you don't want to hear,
but I'm going to finish. Turn away your head. This is for Lady Jessica.
He's at the height of his career, with a great and honourable task in front
of him. If you turn him aside, you'll not only wreck and ruin your
own life and reputation, but you'll wreck and ruin his. You won't!
You won't! His interests, his duty, his honour all lie out there. If you
care for him, don't keep him shuffling and malingering here. Send him
out with me to finish his work like the good, splendid fellow he is.
Set him free, Lady Jessica, and go back to your home. Your husband
has been here. He's sorry for what is past, and he has promised to

treat you more kindly in the future. He's waiting at home to take you out. You missed a very good dinner last night. Don't miss another to-night. I never saw a man in a better temper than your husband. Go to him, and do, once for all, have done with this other folly. Do believe me, my dear Ned, my dear Lady Jessica, before it is too late, do believe me, it wont work, it won't work, it won't work!

[*A little pause.*

LADY JESSICA. I think you're the most horrid man I ever met!

SIR CHRISTOPHER. Because I've told you the truth.

LADY JESSICA. Yes, that's the worst of it! It is the truth.

LADY ROSAMUND. It's exactly what I've been telling her all the afternoon.

FALKNER. Lady Jessica, I want to speak to you alone.

LADY JESSICA. What's the use? We've got to part.

FALKNER. No! No!

LADY JESSICA. Yes, my friend. I won't ruin your career. We've got to part: and the fewer words the better.

FALKNER. I can't give you up.

LADY JESSICA. You must! Perhaps it's best. You can always cherish your fancy portrait of me, and you'll never find out how very unlike me it is. And I shall read about you in the newspapers and be very proud and— Come along, Rosy!

[*Going off. Falkner is going after her.*

SIR CHRISTOPHER (*stopping him*). It can answer no purpose, Ned.

FALKNER. What the devil has it got to do with you? You've taken her from me. Leave her to me for a few minutes. Lady Jessica, I claim to speak to you alone.

LADY JESSICA. It can only be to say "Good-bye."

FALKNER. I'll never say it.

LADY JESSICA. Then I must. Good-bye!

FALKNER. No—say it to me alone.

LADY JESSICA. It can only be that—no more—

FALKNER. Say it to me alone.

[*Pointing to curtains.*

LADY JESSICA. Rosy, wait for me. I won't be a minute.

[*Goes to Falkner. Lady Rosamund makes a little movement to stop her. Sir Christopher by a gesture silences Lady Rosamund and allows Lady Jessica to pass through the curtains where Falkner has preceded her.*

SIR CHRISTOPHER (*to Lady Jessica*). Remember, his future is at stake as well as yours. Only the one word.

LADY JESSICA (*as she passes through the curtain*). Only the one word.

SIR CHRISTOPHER (*to Lady Rosamund*). You'll excuse my packing. I've not a moment to waste.

[*Enter Taplin.*

TAPLIN. Mr. Gilbert Nepean, Sir Christopher; he says he must see you.

SIR CHRISTOPHER. You didn't say Lady Jessica was here?

TAPLIN. No, Sir Christopher.

SIR CHRISTOPHER. I'll come to him.

[*Exit Taplin. Lady Rosamund passes between the curtains. Sir Christopher is going to door; meets Gilbert Nepean, who enters very excitedly.*

GILBERT (*off, left*). Deering! Deering, she's not at home! She's not at her sister's. You don't think she has gone to that fellow?

SIR CHRISTOPHER. Make yourself easy. She is coming back to you.

GILBERT. Where is she?

SIR CHRISTOPHER. Will you let me take a message to her? May I tell her that for the future you will treat her with every kindness and consideration?

GILBERT. Yes—yes. Say—oh—tell her what you please. Say I know I've behaved like a bear. Tell her I'm sorry, and if she'll come home, I'll do my best to make her happy in future.

SIR CHRISTOPHER. And (*taking out watch*) it's rather too late for dinner; may I suggest an invitation to supper?

GILBERT. Yes—yes.

SIR CHRISTOPHER (*calls*). Lady Rosamund—

[*Lady Rosamund enters.*

GILBERT. You—

[*Going toward curtains. Sir Christopher intercepts him.*

LADY ROSAMUND. We stepped over to ask Sir Christopher's advice.

SIR CHRISTOPHER. And, strange to say, they've taken it.

GILBERT (*trying to get to curtains*). Where is Jessica?

SIR CHRISTOPHER (*stopping him*). No. I'm to take the message. Lady Jessica, your husband is waiting to take you to supper. You've only just time to go home and dress.

[*Lady Jessica draws curtains aside, turns and throws a last agonized adieu to Falkner, who stands speechless and helpless. Lady Jessica then controls her features and comes out to Gilbert. The curtains close.*

GILBERT. Will you come home and dress and go to the Savoy to supper?

[*Offering arm.*

LADY JESSICA. Delighted.

[*Taking his arm.*

GILBERT. And you, Rosy?

LADY ROSAMUND. I can't. (*Looking at watch.*) It's nearly ten o'clock! Good-night, Sir Christopher. Good-night, dearest. (*Kissing Lady Jessica.*) Good-night, Gilbert. Take care of her, or you'll lose her. Excuse my running away; I must get back to my poor old Freddie.

[*Exit Lady Rosamund. Falkner's face appears through the curtains. Lady Jessica sees it.*

SIR CHRISTOPHER. Good-night, Lady Jessica, and good-bye!

LADY JESSICA. Good-night, Sir Christopher, and—(*at Falkner*) one last good-bye.

[*She looks towards curtains as if about to break away from Gilbert and go to Falkner.*

SIR CHRISTOPHER. Good-night, Nepean!

GILBERT. Good-night, Deering.

SIR CHRISTOPHER. Try and keep her. She's worth the keeping.

GILBERT. I'll try.

[*Exeunt Lady Jessica and Gilbert. Sir Christopher goes towards door with them; Falkner comes forward in great despair, from curtains, throws himself into chair against table, buries his face in his hands.*

SIR CHRISTOPHER (*goes to him very affectionately*). Come! Come! My dear old Ned! This will never do! And all for a woman! They're not worth it. (*Aside, softly.*) Except one! They're not worth it. Come, buckle on your courage! There's work in front of you, and fame, and honour! And I must take you out and bring you back with flying colours! Come! Come! My dear old fellow!

FALKNER. Let me be for a minute, Kit. Let me be!

[*Enter Beatrice. Sir Christopher goes to her.*

BEATRICE. What's the matter?

SIR CHRISTOPHER. Hush! Poor old chap! He's hard hit! Everybody else seems to be making a great mess of their love affairs. We won't make a mess of ours?

BEATRICE. No. You'll get over this, Ned? We'll help you. You'll get over it?

FALKNER (*rising with great determination*). Yes, I shall pull round. I'll try! I'll try! To-morrow, Kit? We start to-morrow?

SIR CHRISTOPHER (*putting one arm round each affectionately*). To-morrow! My wife! My friend! My two comrades!

CURTAIN

THE NOTORIOUS MRS. EBBSMITH

A DRAMA IN FOUR ACTS
by
SIR ARTHUR WING PINERO

The scene is laid in Venice; firstly at the Palazzo Arconati, a lodging-house on the Grand Canal; afterwards in an apartment in the Campo S. Bartolomeo.

It is Eastertide, a week passing between the events of the first and second acts.

Time: The Present

THE NOTORIOUS MRS. EBBSMITH

Original cast, as first disclosed at the Garrick Theatre, March 13th, 1895.

DUKE OF ST. OLPHERTS	Mr. John Hare
SIR SANDFORD CLEEVE	Mr. Ian Robertson
LUCAS CLEEVE	Mr. Forbes-Robertson
REV. AMOS WINTERFIELD	Mr. C. Aubrey Smith
SIR GEORGE BRODRICK	Mr. Joseph Carne
DR. KIRKE	Mr. Fred Thorne
FORTUNÉ	Mr. Gerald du Maurier
ANTONIO POPPI	Mr. C. F. Caravoglia
AGNES	Mrs. Patrick Campbell
GERTRUDE THORPE	Miss Ellis Jeffreys
SYBIL CLEEVE	Miss Eleanor Calhoun
NELLA	Miss Mary Halsey
HEPHZIBAH	Mrs. Charles Groves

124

THE NOTORIOUS MRS. EBBSMITH

THE FIRST ACT

The scene is a room in the Palazzo Arconati, on the Grand Canal, Venice. The room itself is beautiful in its decayed grandeur, but the furniture and hangings are either tawdry and meretricious or avowedly modern. The three windows at the back open on to a narrow, covered balcony, or loggia, and through them can be seen the west side of the canal. Between the recessed double doors, on either side of the room, is a fireplace out of use, and a marble mantelpiece, but a tiled stove is used for a wood fire. Breakfast things are laid on a table. The sun streams into the room.

ANTONIO POPPI *and* NELLA, *two Venetian servants, with a touch of the picturesque in their attire, are engaged in clearing the breakfast table.*

NELLA [*turning her head*]. Ascolta! (Listen!)

ANTONIO. Una gondola allo scalo. (A gondola at our steps.) [*They open the centre window; go out onto the balcony, and look down below.*] La Signora Thorpe. (The Signora Thorpe.)

NELLA. Con suo fratello. (With her brother.)

ANTONIO [*calling*]. Buon dì, Signor Winterfield! Iddio la benedica! (Good day, Signor Winterfield! The blessing of God be upon you!)

NELLA [*calling*]. Buon dì, Signora! La Madonna l'assista! (Good day, Signora! May the Virgin have you in her keeping!)

ANTONIO [*returning to the room*]. Noi siamo in ritardo di tutto questa mattina. (We are behindhand with everything this morning.)

NELLA [*following him*]. È vero. (That is true.)

ANTONIO [*bustling about*]. La stufa! (The stove!)

NELLA [*throwing wood into the stove*]. Che tu sia benedetta per rammentarmelo! Questi Inglesi non si contentono del sole. (Bless you for remembering it! These English are not content with the sun.)

> [*Leaving only a vase of flowers upon the table, they hurry out with the breakfast things. At the same moment,* FORTUNÉ, *a manservant, enters, showing in* MRS. THORPE *and the* REV. AMOS WINTERFIELD. GERTRUDE THORPE *is a pretty, honest looking young woman of about seven and twenty. She is in mourning, and has sorrowful eyes, and a complexion that is too delicate; but natural cheerfulness and brightness are seen through all.* AMOS *is about forty— big, burly, gruff; he is untidily dressed, and has a pipe in his hand.* FORTUNÉ *is carrying a pair of freshly cleaned, tan-coloured boots upon boot-trees.*

GERTRUDE. Now, Fortuné, you ought to have told us downstairs that Dr. Kirke is with Mrs. Cleeve.

AMOS. Come away, Gerty. Mrs. Cleeve can't want to be bored with us just now.

FORTUNÉ. Mrs. Cleeve give 'er ordares she is always to be bored wiz Madame Thorpe and Mr. Winterfield.

AMOS. Ha, ha!

GERTRUDE [*smiling*]. Fortuné!

FORTUNÉ. Besides, ze doctares vill go in 'alf a minute, you see.

GERTRUDE. Doctors!

AMOS. What, is there another doctor with Dr. Kirke?

FORTUNÉ. Ze great physician, Sir Brodrick.

GERTRUDE. Sir George Brodrick? Amos!

AMOS. Doesn't Mr. Cleeve feel so well?

FORTUNÉ. Oh, yes. But Mrs. Cleeve 'appen to read in a newspapare zat Sir George Brodrick vas in Florence for ze Pâque—ze Eastare. Sir Brodrick vas Mr. Cleeve's doctare in London, Mrs. Cleeve tell me, so 'e is acquainted wiz Mr. Cleeve's inside.

AMOS. Ho, ho!

GERTRUDE. Mr. Cleeve's constitution, Fortuné.

FORTUNÉ. Excuse, madam. Zerefore Mrs. Cleeve she telegraph for Sir Brodrick to come to Venise.

AMOS. To consult with Dr. Kirke, I suppose.

FORTUNÉ [*listening*]. 'Ere is ze doctares.

> [DR. KIRKE *enters, followed by* SIR GEORGE BRODRICK. KIRKE *is a shabby snuff-taking old gentlemen — blunt, hut kind;* SIR GEORGE, *on the contrary, is scrupulously neat in his dress, and has a suave, professional manner.* FORTUNÉ *withdraws.*

KIRKE. Good-morning, Mr. Winterfield. [*To* GERTRUDE.] How do you do, my dear? You're getting some colour into your pretty face, I'm glad to see. [*To* SIR GEORGE.] Mr. Winterfield—Sir George Brodrick.

> [SIR GEORGE *and* AMOS *shake hands.*

KIRKE [*to* SIR GEORGE]. Mrs. Thorpe. [SIR GEORGE *shakes hands with* GERTRUDE. Sir George and I started life together in London years ago; now he finds me here in Venice—well, we can't all win the race, eh?

SIR GEORGE. My dear old friend! [*To* GERTRUDE.] Mr. Cleeve has been telling me, Mrs. Thorpe, how exceedingly kind you and your brother have been to him during his illness.

GERTRUDE. Oh, Mr. Cleeve exaggerates our little services.

AMOS. *I've* done nothing.

GERTRUDE. Nor I.

KIRKE. Now, my dear!

GERTRUDE. Dr. Kirke, you weren't in Florence with us; you're only a tale-bearer.

KIRKE. Well, I've excellent authority for my story of a young woman who volunteered to share the nursing of an invalid at a time when she herself stood greatly in need of being nursed.

GERTRUDE. Nonsense! [*To* SIR GEORGE.] You know, Amos—my big brother over there—Amos and I struck up an acquaintance with Mr. and Mrs. Cleeve at Florence, at the Hotel d'Italie, and occasionally one of us would give Mr. Cleeve his dose while poor Mrs. Cleeve took a little rest or a drive—but positively that's all.

KIRKE. You don't tell us—

GERTRUDE. I've nothing more to tell, except that I'm awfully fond of Mrs. Cleeve—

AMOS. Oh, if you once get my sister on the subject of Mrs. Cleeve— [*Taking up a newspaper.*]

GERTRUDE [*to* SIR GEORGE]. Yes, I always say that if I were a man searching for a wife, I should be inclined to base my ideal on Mrs. Cleeve.

SIR GEORGE [*edging away towards* KIRKE, *with a surprised, uncomfortable smile*]. Eh? Really?

GERTRUDE. You conceive a different ideal, Sir George?

SIR GEORGE. Oh—well—

GERTRUDE. Well, Sir George?

AMOS. Perhaps Sir George has heard that Mrs. Cleeve holds regrettable opinions on some points. If so, he may feel surprised that a parson's sister—

GERTRUDE. Oh, I don't share all Mrs. Cleeve's views, or sympathize with them, of course. But they succeed only in making me sad and sorry. Mrs. Cleeve's opinions don't stop me from loving the gentle, sweet woman; admiring her for her patient, absorbing devotion to her husband; wondering at the beautiful stillness with which she seems to glide through life!—

AMOS [*putting down the newspaper; to* SIR GEORGE *and* KIRKE]. I told you so! [*To* GERTRUDE.] Gertrude, I'm sure Sir George and Dr. Kirke want to be left together for a few minutes.

GERTRUDE [*going up to the window*]. I'll sun myself on the balcony.

AMOS. And I'll go and buy some tobacco. [*To* GERTRUDE.] Don't be long, Gerty. [*Nodding to* SIR GEORGE *and* KIRKE.] Good-morning.

[*They return his nod, and he goes out.*

GERTRUDE [*on the balcony outside the window to* KIRKE *and* SIR GEORGE]. Dr. Kirke, I've heard what doctors' consultations consist of. After looking at the pictures you talk about whist.

[*She closes the window and sits.*

KIRKE [*producing his snuff-box*]. Ha, ha!

SIR GEORGE. Why, this lady and her brother evidently haven't the faintest suspicion of the actual truth, my dear Kirke!

KIRKE [*taking snuff*]. Not the slightest.

SIR GEORGE. The woman made a point of being extremely explicit with you, you tell me?

KIRKE. Yes; she was plain enough with me. At our first meeting she said, "Doctor, I want you to know so-and-so, and so-and-so, and so-and-so."

SIR GEORGE. Really? Well, it certainly isn't fair of Cleeve and his—his associate to trick decent people like Mrs. Thorpe and her brother. Good gracious, the brother is a clergyman too!

KIRKE. The rector of some dull hole in the north of England.

SIR GEORGE. Really?

KIRKE. A bachelor; this Mrs. Thorpe keeps house for him. She's a widow.

SIR GEORGE. Really?

KIRKE. Widow of a captain in the army. Poor thing! She's lately lost her only child, and can't get over it.

SIR GEORGE. Indeed, really, really? . . . But about Cleeve now—he had Roman fever of rather a severe type?

KIRKE. In November. And then that fool of a Bickerstaff at Rome allowed the woman to move him to Florence too soon, and there he had a relapse. However, when she brought him on here the man was practically well.

SIR GEORGE. The difficulty being to convince him of the fact, eh? A highly strung, emotional creature?

KIRKE. You've hit him.

SIR GEORGE. I've known him from his childhood. Are you still giving him anything?

KIRKE. A little quinine, to humour him.

SIR GEORGE. Exactly. [*Looking at his watch.*] Where is she, where is she? I've promised to take my wife shopping in the Merceria this morning. By-the-bye, Kirke,—I must talk scandal, I find—*this* is rather an odd circumstance. Whom do you think I got a bow from as I passed through the hall of the Danieli last night? [KIRKE *grunts and shakes his head.*] The Duke of St. Olpherts.

KIRKE [*taking snuff*]. Ah! I suppose you're in with a lot of swells now, Brodrick.

SIR GEORGE. No, no, you don't understand me. The duke is this young fellow's uncle by marriage. His Grace married a sister of Lady Cleeve's, of Cleeve's mother, you know.

KIRKE. Oh! This looks as if the family are trying to put a finger in the pie.

SIR GEORGE. The duke may be here by mere chance. Still, as you say, it does look— [*Lowering his voice as* KIRKE *rises, eyes an opening door.*] Who's that?

KIRKE. The woman.

> [AGNES *enters. She moves firmly but noiselessly—a placid woman with a sweet, low voice. Her dress is plain to the verge of coarseness; her face, which has little colour, is at the first glance almost wholly unattractive.*

AGNES [*looking from one to the other*]. I thought you would send for me perhaps. [*To* SIR GEORGE.] What do you say about him?

KIRKE. One moment. [*Pointing to the balcony.*] Mrs. Thorpe—

AGNES. Excuse me.

> [*She goes to the window and opens it.*

GERTRUDE. O Mrs. Cleeve! [*Entering the room.*] Am I in the way?

AGNES. You are never that, dear. Run along to my room; I'll call you in a minute or two. [GERTRUDE *nods and goes to the door.*] Take off your hat and sit with me a little while.

GERTRUDE. I'll stay for a bit, but this hat doesn't take off.

[*She goes out.*

AGNES [*to* SIR GEORGE *and* KIRKE]. Yes?

SIR GEORGE. We are glad to be able to give a most favourable report. I may say that Mr. Cleeve has never appeared to be in better health.

AGNES [*drawing a deep breath*]. He will be very much cheered by what you say.

SIR GEORGE [*bowing stiffly*]. I'm glad—

AGNES. His illness left him with a morbid, irrational impression that he would never be quite his former self again.

SIR GEORGE. A nervous man recovering from a scare. I've helped to remove that impression, I believe.

AGNES. Thank you. We have a troublesome, perhaps a hard time before us; we both need all our health and spirits. [*Turning her head, listening.*] Lucas?

[LUCAS *enters the room. He is a handsome, intellectual-looking young man of about eight and twenty.*

LUCAS [*to* AGNES, *excitedly*]. Have you heard what they say of me?

AGNES [*smiling*]. Yes.

LUCAS. How good of you, Sir George, to break up your little holiday for the sake of an anxious, fidgety fellow. [*To* AGNES.] Isn't it?

AGNES. Sir George has rendered us a great service.

LUCAS [*going to* KIRKE, *brightly*]. Yes, and proved how ungrateful I've been to you, doctor.

KIRKE. Don't apologize. People who don't know when they're well are the mainstay of my profession. [*Offering snuff-box.*] Here—

[LUCAS *takes a pinch of snuff, laughingly.*

AGNES [*in a low voice to* SIR GEORGE]. He has been terribly hipped at times. [*Taking up the vase of flowers from the table.*] Your visit will have made him another man.

[*She goes to a table, puts down the vase upon the tray, and commences to cut and arrange the fresh flowers she finds there.*

LUCAS [*seeing that* AGNES *is out of hearing*]. Excuse me, Kirke—just for one moment. [*To* SIR GEORGE.] Sir George— [KIRKE *joins* AGNES.] You still go frequently to Great Cumberland Place?

SIR GEORGE. Your mother's gout has been rather stubborn lately.

LUCAS. Very likely she and my brother Sandford will get to hear of your visit to me here; in that case you'll be questioned pretty closely, naturally.

SIR GEORGE. My position is certainly a little delicate.

LUCAS. Oh, you may be perfectly open with my people as to my present mode of life. Only—[*he motions* SIR GEORGE *to be seated; they sit facing each other*] only I want you to hear me declare again plainly [*looking toward* AGNES] that but for the care and devotion of that good woman over there, but for the solace of that woman's companionship, I should have been dead months ago; I should have died raving in my awful bedroom on the ground-floor of that foul Roman hotel. Malarial fever, of course! Doctors don't admit—do they?—that it is possible for strong men to die of miserable marriages. And yet I was dying in Rome, I truly believe, from *my* bitter, crushing disappointment, from the consciousness of my wretched, irretrievable—

> [FORTUNÉ *enters carrying* LUCAS's *hat, gloves, overcoat, and silk wrap, and, upon a salver, a bottle of medicine and a glass.*

LUCAS [*sharply*]. Qu'y a-t-il, Fortuné?

FORTUNÉ. Sir, you 'ave an appointment.

LUCAS [*rising*]. At the Danieli at eleven. Is it so late?

> [FORTUNÉ *places the things upon the table.* LUCAS *puts the wrap round his throat.* AGNES, *who has turned on* FORTUNÉ's *entrance, goes to* LUCAS *and arranges the wrap for him solicitously.*

SIR GEORGE [*rising*]. I have to meet Lady Brodrick at the Piazzetta. Let me take you in my gondola.

LUCAS. Thanks, delighted.

AGNES [*to* SIR GEORGE]. I would rather Lucas went in the house gondola: I know its cushions are dry. May he take you to the Piazzetta?

SIR GEORGE [*a little stiffly*]. Certainly.

AGNES [*to* FORTUNÉ]. Mettez les coussins dans la gondole.

FORTUNÉ. Bien, madame.

> [FORTUNÉ *goes out.* AGNES *begins to measure a dose of medicine.*

SIR GEORGE [*to* AGNES]. Er—I—ah—

LUCAS [*putting on his gloves*]. Agnes, Sir George—

AGNES [*turning to* SIR GEORGE, *the bottle and glass in her hands*]. Yes?

SIR GEORGE. [*constrainedly*]. We always make a point of acknowledging the importance of nursing as an aid to medical treatment. I—I am sure Mr. Cleeve owes you much in that respect.

AGNES. Thank you.

SIR GEORGE [*to* LUCAS]. I have to discharge my gondola; you'll find me at the steps, Cleeve. [AGNES *shifts the medicine bottle from one hand to the other so that her right hand may be free, but* SIR GEORGE *simply bows in a formal way and moves towards the door.*] You are coming with us, Kirke?

KIRKE. Yes.

SIR GEORGE. Do you mind seeing that I'm not robbed by my gondolier?

> [*He goes out.*

AGNES [*giving the medicine to* LUCAS, *undisturbed*]. Here, dear.

KIRKE. [*to* AGNES]. May I pop in to-night for my game of chess?

AGNES. Do, doctor; I shall be very pleased.

KIRKE [*shaking her hand in a marked way*]. Thank you.

> [*He follows* SIR GEORGE.

AGNES [*looking after him*]. Liberal little man.

> [*She has* LUCAS's *overcoat in her hand; a small pen-and-ink drawing of a woman's head drops from one of the pockets. They pick it up together.*

AGNES. Isn't that the sketch you made of me in Florence?

LUCAS [*replacing it in the coat pocket*]. Yes.

AGNES. You are carrying it about with you?

LUCAS. I slipped it into my pocket thinking it might interest the duke.

AGNES [*assisting him with his overcoat*]. Surely I am too obnoxious in the abstract for your uncle to entertain such a detail as a portrait.

LUCAS. It struck me it might serve to correct certain preconceived notions of my people's.

AGNES. Images of a beautiful temptress with peach-blossom cheeks and stained hair?

LUCAS. That's what I mean; I assume they suspect a decline of taste on my part of that sort. Good-by, dear.

AGNES. Is this mission of the Duke of St. Olpherts the final attempt to part us, I wonder? [*Angrily, her voice hardening.*] Why should they harass and disturb you as they do?

LUCAS [*kissing her*]. Nothing disturbs me now that I *know* I am strong and well. Besides everybody will soon tire of being shocked. Even conventional morality must grow breathless in the chase.

> [*He leaves her. She opens the door and calls.*

AGNES. Mrs. Thorpe! I am alone now.

> [*She goes on to the balcony through the centre window, and looks down below.* GERTRUDE *enters and joins her.*

GERTRUDE. How well your husband is looking!

AGNES. Sir George Brodrick pronounces him quite recovered.

GERTRUDE. Isn't that splendid! [*Waving her hand and calling.*] Buon giorno, Signor Cleeve! Come molto meglio voi state! [*Leaving the balcony, laughing*]. Ha, ha! my Italian!

> [AGNES *waves finally to the gondola below, returns to the room, and slips her arm through* GERTRUDE's.

AGNES. Two whole days since I've seen you.

GERTRUDE. They've been two of my bad days, dear.

AGNES [*looking into her face*]. All right now?

GERTRUDE. Oh, "God's in His heaven" this morning! When the sun's out I feel that my little boy's bed in Ketherick Cemetery is warm and cosy.

AGNES [*patting* GERTRUDE's *hand*]. Ah!—

GERTRUDE. The weather's the same all over Europe, according to the papers. Do you think it's really going to settle at last? To me these chilly, showery nights are terrible. You know, I still tuck my child up at night-time, still have my last peep at him before going to my own bed; and it is awful to listen to these cold rains—drip, drip, drip upon that little green coverlet of his!

[*She goes and stands by the window silently.*

AGNES. This isn't strong of you, dear Mrs. Thorpe. You mustn't—you mustn't.

[AGNES *brings the tray with the cut flowers to the nearer table; calmly and methodically she resumes trimming the stalks.*

GERTRUDE. You're quite right. That's over. Now, then, I'm going to gabble for five minutes gaily. [*Settling herself comfortably in an armchair.*] What jolly flowers you've got there! What have you been doing with yourself? Amos took me to the Caffè Quadri yesterday to late breakfast, to cheer me up. Oh, I've something to say to you! At the Caffè, at the next table to ours, there were three English people —two men and a girl—home from India, I gathered. One of the men was looking out of the window, quizzing the folks walking in the Piazza, and suddenly he caught sight of your husband. [AGNES'S *hands pause in their work.*] "I do believe that's Lucas Cleeve," he said. And then the girl had a peep, and said, "Certainly it is." And the man said," I must find out where he's stopping; if Minerva is with him, you must call." "Who's Minerva?" said the second man. "Minerva is Mrs. Lucas Cleeve," the girl said; "it's a pet-name—he married a chum of mine, a daughter of Sir John Steyning's, a year or so after I went out." [*Rising and coming down.*] Excuse me, dear. Do these people really know you and your husband, or were they talking nonsense?

[AGNES *takes the vase of faded flowers, goes on to the balcony and empties the contents of the vase into the canal. Then she stands by the window, her back towards* GERTRUDE.

AGNES. No; they evidently know Mr. Cleeve.

GERTRUDE. Your husband never calls you by that pet-name of yours. Why is it you haven't told me you're a daughter of Admiral Steyning's?

AGNES. Mrs. Thorpe—

GERTRUDE [*warmly*]. Oh, I must say what I mean! I have often pulled myself up short in my gossips with you, conscious of a sort of wall between us. [AGNES *comes slowly from the window.*] Somehow, I feel now that you haven't in the least made a friend of me. I'm hurt. It's stupid of me; I can't help it.

AGNES [*after a moment's pause*]. I am not the lady these people were speaking of yesterday.

GERTRUDE. Not?—

AGNES. Mr. Cleeve is no longer with his wife; he has left her.

GERTRUDE. Left—his wife!

AGNES. Like yourself, I am a widow. I don't know whether you've ever heard my name—Ebbsmith. [GERTRUDE *stares at her blankly.*] I beg your pardon sincerely. I never meant to conceal my true position; such a course is opposed to every principle of mine. But I grew so attached to you in Florence and—well, it was contemptibly weak; I'll never do such a thing again.

[*She goes back to the table and commences
to refill the vase with the fresh flowers.*

GERTRUDE. When you say that Mr. Cleeve has left his wife, I suppose
you mean to tell me you have taken her place?

AGNES. Yes, I meant that.

[GERTRUDE *rises and walks to the door.*

GERTRUDE [*at the door*]. You knew that I could not speak to you again
after hearing this?

AGNES. I thought it almost certain you would not.

[*After a moment's irresolution.* GERTRUDE
returns, and stands by the settee.

GERTRUDE. I can hardly believe you.

AGNES. I should like you to hear more than just the bare facts.

GERTRUDE. [*drumming on the back of the settee*]. Why don't you tell
me more?

AGNES. You were going, you know.

GERTRUDE [*sitting*]. I won't go quite like that. Please tell me.

AGNES [*calmly*]. Well, did you ever read of John Thorold—"Jack Thorold,
the demagogue"? [GERTRUDE *shakes her head.*] I daresay not. John
Thorold, once a school-master, was my father. In my time he used to
write for the two or three so-called inflammatory journals, and hold
forth in small lecture halls, occasionally even from the top of a wooden
stool in the Park, upon trade and labour questions, division of wealth,
and the rest of it. He believed in nothing that people who go to
church are credited with believing in, Mrs. Thorpe; his scheme for
the re-adjustment of things was Force, his pet doctrine the ultimate
healthy healing that follows the surgery of revolution. But to me he
was the gentlest creature imaginable; and I was very fond of him, in
spite of his—as I then thought—strange ideas. Strange ideas! Hah,
many of 'em luckily don't sound quite so irrational to-day!

GERTRUDE [*under her breath*]. Oh!—

AGNES. My home was a wretched one. If dad was violent out of the
house, mother was violent enough in it; with her it was rave, sulk,
storm, from morning till night; till one day father turned a deaf ear
to mother and died in his bed. That was my first intimate experience
of the horrible curse that falls upon so many.

GERTRUDE. Curse?

AGNES. The curse of unhappy marriage. Though really I'd looked on
at little else all my life. Most of our married friends were cursed in a
like way; and I remember taking an oath, when I was a mere child,
that nothing should ever push me over into the choked up, seething
pit. Fool! When I was nineteen I was gazing like a pet sheep into a
man's eyes; and one morning I was married, at St. Andrew's Church
in Holborn, to Mr. Ebbsmith, a barrister.

GERTRUDE. In church?

AGNES. Yes, in church—in church. In spite of father's unbelief and
mother's indifference, at the time I married I was as simple—ay, in my
heart as devout—as any girl in a parsonage. The other thing hadn't
soaked into me. Whenever I could escape from our stifling rooms at

home, and slam the front door behind me, the air blew away uncertainty and scepticism; I seemed only to have to take a long, deep breath to be full of hope and faith. And it was like this till that man married me.

GERTRUDE. Of course, I guess your marriage was an unfortunate one.

AGNES. It lasted eight years. For about twelve months he treated me like a woman in a harem, for the rest of the time like a beast of burden. Oh! when I think of it! [*Wiping her brow with her handkerchief.*] Phew!

GERTRUDE. It changed you?

AGNES. Oh, yes, it changed me.

GERTRUDE. You spoke of yourself just now as a widow. He's dead?

AGNES. He died on our wedding day—the eighth anniversary.

GERTRUDE. You were free then—free to begin again.

AGNES. Eh? [*Looking at* GERTRUDE.] Yes, but you don't begin to believe all over again. [*She gathers up the stalks of flowers from the tray, and, kneeling, crams them into the stove.*] However, this is an old story. I'm thirty-three now.

GERTRUDE [*hesitatingly*]. You and Mr. Cleeve?—

AGNES. We've known each other since last November, no longer. Six years of my life unaccounted for, eh? Well, for a couple of years or so I was lecturing.

GERTRUDE. Lecturing?

AGNES. Ah, I'd become an out-and-out child of my father by that time—spouting perhaps you'd call it, standing on the identical little platforms he used to speak from, lashing abuses with my tongue as he had done. Oh, and I was fond, too, of warning women.

GERTRUDE. Against what?

AGNES. Falling into the pit.

GERTRUDE. Marriage?

AGNES. The choked-up, seething pit—until I found my bones almost through my skin, and my voice too weak to travel across a room.

GERTRUDE. From what cause?

AGNES. Starvation, my dear. So, after lying in a hospital for a month or two, I took up nursing for a living. Last November I was sent for by Dr. Bickerstaff to go through to Rome to look after a young man who'd broken down there; and who declined to send for his friends. My patient was Mr. Cleeve—[*taking up the tray*] and that's where his fortunes join mine.

> [*She crosses the room and puts the tray upon the cabinet.*

GERTRUDE. And yet, judging from what that girl said yesterday, Mr. Cleeve married quite recently?

AGNES. Less than three years ago. Men don't suffer as patiently as women. In many respects his marriage story is my own reversed—the man in place of the woman. I endured my hell, though; he broke the gates of his.

GERTRUDE. I have often seen Mr. Cleeve's name in the papers. His future promised to be brilliant, didn't it?

AGNES [*tidying the table, folding the newspapers, etc.*]. There's a great career for him still.

GERTRUDE. In Parliament—*now?*

AGNES. No; he abandons that and devotes himself to writing. We shall write much together, urging our views on this subject of Marriage. We shall have to be poor, I expect, but we shall be content.

GERTRUDE. Content!

AGNES. Quite content. Don't judge us by my one piece of cowardly folly in keeping the truth from you, Mrs. Thorpe. Indeed, it's our great plan to live the life we have mapped out for ourselves, fearlessly, openly; faithful to each other, helpful to each other, for as long as we remain together.

GERTRUDE. But tell me—you don't know how—how I have liked you!—tell me, if Mr. Cleeve's wife divorces him he will marry you?

AGNES. No.

GERTRUDE. No!

AGNES. No. I haven't made you quite understand—Lucas and I don't desire to marry, in your sense.

GERTRUDE. But you are devoted to each other!

AGNES. Thoroughly.

GERTRUDE. What, is that the meaning of "for as long as you are together"! You would go your different ways if ever you found that one of you was making the other unhappy?

AGNES. I do mean that. We remain together only to help, to heal, to console. Why should men and women be so eager to grant to each other the power of wasting life? That is what marriage gives—the right to destroy years and years of life. And the right once given, it *attracts, attracts!* We have both suffered from it. So many rich years of my life have been squandered by it. And out of his life, so much force, energy—spent in battling with the shrew, the termagant he has now fled from; strength never to be replenished, never to be repaid—all wasted, wasted!

GERTRUDE. Your legal marriage with him might not bring further miseries.

AGNES. Too late! We have done with Marriage; we distrust it. We are not now among those who regard Marriage as indispensable to union. We have done with it!

GERTRUDE [*advancing to her*]. You know, it would be impossible for me, if I would do so, to deceive my brother as to all this.

AGNES. Why, of course, dear.

GERTRUDE [*looking at her watch*]. Amos must be wondering—

AGNES. Run away, then.

[GERTRUDE *crosses quickly towards to door.*

GERTRUDE [*retracing a step or two*]. Shall I see you?—Oh!

AGNES [*shaking her head*]. Ah!

GERTRUDE [*going to her constrainedly*]. When Amos and I have talked this over, perhaps—perhaps—

AGNES. No. no, I fear not. Come, my dear friend, [*with a smile*] give me a shake of the hand.

GERTRUDE [*taking her hand*]. What you've told me is dreadful. [*Looking into* AGNES's *face.*] And yet you're not a wicked woman! [*Kissing* AGNES.] In case we don't meet again.

> [*The women separate quickly, looking towards the door as* LUCAS *enters.*

LUCAS [*shaking hands with* GERTRUDE]. How do you do, Mrs. Thorpe? I've just had a wave of the hand from your brother.

GERTRUDE. Where is he?

LUCAS. On his back in a gondola, a pipe in his mouth as usual, gazing skywards. [*Going on the balcony.*] He's within hail.

> [GERTRUDE *goes quickly to the door, followed by* AGNES.

LUCAS. There! by the Palazzo Sforza.

> [*He re-enters the room;* GERTRUDE *has disappeared.*

LUCAS [*going towards the door*]. Let me get hold of him, Mrs. Thorpe.

AGNES [*standing before* LUCAS, *quietly*]. She knows, Lucas, dear.

LUCAS. Does she?

AGNES. She overheard some gossip at the Caffè Quadria yesterday, and began questioning me, so I told her.

LUCAS [*taking off his coat*]. Adieu to them, then, eh?

AGNES [*assisting him*]. Adieu.

LUCAS. I intended to write to the brother directly they had left Venice, to explain.

AGNES. Your describing me as "Mrs. Cleeve" at the hotel in Florence helped to lead us into this; after we move from here, I must always be, frankly, "Mrs. Ebbsmith."

LUCAS. These were decent people. You and she had formed quite an attachment.

AGNES. Yes.

> [*She places his coat, etc., on a chair, then fetches her work-basket from the cabinet.*

LUCAS. There's something of the man in your nature, Agnes.

AGNES. I've anathematized my womanhood often enough.

> [*She sits at the table, taking out her work composedly.*

LUCAS. Not that every man possesses the power you have acquired—the power of going through life with compressed lips.

AGNES [*looking up smiling*]. A propos?

LUCAS. These people—this woman you've been so fond of. You see them shrink away with the utmost composure.

AGNES [*threading a needle*]. You forget, dear, that you and I have prepared ourselves for a good deal of this sort of thing.

LUCAS. Certainly, but at the moment—

AGNES. One must take care that the regret lasts no longer than a moment. Have you seen your uncle?

LUCAS. A glimpse. He hadn't long risen.

AGNES. He adds sluggishness to other vices, then?

LUCAS [*lighting a cigarette*]. He greeted me through six inches of open door. His toilet has its mysteries.

AGNES. A stormy interview?

LUCAS. The reverse. He grasped my hand warmly, declared I looked the picture of health, and said it was evident I had been most admirably nursed.

AGNES [*frowning*]. That's a strange utterance. But he's an eccentric, isn't he?

LUCAS. No man has ever been quite satisfied as to whether his oddities are ingrained or affected.

AGNES. No man. What about women?

LUCAS. Ho, they have had opportunities of closer observation.

AGNES. Hah! And they report?—

LUCAS. Nothing. They become curiously reticent.

AGNES [*scornfully, as she is cutting a thread*]. These noblemen!

LUCAS. [*taking a packet of letters from his pocket*]. Finally he presented me with these, expressed a hope that he'd see much of me during the week, and dismissed me with a fervent God bless you.

AGNES [*surprised*]. He remains here then?

LUCAS. It seems so.

AGNES. What are those, dear?

LUCAS. The duke has made himself the bearer of some letters from friends. I've only glanced at them—reproaches—appeals—

AGNES. Yes, I understand.

> [*He sits looking through the letters impatiently, then tearing them up and throwing the pieces upon the table.*

LUCAS. Lord Warminster—my godfather. "My dear boy. For God's sake!"—[*Tearing up the letter and reading another.*] Sir Charles Littlecote. "Your brilliant future . . . blasted. . . ." [*Another letter.*] Lord Froom. "Promise of a useful political career unfulfilled . . . cannot an old friend . . . ?" [*Another letter.*] Edith Heytesbury. I didn't notice a woman had honoured me. [*In an undertone.*] Edie!—[*Slipping the letter into his pocket and opening another.*] Jack Brophy. "Your great career"—Major Leete. "Your career"—[*Destroying the rest of the letters without reading them.*] My career! my career! That's the chorus, evidently. Well, there goes my career!

> [*She lays her work aside and goes to him.*

AGNES. Your career? [*Pointing to the destroyed letters.*] True, that one is over. But there's the other, you know—*ours.*

LUCAS [*touching her hand*]. Yes, yes. Still, it's just a little saddening, the saying good-by [*disturbing the scraps of paper*] to all this.

AGNES. Saddening, dear? Why, this political career of yours—think what it would have been at best! Accident of birth sent you to the wrong side of the House, influence of family would always have kept you there.

LUCAS [*partly to himself*]. But I made my mark. I did make my mark.

AGNES. Supporting the Party that retards; the Party that preserves for the rich, palters with the poor. [*Pointing to the letter again.*] Oh, there's not much to mourn for there.

LUCAS. Still it was—success.

AGNES. Success!

LUCAS. I was talked about, written about, as a Coming Man—*the* Coming Man!

AGNES. How many "coming men" has one known! Where on earth do they all go to?

LUCAS. Ah, yes, but I allowed for the failures and carefully set myself to discover the causes of them. And, as I put my finger upon the causes and examined them, I congratulated myself and said, "Well, I haven't *that* weak point in my armour, or *that;*" and, Agnes, at last I was fool enough to imagine I had no weak point, none whatever.

AGNES. It was weak enough to believe that.

LUCAS. I couldn't foresee that I was doomed to pay the price all nervous men pay for success; that the greater my success became, the more cancer-like grew the fear of never being able to continue it, to excel it; that the triumph of to-day was always to be the torture of to-morrow! Oh, Agnes, the agony of success to a nervous, sensitive man; the dismal apprehension that fills his life and gives each victory a voice to cry out, "Hear, hear! Bravo, bravo, bravo! but this is to be your last—you'll never overtop it!" Ha, yes! I soon found out the weak spot in my armour—the need of constant encouragement, constant reminder of my powers; [*taking her hand*] the need of that subtle sympathy which a sacrificing, unselfish woman alone possesses the secret of. [*Rising.*] Well, my very weakness might have been a source of greatness if, three years ago, it had been to such a woman that I had bound myself—a woman of your disposition; instead of to!— Ah!—

> [*She lays her hand upon his arm soothingly.*

LUCAS. Yes, yes, [*taking her in his arms.*] I know I have such a companion now.

AGNES. Yes—now—

LUCAS. You must be everything to me, Agnes—a double faculty, as it were. When my confidence in myself is shaken, you must try to keep the consciousness of my poor powers alive in me.

AGNES. I shall not fail you in that, Lucas.

LUCAS. And yet, whenever disturbing recollections come uppermost, when I catch myself mourning for those lost opportunities of mine; it is your love that must grant me oblivion—[*kissing her upon the lips*] your love!

> [*She makes no response, and, after a pause,
> gently releases herself and retreats a step
> or two.*

LUCAS [*his eyes following her*]. Agnes, you seem to be changing towards me, growing colder to me. At times you seem to positively shrink from me. I don't understand it. Yesterday I thought I saw you look at me as if I—frightened you!

AGNES. Lucas—Lucas dear, for some weeks, now, I've wanted to say this to you.

LUCAS. What?

AGNES. Don't you think that such a union as ours would be much braver, much more truly courageous, if it could but be—be—

LUCAS. If it could but be—what?

AGNES [*averting her eyes*]. Devoid of passion, if passion had no share in it.

LUCAS. Surely this comes a little late, Agnes, between you and me.

AGNES [*leaning upon the back of a chair, staring before her, and speaking in a low, steady voice*]. What has been was inevitable, I suppose. Still, we have hardly yet set foot upon the path we've agreed to follow. It is not too late for us, in our own lives, to put the highest interpretation upon that word—Love. Think of the inner sustaining power it would give us! [*More forcibly.*] We agree to go through the world together, preaching the lessons taught us by our experiences. We cry out to all people, "Look at us! Man and woman who are in the bondage of neither law nor ritual! Linked simply by mutual trust! Man and wife, but something better than man and wife! Friends, but even something better than friends!" I say there is that which is noble, finely defiant, in the future we have mapped out for ourselves, if only—if only—

LUCAS. Yes!

AGNES [*turning from him*]. If only it could be free from passion!

LUCAS [*in a low voice*]. Yes, but—is that possible?

AGNES [*in the same tone, watching him askance, a frightened look in her eyes*]. Why not?

LUCAS. Young man and woman . . . youth and love . . . ? Scarcely upon this earth, my dear Agnes, such a life as you have pictured.

AGNES. I say it can be, it can be!—

[FORTUNÉ *enters, carrying a letter, upon a salver, and a beautiful bouquet of white flowers. He hands the note to* LUCAS.

LUCAS [*taking the note, glancing at* AGNES]. Eh! [*To* FORTUNÉ, *pointing to the bouquet.*] Qu'avez-vous là?

FORTUNÉ. Ah, excuse. [*Presenting the bouquet to* AGNES.] Wiz compliment. [AGNES *takes the bouquet wonderingly.*] Tell Madame ze Duke of St. Olpherts bring in person, 'e says.

LUCAS [*opening the note*]. Est-il parti?

FORTUNÉ. 'E did not get out of 'is gondola.

LUCAS. Bien. [FORTUNÉ *withdraws. Reading the note aloud.*] "While brushing my hair, my dear boy, I became possessed of a strong desire to meet the lady with whom you are now improving the shining hour. Why the devil shouldn't I, if I want to! Without prejudice, as my lawyer says, let me turn-up this afternoon and chat pleasantly to her of Shakespeare, also the musical glasses. Pray hand her this flag of truce—I mean my poor bunch of flowers—and believe me yours, with a touch of gout, ST. OLPHERTS." [*Indignantly crushing the note.*] Ah!

AGNES [*frowning at the flowers*]. A taste of the oddities, I suppose!

LUCAS. He is simply making sport of us. [*Going on to the balcony, and looking out.*] There he is. Damn that smile of his!

AGNES. Where? [*She joins him.*]

LUCAS. With the two gondoliers.

AGNES. Why— that's a beautiful face! How strange!

LUCAS [*drawing her back into the room*]. Come away. He is looking up at us.

AGNES. Are you sure he sees us?

LUCAS. He did.

AGNES. He will want an answer—

> [*She deliberately flings the bouquet over the balcony into the canal, then returns to the table and picks up her work.*

LUCAS [*looking out again cautiously*]. He throws his head back and laughs heartily. [*Re-entering the room.*] Oh, of course, his policy is to attempt to laugh me out of my resolves. They send him here merely to laugh at me, Agnes, to laugh at me— [*Coming to* AGNES *angrily*] laugh at me!

AGNES. He must be a man of small resources. [*Threading her needle.*] It is so easy to mock.

END OF THE FIRST ACT.

THE SECOND ACT.

The scene is the same as that of the previous act. Through the windows some mastheads and flapping sails are seen in the distance. The light is that of late afternoon.

AGNES, *very plainly dressed, is sitting at the table, industriously copying from a manuscript. After a moment or two,* ANTONIO *and* NELLA *enter the room, carrying a dressmaker's box which is corded and labelled.*

NELLA. È permesso, Signora. (Permit us, Signora.)

ANTONIO. Uno scatolone per la Signora. (An enormous box for the Signora.)

AGNES [*turning her head*]. Eh?

NELLA. È venuto colla ferrovia—(It has come by the railway—)

ANTONIO [*consulting the label*]. Da Firenze. (From Florence.)

AGNES. By railway, from Florence?

NELLA [*reading from the label*]. "Emilia Bardini, Via Rondinelli."

AGNES. Bardini? That's the dressmaker. There must be some mistake. Non è per me, Nella. (It isn't for me.)

> [ANTONIO *and* NELLA *carry the box to her animatedly.*

NELLA. Ma guardi, Signora! (But look, Signora!)

ANTONIO. Alla Signora Cleeve!

NELLA. E poi abbiamo pagato il porto della ferrovia. (Besides, we have paid the railway dues upon it.)

AGNES [*collecting her sheets of paper*]. Hush, hush! don't trouble me just now. Mettez-la, n'importe où.

> [*They place the box on another table.*

NELLA. La corda intaccherebbe la forbice della Signora. Vuole che Antonio la tagli? (The cord would blunt the Signora's scissors. Shall Antonio cut the cord?)

AGNES [*pinning her sheets of paper together*]. I'll see about it by and by. Laissez-moi!

NELLA [*softly to* ANTONIO]. Taglia, taglia! (Cut, cut!)

> [ANTONIO *produces a knife and cuts the cord, whereupon* NELLA *utters a little scream.*

AGNES [*turning, startled*]. What is it?

NELLA [*pushing* ANTONIO *away*]. Questo stupido non ha capito la Signora e ha tagliata la corda. (The stupid fellow misunderstood the Signora and has severed the cord.)

AGNES [*rising*]. It doesn't matter. Be quiet!

NELLA [*removing the lid from the box angrily*]. Ed ecco la scatola aperta contro voglia della Signora! (And now here is the box open against the Signora's wish!) [*Inquisitively pushing aside the paper which covers the contents of the box.*] Oh, Dio! Si vede tutto quel che vi è! (Oh, God, and all the contents exposed!)

> [*When the paper is removed, some beautiful material trimmed with lace, etc., is seen.*

NELLA. Guardi, guardi, Signora! (Signora, look, look!) [AGNES *examines the contents of the box with a puzzled air.*] Oh, che bellezza! (How beautiful!)

> [LUCAS *enters.*

ANTONIO [*to* NELLA]. Il padrone. (The master.)

> [NELLA *courtesies to* LUCAS, *then withdraws with* ANTONIO.

AGNES. Lucas, the dressmaker in the Via Rondinelli at Florence—the woman who ran up the little gown I have on now—

LUCAS [*with a smile*]. What of her?

AGNES. This has just come from her. Phuh! What does she mean by sending the showy thing to me?

LUCAS. It is my gift to you.

AGNES [*producing enough of the contents of the box to reveal a very handsome dress*]. This!

LUCAS. I knew Bardini had your measurements; I wrote to her instructing her to make that. I remember Lady Heytesbury in something similar last season.

AGNES [*examining the dress*]. A mere strap for the sleeve, and sufficiently décolletée, I should imagine.

LUCAS. My dear Agnes, I can't understand your reason for trying to make yourself a plain-looking woman when nature intended you for a pretty one.

AGNES. Pretty!

LUCAS [*looking hard at her*]. You *are* pretty.

AGNES. Oh, as a girl I may have been [*disdainfully*] pretty. What good did it do anybody? [*Fingering the dress with aversion.*] And when would you have me hang this on my bones?

LUCAS. Oh, when we are dining, or—

AGNES. Dining in a public place?

LUCAS. Why not look your best in a public place?

AGNES. Look my best! You know, I don't think of this sort of garment in connection with our companionship, Lucas.

LUCAS. It is not an extraordinary garment for a lady.

AGNES. Rustle of silk, glare of arms and throat—they belong, in my mind, to such a very different order of things from that we have set up.

LUCAS. Shall I appear before you in ill-made clothes, clumsy boots—

AGNES. Why? We are just as we always have been, since we've been together. I don't tell you that your appearance is beginning to offend.

LUCAS. Offend! Agnes, you—you pain me. I simply fail to understand why you should allow our mode of life to condemn you to perpetual slovenliness.

AGNES. Slovenliness!

LUCAS. No, no, shabbiness.

AGNES [*looking down upon the dress she is wearing*]. Shabbiness!

LUCAS [*with a laugh*]. Forgive me, dear; I'm forgetting you are wearing a comparatively new afternoon gown.

AGNES. At any rate, I'll make this brighter to-morrow with some trimmings, willingly. [*Pointing to the dressmaker's box.*] Then you won't insist on my decking myself out in rags of that kind, eh? There's something in the idea—I needn't explain.

LUCAS [*fretfully*]. Insist! I'll not urge you again. [*Pointing to the box.*] Get rid of it somehow. Are you copying that manuscript of mine?

AGNES. I had just finished it.

LUCAS. Already! [*Taking up her copy.*] How beautifully you write! [*Going to her eagerly.*] What do you think of my Essay?

AGNES. The subject bristles with truth; it's vital.

LUCAS. My method of treating it?

AGNES. Hardly a word out of place.

LUCAS [*chilled*]. Hardly a word?

AGNES. Not a word, in fact.

LUCAS. No, dear, I daresay your "hardly" is nearer the mark.

AGNES. I assure you it is brilliant, Lucas.

LUCAS. What a wretch I am ever to find the smallest fault in you! Shall we dine out to-night?

AGNES. As you wish, dear.

LUCAS. At the Grünwald? [*He goes to the table to pick up his manuscript; when his back is turned she looks at her watch quickly.*] We'll solemnly toast this, shall we in Montefiascone?

AGNES [*eyeing him askance*]. You are going out for your chocolate this afternoon as usual, I suppose?

LUCAS. Yes; but I'll look through your copy first, so that I can slip it into the post at once. You are not coming out?

AGNES. Not till dinner-time.

LUCAS [*kissing her on the forehead*]. I talked over the points of this [*tapping the manuscript*] with a man this morning; he praised some of the phrases warmly.

AGNES. A man? [*In an altered tone.*] The duke?

LUCAS. Er—yes.

AGNES [*with assumed indifference, replacing the lid on the dressmaker's box.*] You have seen him again to-day, then?

LUCAS. We strolled about together for half an hour on the Piazza.

AGNES [*replacing the cord round the box*]. You—you don't dislike him as much as you did?

LUCAS. He's somebody to chat to. I suppose one gets accustomed even to a man one dislikes.

AGNES [*almost inaudibly*]. I suppose so.

LUCAS. As a matter of fact, he has the reputation of being rather a pleasant companion; though I—I confess—I—I don't find him very entertaining.

> [*He goes out. She stands staring at the door through which he has disappeared. There is a knock at the opposite door.*

AGNES [*rousing herself*]. Fortuné! [*Raising her voice.*] Fortuné!

> [*The door opens and* GERTRUDE *enters hurriedly.*

GERTRUDE. Fortuné is complacently smoking a cigarette in the Campo.

AGNES. Mrs. Thorpe!

GERTRUDE [*breathlessly*]. Mr. Cleeve is out, I conclude?

AGNES. No. He is later than usual going out this afternoon.

GERTRUDE [*irresolutely*]. I don't think I'll wait then.

AGNES. But do tell me—you have been crossing the streets to avoid me during the past week—what has made you come to see me now?

GERTRUDE. I *would* come. I've given poor Amos the slip; he believes I'm buying beads for the Ketherick school-children.

AGNES [*shaking her head*]. Ah, Mrs. Thorpe!—

GERTRUDE. Of course, it's perfectly brutal to be underhanded. But we're leaving for home to-morrow; I couldn't resist it.

AGNES [*coldly*]. Perhaps I'm very ungracious—

GERTRUDE [*taking* AGNES's *hand*]. The fact is, Mrs. Cleeve—oh, what do you wish me to call you?

AGNES [*withdrawing her hand*]. Well, you're off tomorrow. Agnes will do.

GERTRUDE. Thank you. The fact is, it's been a bad week with me—restless, fanciful. And I haven't been able to get you out of my head.

AGNES. I'm sorry.

GERTRUDE. Your story, your present life; you, yourself—such a contradiction to what you profess!—well, it all has a sort of fascination for me.

AGNES. My dear, you're simply not sleeping again. [*Turning away.*] You'd better go back to the ammonia Kirke prescribed for you.

GERTRUDE [*taking a card from her purse, with a little light laugh*]. You want to physic me, do you, after worrying my poor brain as you've done? [*Going to her.*] "The Rectory, Daleham, Ketherick Moor." Yorkshire, you know. There can be no great harm in your writing to me sometimes.

AGNES [*refusing the card*]. No; under the circumstances I can't promise that.

GERTRUDE [*wistfully*]. Very well.

AGNES [*facing her*]. Oh, can't you understand that it can only be—disturbing to both of us for an impulsive, emotional creature like yourself to keep up acquaintanceship with a woman who takes life as I do? We'll drop each other, leave each other alone.

> [*She walks away, and stands leaning upon the stove, her back towards* GERTRUDE.

GERTRUDE [*replacing the card in her purse*]. As you please. Picture me, sometimes, in that big, hollow shell of a rectory at Ketherick, strolling about my poor dead little chap's empty room.

AGNES [*under her breath*]. Oh!

GERTRUDE [*turning to go*]. God bless you.

AGNES. Gertrude! [*With altered manner.*] You—you have the trick of making me lonely also. [*Going to* GERTRUDE, *taking her hands, and fondling them.*] I'm tired of talking to the walls! And your blood is warm to me! Shall I tell you, or not—or not?

GERTRUDE. Do tell me.

AGNES. There is a man here, in Venice, who is torturing me—flaying me alive.

GERTRUDE. Torturing you?

AGNES. He came here about a week ago; he is trying to separate us.

GERTRUDE. You and Mr. Cleeve?

AGNES. Yes.

GERTRUDE. You are afraid he will succeed?

AGNES. Succeed! What nonsense you talk!

GERTRUDE. What upsets you then?

AGNES. After all, it's difficult to explain—the feeling is so indefinite. It's like—something in the air. This man is influencing us both oddly. Lucas is as near illness again as possible; I can *hear* his nerves vibrating. And I—you know what a fish-like thing I am as a rule—just look at me now, as I'm speaking to you.

GERTRUDE. But don't you and Mr. Cleeve—talk to each other?

AGNES. As children do when the lights are put out—of everything but what's uppermost in their minds.

GERTRUDE. You have met the man?

AGNES. I intend to meet him.

GERTRUDE. Who is he?

AGNES. A relation of Lucas's—the Duke of St. Olpherts.

GERTRUDE. He has right on his side then?

AGNES. If you choose to think so.

GERTRUDE [*deliberately*]. Supposing he *does* succeed in taking Mr. Cleeve away from you?

AGNES [*staring at* GERTRUDE]. What, *now*, do you mean?

GERTRUDE. Yes.

> [*There is a brief pause; then* AGNES *walks across the room wiping her brow with her handkerchief.*

AGNES. I tell you, that idea's—preposterous.

GERTRUDE. Oh, I can't understand you!

AGNES. You'll respect my confidence?

GERTRUDE. Agnes!

AGNES [*sitting*]. Well, I fancy this man's presence here has simply started me thinking of a time—oh, it may never come!—a time when I may cease to be—necessary to Mr. Cleeve. Do you understand?

GERTRUDE. I remember what you told me of your being prepared to grant each other freedom if—

AGNES. Yes, yes—and for the past few days this idea has filled me with a fear of the most humiliating kind.

GERTRUDE. What fear?

AGNES. The fear lest, after all my beliefs and protestations, I should eventually find myself loving Lucas in the helpless, common way of women—

GERTRUDE [*under her breath*]. I see.

AGNES. The dread that the moment may arrive some day when, should it be required of me, *I sha'n't feel myself able to give him up easily.* [*Her head drooping, uttering a low moan.*] Oh!—

> [LUCAS, *dressed for going out, enters, carrying* AGNES'S *copy of his manuscript, rolled and addressed for the post.* AGNES *rises.*

AGNES [*to* LUCAS]. Mrs. Thorpe starts for home to-morrow; she has called to say good-by.

LUCAS [*to* GERTRUDE]. It is very kind. Is your good brother quite well?

GERTRUDE [*embarrassed*]. Thanks, quite.

LUCAS [*smiling*]. I believe I have added to his experience of the obscure corners of Venice, during the past week.

GERTRUDE. I—I don't—why?

LUCAS. By so frequently putting him to the inconvenience of avoiding me.

GERTRUDE. Oh, Mr. Cleeve, we—I—I—

LUCAS. Please tell your brother I asked after him.

GERTRUDE. I—I can't; he—doesn't know I've—I've—

LUCAS. Ah! really? [*With a bow.*] Good-by.

> [*He goes out,* AGNES *accompanying him to the door.*

GERTRUDE [*to herself*]. Brute! [*To* AGNES.] Oh, I suppose Mr. Cleeve has made me look precisely as I feel.

AGNES. How?

GERTRUDE. Like people deserve to feel, who do godly, mean things.

> [FORTUNÉ *appears.*

FORTUNÉ [*To* AGNES, *significantly.*] Mr. Cleeve 'as jus' gone out.

AGNES. Vous savez, n'est-ce pas.

FORTUNÉ [*glancing at* GERTRUDE]. But Madame is now engage.

GERTRUDE [*to* AGNES]. Oh, I am going.

AGNES [*to* GERTRUDE]. Wait. [*Softly to her.*] I want you to hear this little comedy. Fortuné shall repeat my instructions. [*To* FORTUNÉ.] Les ordres que je vous ai donnés, répétez-les.

FORTUNÉ [*speaking in an undertone*]. On ze left 'and side of ze Campo—

AGNES. Non, non—tout haut.

FORTUNÉ [*aloud, with a slight shrug of the shoulders*]. On ze left 'and side of ze Campo—

AGNES. Yes.

FORTUNÉ. In one of ze doorways—between Fiorentini's and ze leetle lamp shop ze—ze—h'm—ze person.

AGNES. Precisely. Dépêchez-vous. [FORTUNÉ *bows and retires.*] Fortuné flatters himself he is engaged in some horrid intrigue. You guess whom I am expecting?

GERTRUDE. The duke?

AGNES [*ringing a bell*]. I've written to him asking him to call upon me this afternoon while Lucas is at Florian's. [*Referring to her watch.*] He is to kick his heels about the Campo till I let him know I am alone.

GERTRUDE. Will he obey you?

AGNES. A week ago he was curious to see the sort of animal I am. If he holds off now I'll hit upon some other plan. I will come to close quarters with him, if only for five minutes.

GERTRUDE. Good-by. [*They embrace, then walk together to the door.*] You still refuse my address?

AGNES. You bat! Didn't you see me make a note of it?

GERTRUDE. You!

AGNES [*her hand on her heart*]. Here.

GERTRUDE [*gratefully*]. Ah!

[*She goes out.*

AGNES [*at the open door*]. Gertrude!

GERTRUDE [*outside*]. Yes?

AGNES [*in a low voice*]. Remember, in my thoughts I pace that lonely little room of yours with you. [*As if to stop* GERTRUDE *from re-entering.*] Hush! No, no.

[*She closes the door sharply.* NELLA *appears.*

AGNES [*pointing to the box on the table*]. Portez ce carton dans ma chambre.

NELLA [*trying to peep into the box as she carries it*]. Signora, se Ella si mettesse questo magnifico abito! Oh! quanto sarebbe più bella! (Signora, if you were to wear this magnificent dress! Oh! how much more beautiful you would be!)

AGNES [*listening*]. Sssh! Sssh! [NELLA *goes out.* FORTUNÉ *enters.*] Eh, bien?

[FORTUNÉ *glances over his shoulder. The* DUKE OF ST. OLPHERTS *enters; the wreck of a very handsome man, with delicate features, a transparent complexion, a polished manner, and a smooth, weary voice. He limps, walking with the aid of a cane.* FORTUNÉ *retires.*

AGNES. Duke of St. Olpherts?

ST. OLPHERTS [*bowing*]. Mrs. Ebbsmith?

AGNES. Mr. Cleeve would have opposed this rather out-of-the-way proceeding of mine. He doesn't know I have asked you to call on me to-day.

ST. OLPHERTS. So I conclude. It gives our meeting a pleasant air of adventure.

AGNES. I shall tell him directly he returns.

ST. OLPHERTS [*gallantly*]. And destroy a cherished secret.

AGNES. You are an invalid; [*motioning him to be seated*] pray don't stand. [*Sitting.*] Your Grace is a man who takes life lightly. It will relieve you to hear that I wish to keep sentiment out of any business we have together.

ST. OLPHERTS. I believe I haven't the reputation of being a sentimental man. [*Seating himself.*] You send for me, Mrs. Ebbsmith—

AGNES. To tell you I have come to regard the suggestion you were good enough to make a week ago—

ST. OLPHERTS. Suggestion?

AGNES. Shakespeare, the musical glasses, you know—

ST. OLPHERTS. Oh, yes. Ha! ha!

AGNES. I've come to think it a reasonable one. At the moment I considered it a gross impertinence.

ST. OLPHERTS. Written requests are so dependent on a sympathetic reader.

AGNES. That meeting might have saved you time and trouble.

ST. OLPHERTS. I grudge neither.

AGNES. It might perhaps have shown your Grace that your view of life is too narrow; that your method of dealing witih its problems wants variety; that, in point of fact, your employment upon your present mission is distinctly inappropriate. Our meeting to-day may serve the same purpose.

ST. OLPHERTS. My view of life?

AGNES. That all men and women may safely be judged by the standards of the casino and the dancing-garden.

ST. OLPHERTS. I have found those standards not altogether untrustworthy. My method—?

AGNES. To scoff, to sneer, to ridicule.

ST. OLPHERTS. Ah! And how much is there, my dear Mrs. Ebbsmith, belonging to humanity that survives being laughed at?

AGNES. More than you credit, duke. For example, I—I think it possible you may not succeed in grinning away the compact between Mr. Cleeve and myself.

ST. OLPHERTS. Compact?

AGNES. Between serious man and woman.

ST. OLPHERTS. Serious *woman*.

AGNES. Ah, at least you must see that—serious woman. [*Rising, facing him.*] You can't fail to realize, even from this slight personal knowledge of me, that you are not dealing just now with some poor, feeble ballet-girl.

ST. OLPHERTS. But how well you put it! [*Rising.*] And how frank of you to furnish, as it were, a plan of the fortfications to the—the—

AGNES. Why do you stick at "enemy"?

ST. OLPHERTS. It's not the word. Opponent! For the moment, perhaps, opponent. I am never an enemy, I hope, where your sex is concerned.

AGNES. No, I am aware that you are not overnice in the bestowal of your patronage—where my sex is concerned.

ST. OLPHERTS. You regard my appearance in an affair of morals as a quaint one.

AGNES. Your Grace is beginning to know me.

ST. OLPHERTS. Dear lady, you take pride, I hear, in belonging to—The People. You would delight me amazingly by giving me an inkling of the popular notion of my career.

AGNES [*walking away*]. Excuse me.

ST. OLPHERTS [*following her*]. Please! It would be instructive, perhaps chastening. I entreat.

AGNES. No.

ST. OLPHERTS. You are letting sentiment intrude itself. [*Sitting, in pain.*] I challenge you.

AGNES. At Eton you were curiously precocious. The head-master, referring to your aptitude with books, prophesied a brilliant future for you; your tutor, alarmed by your attachment to a certain cottage at Ascot which was minus a host, thanked his stars to be rid of you. At Oxford you closed all books, except, of course, betting-books.

ST. OLPHERTS. I detected the tendency of the age—scholarship for the masses. I considered it my turn to be merely intuitively intelligent.

AGNES. You left Oxford a gambler and spendthrift. A year or two in town established you as an amiable, undisguised debauchee. The rest is modern history.

ST. OLPHERTS. Complete your sketch. Don't stop at the—rude outline.

AGNES. Your affairs falling into disorder, you promptly married a wealthy woman—the poor, rich lady who has for some years honoured you by being your duchess at a distance. This burlesque of marriage helped to reassure your friends, and actually obtained for you an ornamental appointment for which an over-taxed nation provides a handsome stipend. But, to sum up, you must always remain an irritating source of uneasiness to your own order, as, luckily, you will always be a sharp-edged weapon in the hands of mine.

ST. OLPHERTS [*with a polite smile*]. Yours! Ah, to that small, unruly section to which I understand you particularly attach yourself. To the—

AGNES [*with changed manner, flashing eyes, harsh voice, and violent gestures*]. The sufferers, the toilers; that great crowd of old and young—old and young stamped by excessive labour and privation all of one pattern—whose backs bend under burdens, whose bones ache and grow awry, whose skins, in youth and in age, are wrinkled and yellow; those from whom a fair share of the earth's space and of the light of day is withheld. [*Looking down upon him fiercely.*] The half-starved who are bidden to stand with their feet in the kennel to watch gay processions in which you and your kind are borne high. Those who would strip the robes from a dummy aristocracy and cast the broken dolls into the limbo of a nation's discarded toys. Those who—mark me!—are already upon the highway, marching, marching; whose time is coming as surely as yours is going!

ST. OLPHERTS [*clapping his hands gently*]. Bravo! bravo! Really, a flash of the old fire. Admirable! [*She walks away to the window with an impatient exclamation.*] Your present *affaire du coeur* does not wholly absorb you then, Mrs. Ebbsmith. Even now the murmurings of love have not entirely superseded the thunderous denunciations of—h'm—you once bore a nickname, my dear.

AGNES [*turning sharply*]. Ho, so you've heard *that*, have you!

ST. OLPHERTS. Oh, yes.

AGNES. Mad—Agnes? [*He bows deprecatingly.*] We appear to have studied each other's history pretty closely.

ST. OLPHERTS. Dear lady, this is not the first time the same roof has covered us.

AGNES. No?

ST. OLPHERTS. Five years ago, on a broiling night in July, I joined a party of men who made an excursion from a club-house in St. James's Street to the unsavoury district of St. Luke's.

AGNES. Oh, yes.

ST. OLPHERTS. A depressin' building; the Iron Hall, Barker Street—no—Carter Street.

AGNES. Precisely.

ST. OLPHERTS. We took our places amongst a handful of frowsy folks who cracked nuts and blasphemed. On the platform stood a gaunt, white-faced young lady resolutely engaged in making up by extravagance of gesture for the deficiencies of an exhausted voice. "There," said one of my companions, "that is the notorious Mrs. Ebbsmith." Upon which a person near us, whom I judged from his air of leaden laziness to be a British working man, blurted out, "Notorious Mrs. Ebbsmith! Mad Agnes! That's the name her sanguinary friends give her—Mad Agnes!" At that moment the eye of the panting oratress caught mine for an instant and you and I first met.

AGNES [*passing her hand across her brow, thoughtfully*]. Mad—Agnes . . . [*To him, with a grim smile.*] We have both been criticised, in our time, pretty sharply, eh, duke?

ST. OLPHERTS. Yes. Let that reflection make you more charitable to a poor peer.

> [*A knock at the door.*

AGNES. Entrez!

> [FORTUNÉ *and* ANTONIO *enter,* ANTONIO *carrying tea, etc., upon a tray.*

AGNES [*to* ST. OLPHERTS]. You drink tea—fellow-sufferer?

> [*He signifies assent.* FORTUNÉ *places the tray on the table, then withdraws with* AN-TONIO. AGNES *pours out tea.*

ST. OLPHERTS [*producing a little box from his waistcoat pocket*]. No milk, dear lady. May I be allowed—saccharine?

> [*She hands him his cup of tea; their eyes meet.*

AGNES [*scornfully*]. Tell me now—really—why do the Cleeves send a rip like you to do their serious work?

ST. OLPHERTS [*laughing heartily*]. Ha, ha, ha! Rip! ha, ha! Poor solemn family! Oh, set a thief to catch a thief, you know. That, I presume, is their motive.

AGNES [*pausing in the act of pouring out tea and staring at him*]. What do you mean?

ST. OLPHERTS [*sipping his tea*]. Set a thief to catch a thief. And, by deduction, set one sensualist who, after all, doesn't take the trouble to deceive himself, to rescue another who does.

AGNES. If I understand you, that is an insinuation against Mr. Cleeve.

ST. OLPHERTS. Insinuation!—

AGNES [*looking at him fixedly*]. Make yourself clearer.

ST. OLPHERTS. You have accused me, Mrs. Ebbsmith, of narrowness of outlook. In the present instance dear lady, it is *your* judgment which is at fault.

AGNES. Mine?

ST. OLPHERTS. It is not I who fall into the error of confounding you with the designing *danseuse* of commerce; it is, strangely enough, you who have failed in your estimate of Mr. Lucas Cleeve.

AGNES. What is my estimate?

ST. OLPHERTS. I pay you the compliment of believing that you have looked upon my nephew as a talented young gentleman whose future was seriously threatened by domestic disorder; a young man of a certain courage and independence, with a share of the brain and spirit of those terrible human pests called reformers; the one young gentleman, in fact, most likely to aid you in advancing your vivacious social and political tenets. You have had such thoughts in your mind?

AGNES. I don't deny it.

ST. OLPHERTS. Ah! But what is the real, the actual Lucas Cleeve?

AGNES. Well—what is the real Lucas Cleeve?

ST. OLPHERTS. Poor dear fellow! I'll tell you. [*Going to the table to deposit his cup there; while she watches him, her hands tightly clasped, a frightened look in her eyes.*] The real Lucas Cleeve. [*Coming back to her.*] An egoist. An egoist.

AGNES. An egoist. Yes.

ST. OLPHERTS. Possessing ambition without patience, self-esteem without self-confidence.

AGNES. Well?

ST. OLPHERTS. Afflicted with a desperate craving for the opium-like drug, adulation; persistently seeking the society of those whose white, pink-tipped fingers fill the pernicious pipe most deftly and delicately. Eh?

AGNES. I didn't— Pray go on.

ST. OLPHERTS. Ha, I remember they looked to his marriage to check his dangerous fancy for the flutter of lace, the purr of pretty women. And now here he is—loose again.

AGNES [*suffering*]. Oh!—

ST.OLPHERTS. In short, in intellect still nothing but a callow boy; in body, nervous, bloodless, hysterical; in morals—an Epicure.

AGNES. Have done! Have done!

ST. OLPHERTS. "Epicure" offends you. A vain woman would find consolation in the word.

AGNES. Enough of it! Enough! Enough!

> [*She turns away, beating her hands together. The light in the room has gradually become subdued; the warm tinge of sunset now colours the scene outside the windows.*

ST. OLPHERTS [*with a shrug of his shoulders*]. The real Lucas Cleeve.

AGNES. No, no! untrue! untrue! [LUCAS *enters. The three remain silent for a moment.*] The Duke of St. Olpherts calls in answer to a letter I wrote to him yesterday. I wanted to make his acquaintance.

> [*She goes out.*

LUCAS [*after a brief pause*]. By a lucky accident the tables were crowded at Florian's; I might have missed the chance of welcoming you. In God's name, duke, why must you come here?

ST. OLPHERTS [*fumbling in his pockets for a note*]. In God's name? You bring the orthodoxy into this queer firm then, Lucas? [*Handing the note to* LUCAS.] A peremptory summons.

LUCAS. You need not have obeyed it. [ST. OLPHERTS *takes a cigarette from his case and limps away.*] I looked about for you just now. I wanted to see you.

ST. OLPHERTS [*lighting the cigarette*]. How fortunate!—

LUCAS. To tell you that this persecution must come to an end. It has made me desperately wretched for a whole week.

ST. OLPHERTS. Persecution?

LUCAS. Temptation.

ST. OLPHERTS. Dear Lucas, the process of inducing a man to return to his wife isn't generally described as temptation.

LUCAS. Ah, I won't hear another word of that proposal. [ST. OLPHERTS *shrugs his shoulders.*] I say my people are offering me, through you, a deliberate temptation to be a traitor. To which of these two women —my wife or [*pointing to the door*] to her—am I really bound now? It may be regrettable, scandalous, but the common rules of right and wrong have ceased to apply here. Finally, duke—and this is my message—I intend to keep faith with the woman who sat by my bedside in Rome, the woman to whom I shouted my miserable story in my delirium, the woman whose calm, resolute voice healed me, hardened me, renewed in me the desire to live.

ST. OLPHERTS. Ah! Oh, these modern nurses, in their greys, or browns, and snowy bibs! They have much to answer for, dear Lucas.

LUCAS. No, no! Why will you persist, all of you, in regarding this as a mere morbid infatuation bred in the fumes of pastilles? It isn't so! Laugh if you care to!—but this is a meeting of affinities, of the solitary man and the truly sympathetic woman.

ST. OLPHERTS. And oh, oh, these sympathetic women!

LUCAS. No! Oh, the unsympathetic women! There you have the cause of half the world's misery. The unsympathetic women—you should have loved one of them.

ST. OLPHERTS. I daresay I've done that in my time.

LUCAS. Love one of these women—*I* know!—worship her, yield yourself to the intoxicating day-dreams that make the grimy world sweeter than any heaven ever imagined. How your heart leaps with gratitude for your good fortune; how compassionately you regard your unblest fellow-men! What may you not accomplish with such a mate beside you; how high will be your aims, how paltry every obstacle that bars your way to them; how sweet is to be the labour, how divine the rest! Then— you marry her. Marry her, and in six months, if you've pluck enough to do it, lag behind your shooting-party and blow your brains out by accident, at the edge of a turnip-field. You have found out by that time all that there is to look for— the daily diminishing interest in your doings, the poorly assumed attention as you attempt to talk over some plan for the future; then the yawn and, by degrees, the covert sneer, the little sarcasm, and, finally, the frank, open stare of boredom. Ah, duke, when you all carry out your repressive legislation against women of evil lives, don't fail to include in your schedule the Unsympathetic Wives. They are the women whose victims show the sorriest scars; they are the really "bad women" of the world—all the others are snow-white in comparison!

ST. OLPHERTS. Yes, you've got a great deal of this in that capital Essay you quoted from this morning. Dear fellow, I admit your home discomforts. But to jump out of that frying-pan into this confounded—what does she call it?—Compact!

LUCAS. Compact?

ST. OLPHERTS. A vague reference, as I understand, to your joint crusade against the blessed institution of Marriage.

LUCAS [an alteration in his manner]. Oh—ho, that idea! What— what has she been saying to you?

ST. OLPHERTS. Incidentally she pitched into me, dear Lucas; she attacked my moral character. You must have been telling tales.

LUCAS.   Oh, I—I hope not. Of course, we—

ST. OLPHERTS. Yes, yes—a little family gossip, to pass the time while she has been dressing her hair, or—by-the-bye, she doesn't appear to spend much time in dressing her hair.

LUCAS [biting his lip]. Really?

ST. OLPHERTS. Then she denounced the gilded aristocracy generally. Our day is over; we're broken wooden dolls and are going to be chucked. The old tune, but I enjoyed the novelty of being so near the instrument. I assure you, dear fellow, I was within three feet of her when she deliberately Trafalgar Squared me.

LUCAS [with an uneasy laugh]. You're the red rag, duke. This spirit of revolt in her—it's ludicrously extravagant; but it will die out in time, when she has become used to being happy and cared for— [partly to himself, with clenched hands] yes, cared for.

ST. OLPHERTS.   Die out? Bred in the bone, dear Lucas.

LUCAS. On some topics she's a mere echo of her father—if you mean that.

ST. OLPHERTS. The father—one of these public-park vermin, eh?

LUCAS. Dead years ago.

ST. OLPHERTS. I once heard her bellowing in a dirty little shed in St. Luke's. I told you?

LUCAS. Yes; you've told me.

ST. OLPHERTS. I sat there again, it seemed, this afternoon. The orator not quite so lean, perhaps; a little less witch-like, but—

LUCAS. She was actually in want of food in those days. Poor girl! [*Partly to himself.*] I mean to remind myself of that constantly. Poor girl!

ST. OLPHERTS. *Girl!* Let me see—you're considerably her junior?

LUCAS. No, no; a few months perhaps.

ST. OLPHERTS. Oh, come!

LUCAS. Well, years—two or three.

ST. OLPHERTS. The voice remains rather raucous.

LUCAS. By God, the voice is sweet.

ST. OLPHERTS. Well—considering the wear and tear. Really, my dear fellow, I do believe this—I do believe that if you gowned her respectably—

LUCAS [*impulsively*]. Yes, yes, I say so. I tell her that.

ST. OLPHERTS [*with a smile*]. Do you! That's odd now.

LUCAS. What a topic! Poor Agnes's dress!

ST. OLPHERTS. Your taste used to be rather aesthetic. Even your own wife is one of the smartest women in London.

LUCAS. Ha, well, I must contrive to smother these aesthetic tastes of mine.

ST. OLPHERTS. It's a pity that other people will retain their sense of the incongruous.

LUCAS [*snapping his fingers*]. Other people!—

ST. OLPHERTS. The public.

LUCAS. The public?

ST. OLPHERTS. Come, you know well enough that unostentatious immodesty is no part of your partner's programme. Of course, you will find yourself by and by in a sort of perpetual public parade with your crack-brained visionary—

LUCAS. You shall not speak of her so! You shall not.

ST. OLPHERTS [*unconcernedly*]. Each of you bearing a pole of the soiled banner of Free Union. Free Union for the People! Ho, my dear Lucas!

LUCAS. Good heavens, duke, do you imagine, now that I am in sound health and mind again, that I don't see the hideous absurdity of these views of hers!

ST. OLPHERTS. Then why the deuce don't you listen a little more patiently to *my* views?

LUCAS. No, no. I tell you I intend to keep faith with her, as far as I am able. She's so earnest, so pitiably earnest. If I broke faith with her entirely it would be too damnably cowardly.

ST. OLPHERTS. Cowardly?

LUCAS [*pacing the room agitatedly*]. Besides, we shall do well together, after all, I believe—she and I. In the end we shall make concessions to each other and settle down, somewhere abroad, peacefully.

st. olpherts. Hah! And they called you a Coming Man at one time, didn't they?

lucas. Oh, I—I shall make as fine a career with my pen as that other career would have been. At any rate, I ask you to leave me to it all—to leave me.

> [fortuné *enters. The shades of evening have now deepened; the glow of sunset comes into the room.*

fortuné. I beg your pardon, sir.

lucas. Well?

fortuné. It is pas' ze time for you to dress for dinner.

lucas. I'll come.

> [fortuné *goes out.*

st. olpherts. When do we next meet, dear fellow?

lucas. No, no—please not again.

> [nella *enters, excitedly.*

nella [*speaking over her shoulder*]. Si, Signora; ecco il Signore. (Yes, Signora; here is the Signor). [*To* cleeve]. Scusi, Signore. Quando la vedrá come é cara!— (Pardon, Signor. When you see her you'll see how sweet she looks!—) [agnes's *voice is heard.*

agnes [*outside*]. Am I keeping you waiting, Lucas?

> [*She enters, handsomely gowned, her throat and arms bare, the fashion of her hair roughly altered. She stops abruptly upon seeing* st. olpherts; *a strange light comes into her eyes; voice, manner, bearing, all express triumph. The two men stare at her blankly. She appears to be a beautiful woman.*

agnes [*to* nella]. Un petit châle noir tricoté—cherchez-le [nella *withdraws*]. Ah, you are not dressed, Lucas dear.

lucas. What—what time is it?

> [*He goes towards the door still staring at* agnes.

st. olpherts [*looking at her and speaking in an altered tone*]. I fear my gossiping has delayed him. You—you dine out?

agnes. At the Grünwald. Why don't you join us? [*Turning to* lucas *lightly*]. Persuade him, Lucas.

> [lucas *pauses at the door.*

st. olpherts. Er—impossible. Some—friends of mine may arrive to-night. [lucas *goes out*]. I am more than sorry.

agnes [*mockingly*]. Really? You are sure you are not shy of being seen with a notorious woman?

st. olpherts. My dear Mrs. Ebbsmith!—

agnes. No, I forget—that would be unlike you. *Mad* people scare you, perhaps?

st. olpherts. Ha, ha! don't be too rough.

AGNES. Come, duke, confess—isn't there more sanity in me than you suspected?

ST. OLPHERTS [*in a low voice, eyeing her*]. Much more. I think you are very clever.

> [LUCAS *quietly re-enters the room; he halts upon seeing that* ST. OLPHERTS *still lingers.*]

ST. OLPHERTS [*with a wave of the hand to* LUCAS]. Just off, dear fellow. [*He offers his hand to* AGNES; *she quickly places hers behind her back*]. You—you are charming. [*He walks to the door, then looks round at the pair*]. Au 'voir!

AGNES. Au 'voir! [ST. OLPHERTS *goes out. Her head drooping suddenly, her voice hard and dull*]. You had better take me to Fulici's before we dine and buy me some gloves.

LUCAS [*coming to her and seizing her hand*]. Agnes dear!

AGNES [*Releasing herself and sitting with a heavy, almost sullen, look upon her face*]. Are you satisfied?

LUCAS [*by her side*]. You have delighted me! how sweet you look!

AGNES. Ah—

LUCAS. You shall have twenty new gowns now; you shall see the women envying you, the men envying me. Ah, ha! fifty new gowns! you will wear them?

AGNES. Yes.

LUCAS. Why, what has brought about this change in you?

AGNES. What!

LUCAS. What?

AGNES. I—know—

LUCAS. You know.

AGNES. Exactly how you regard me.

LUCAS. I don't understand you—

AGNES. Listen. Long ago, in Florence, I began to suspect that we had made a mistake, Lucas. Even there I began to suspect that your nature was not one to allow you to go through life sternly, severely, looking upon me more and more each day as a fellow-worker, and less and less as—a woman. I suspected this—oh, proved it!—but still made myself believe that this companionship of ours would gradually become, in a sense, colder—more temperate, more impassive. [*Beating her brow*]. Never! never! Oh, a few minutes ago this man, who means to part us if he can, drew your character, disposition, in a dozen words!

LUCAS. You believe *him*! You credit what *he* says of me!

AGNES. I declared it to be untrue. Oh, but—

LUCAS. But—but—!

AGNES [*rising, seizing his arm*]. The picture he paints of you is not wholly a false one. Sssh! Lucas, hark, attend to me! I resign myself to it all! Dear, I must resign myself to it!

LUCAS. Resign yourself? Has life with me become so distasteful?

AGNES. Has it? Think! Why, when I realized the actual conditions of our companionship—why didn't I go on my own way stoically? Why don't I go at this moment?

LUCAS. You really *love* me, do you mean—as simple, tender women are content to love? [*She looks at him, nods slowly, then turns away and droops over the table. He raises her and takes her in his arms*]. My dear girl! My dear, cold, warm-hearted girl! Ha! You couldn't bear to see me packed up in one of the duke's travelling-boxes and borne back to London, eh? [*She shakes her head; her lips form the word "No."*] No fear of that, my—my sweetheart!

AGNES [*gently pushing him from her*]. Quick—dress—take me out.

LUCAS. You are shivering; go and get your thickest wrap.

AGNES. That heavy brown cloak of mine?

LUCAS. Yes.

AGNES. It's an old friend, but—dreadfully *shabby*. You will be ashamed of me again.

LUCAS. Ashamed!—

AGNES. I'll write to Bardini about a new one to-morrow. I won't oppose you—I won't repel you any more.

LUCAS. Repel me! I only urged you to reveal yourself as what you are—a beautiful woman.

AGNES. Ah! Am I—that?

LUCAS [*kissing her*]. Beautiful—beautiful!

AGNES [*with a gesture of abandonment*]. I—I'm glad.

> [*She leaves him and goes out. He looks after her for a moment thoughtfully, then suddenly passes his hands across his brow and opens his arms widely as if casting a burden from him.*

LUCAS. Oh!—oh!—[*Turning away alertly*]. Fortuné——!

END OF THE SECOND ACT.

THE THIRD ACT.

The scene is the same as before, but it is evening, and the lamps are lighted within the room, while outside is bright moonlight. AGNES, *dressed as at the end of the preceding Act, is lying upon the settee propped up by pillows. A pretty silk shawl, which she plays with restlessly, is over her shoulders. Her face is pale, but her eyes glitter, and her voice has a bright ring in it.* KIRKE *is seated at a table, writing.* GERTRUDE, *without hat or mantle, is standing behind the settee, looking down smilingly upon* AGNES.

KIRKE [*writing*]. H'm— [*To* AGNES]. Are you often guilty of this sort of thing?

AGNES [*laughing*]. I've never fainted before in my life; I don't mean to do so again.

KIRKE [*writing*]. Should you alter your mind about that, do select a suitable spot on the next occasion. What was it your head came against?

GERTRUDE. A wooden chest, Mr. Cleeve thinks.

AGNES. With beautiful, rusty, iron clamps. [*Putting her hand to her head, and addressing* GERTRUDE.] The price of vanity.

KIRKE. Vanity?

AGNES. Lucas was to take me out to dinner. While I was waiting for him to dress I must needs stand and survey my full length in a mirror.

KIRKE [*glancing at her*]. A very excusable proceeding.

AGNES. Suddenly the room sank and left me—so the feeling was—in air.

KIRKE. Well, most women can manage to look into their pier-glasses without swooning—eh, Mrs. Thorpe?

GERTRUDE [*smiling*]. How should I know, doctor?

KIRKE [*blotting his writing*]. There. How goes the time?

GERTRUDE. Half-past eight.

KIRKE. I'll leave this prescription at Mantovani's myself. I can get it made up to-night.

AGNES [*taking the prescription out of his hand, playfully*]. Let me look.

KIRKE [*protesting*]. Now, now.

AGNES [*reading the prescription*]. Ha, ha! After all, what humbugs doctors are !

KIRKE. You've never heard me deny it.

AGNES [*returning the prescription to him*]. But I'll swallow it—for the dignity of my old profession.

[*She reaches out her hand to take a cigarette.*

KIRKE. Don't smoke too many of those things.

AGNES. They never harm me. It's a survival of the time in my life when the cupboard was always empty. [*Striking a match*]. Only it had to be stronger tobacco in those days, I can tell you.

[*She lights her cigarette.* GERTRUDE *is assisting* KIRKE *with his overcoat.* LUCAS *enters in evening dress, and looking younger, almost boyish.*

LUCAS [*brightly*]. Well?

KIRKE. She's to have a cup of good *bouillon* — Mrs. Thorpe is going to look after that—and anything else she fancies. She's all right. [*Shaking hands with* AGNES]. The excitement of putting on that pretty frock—[AGNES *gives a hard little laugh. Shaking hands with* LUCAS.] I'll look in to-morrow. [*Turning to* GERTRUDE]. Oh, just a word with you, nurse.

[LUCAS *has been bending over* AGNES *affectionately; he now sits by her, and they talk in under tones; he lights a cigarette from hers.*

KIRKE [*to* GERTRUDE]. There's many a true word, et cetera.

GERTRUDE. Excitement?

KIRKE. Yes; and that smart gown's connected with it too.

GERTRUDE. It is extraordinary to see her like this.

KIRKE. Not the same woman.

GERTRUDE. No, nor is he quite the same man.

KIRKE. How long can you remain with her?

GERTRUDE. Till eleven—if you will let my brother know where I am.

KIRKE. What, doesn't he know?

GERTRUDE. I simply sent word, about an hour ago, that I shouldn't be back to dinner.

KIRKE. Very well.

GERTRUDE. Look here! I'll get you to tell him the truth.

KIRKE. The truth—oh?

GERTRUDE. I called here this afternoon, unknown to Amos, to bid her good-by. Then I pottered about, rather miserably, spending money. Coming out of Naya's the photographer's, I tumbled over Mr. Cleeve, who had been looking for you, and he begged me to come round here again after I had done my shopping.

KIRKE. I understand.

GERTRUDE. Doctor, have you ever seen Amos look dreadfully stern and knit about the brows—like a bishop who is put out?

KIRKE. No.

GERTRUDE. Then you will.

KIRKE. Well, this is a pretty task!—

[*He goes out.* GERTRUDE *comes to* AGNES. LUCAS *rises.*

GERTRUDE. I'm going down into the kitchen to see what these people can do in the way of strong soup.

LUCAS. You are exceedingly good to us, Mrs. Thorpe. I can't tell you how ashamed I am of my bearishness this afternoon.

GERTRUDE [*arranging the shawl about* AGNES's *shoulders*]. Hush, please!

AGNES. Are you looking at my shawl? Lucas brought it in with him, as a reward for my coming out of that stupid faint. I—I have always refused to be—spoilt in this way, but now—now—

LUCAS [*breaking in deliberately*]. Pretty work upon it, is there not, Mrs. Thorpe?

GERTRUDE. Charming. [*Going to the door which* LUCAS *opens for her.*] Thank you.
[*She passes out.* AGNES *rises.*

LUCAS. Oh, my dear girl!—

AGNES [*throwing her cigarette under the stove*]. I'm quite myself again, Lucas dear. Watch me—look! [*Walking firmly.*

LUCAS. No trembling?

AGNES. Not a flutter. [*Watching her open hand.*] My hand is absolutely steady. [*He takes her hand and kisses it upon the palm.*] Ah!—

LUCAS [*looking at her hand*]. No, it is shaking.

AGNES. Yes when you—when you—oh, Lucas!—
[*She sinks into a chair, turning her back upon him, and covering her face with her hands; her shoulders heaving.*

LUCAS [*going to her*]. Agnes, dear!

AGNES [*taking out her handkerchief*]. Let me—let me—

LUCAS [*bending over her*]. I've never seen you—

AGNES. No; I've never been a crying woman. But some great change has befallen me, I believe. What is it? That swoon—it wasn't mere faintness, giddiness; it was this change coming over me!

LUCAS. You are not unhappy?

AGNES [*wiping her eyes*]. No, I—I don't think I am. Isn't that strange?

LUCAS. My dearest, I'm glad to hear you say that, for you've made me very happy.

AGNES. Because I—?

LUCAS. Because you love me—naturally, that's one great reason.

AGNES. I have always loved you.

LUCAS. But never so utterly, so absorbingly, as you confess you do now. Do you fully realize what your confession does? It strikes off the shackles from me, from us—sets us free. [*With a gesture of freedom.*] Oh, my dear Agnes, free!

AGNES [*staring at him*]. Free?

LUCAS. Free from the burden of that crazy plan of ours of trumpeting our relations to the world. Forgive me—crazy is the only word for it. Thank heaven, we've at last admitted to each other that we're ordinary man and woman! Of course, I was ill—off my head. I didn't know what I was entering upon. And you, dear—living a pleasureless life, letting your thoughts dwell constantly on old troubles; that is how cranks are made. Now that I'm strong again, body and mind, I can protect you, keep you right. Ha, ha! What were we to pose as? Examples of independence of thought and action! [*Laughing.*] Oh, my darling, we'll be independent in thought and action still—but we won't make examples of ourselves, eh?

AGNES [*who has been watching him with wide-open eyes*]. Do you mean that all idea of our writing together, working together, defending our position, and the positions of such as ourselves, before the world, is to be abandoned?

LUCAS. Why, of course.

AGNES. I—I didn't quite mean that.

LUCAS. Oh, come, come! We'll furl what my uncle calls the banner of Free Union finally. [*Going to her, and kissing her hair lightly.*] For the future, mere man and woman. [*Pacing the room excitedly.*] The future! I've settled everything already. The work shall fall wholly on *my* shoulders. My poor girl, you shall enjoy a little rest and pleasure.

AGNES [*in a low voice*]. Rest and pleasure—

LUCAS. We'll remain abroad. One can live unobserved abroad, without actually hiding. [*She rises slowly.*] We'll find an ideal retreat. No more English tourists prying round us! And there, in some beautiful spot, alone except for your company, I'll work! [*As he paces the room, she walks slowly to and fro, listening, staring before her.*] I'll work. My new career! I'll write under a *nom de plume*. My books, Agnes, shall never ride to popularity on the back of a scandal. Our life! The mornings I must spend by myself, of course, shut up in my room. In the afternoon we will walk together. After dinner you shall hear what I've written in the morning; and then a few turns round our pretty garden, a glance at the stars with my arm about your waist—[*She stops abruptly, a look of horror on her face.*] While you whisper to me words of tenderness, words of—[*There is the distant sound of music of mandolin and guitar.*] Ah? [*To* AGNES.] Keep your shawl over your shoulders. [*Opening the window and stepping out; the music becoming louder.*] Some mandolinisti, in a gondola. [*Listening at the window, his head turned from her.*] How pretty, Agnes! Now, don't those mere sounds, in such surroundings, give you a sensation of hatred for revolt and turmoil! Don't they conjure up alluringly pictures of peace and pleasure, of golden days and star-lit nights— pictures of beauty and of love?

AGNES [*sitting on the settee, staring before her, speaking to herself*]. My marriage—the early days of my marriage—all over again!

LUCAS [*turning to her*]. Eh? [*Closing the window, and coming down to her as the music dies away.*] Tell me that those sounds thrill you.

AGNES. Lucas—

LUCAS [*sitting beside her*]. Yes?

AGNES. For the first few months of my marriage—[*Breaking off abruptly, and looking into his face wonderingly.*] Why, how young you seem to have become; you look quite boyish!

LUCAS [*laughing*]. I believe that this return of our senses will make us both young again.

AGNES. Both? [*With a little shudder.*] You know, I'm older than you.

LUCAS. Tsch!

AGNES [*passing her hand through his hair*]. Yes, I shall feel that *now*. [*Stroking his brow tenderly.*] Well—so it has come to this.

LUCAS. I declare you have colour in your cheeks already.

AGNES. The return of my senses?

LUCAS. My dear Agnes, we've both been to the verge of madness, you and I—driven there by our troubles. [*Taking her hand.*] Let us agree, in so many words, that we have completely recovered. Shall we?

AGNES. Perhaps mine is a more obstinate case. My enemies called me mad years ago.

LUCAS [*with a wave of the hand*]. Ah, but the future, the future. No more thoughts of reforming unequal laws from public platforms, no more shrieking in obscure magazines. No more beating of bare knuckles against stone walls. Come, say it!

AGNES [*with an effort*]. Go on.

LUCAS [*looking before him—partly to himself, his voice hardening*]. I'll never be mad again—never. [*Throwing his head back*]. By heavens! [*To her, in an altered tone*]. You don't say it!

AGNES [*after a pause*]. I—I will never be mad again.

LUCAS [*triumphantly*]. Hah! ha, ha! [*She deliberately removes the shawl from about her shoulders and, putting her arms round his neck, draws him to her*]. Ah, my dear girl!

AGNES [*in a whisper with her head on his breast*]. Lucas.

LUCAS. Yes.

AGNES. Isn't *this* madness?

LUCAS. I don't think so.

AGNES. Oh! oh! oh! I believe, to be a woman is to be mad.

LUCAS. No, to be a woman trying not to be a woman—*that* is to be mad.

> [*She draws a long, deep breath, then, sitting away from him, resumes her shawl mechanically.*

AGNES. Now, you promised me to run out to the Capello Nero to get a little food.

LUCAS. Oh, I'd rather—

AGNES [*rising*]. Dearest, you need it.

LUCAS [*rising*]. Well—Fortuné shall fetch my hat and coat.

AGNES. Fortuné! Are you going to take *all* my work from me?

> [*She is walking towards the door; the sound of his voice stops her.*

LUCAS. Agnes! [*She returns*]. A thousand thoughts have rushed through my brain this last hour or two. I've been thinking—my wife—

AGNES. Yes?

LUCAS. My wife—she will soon get tired of her present position. If, by and by, there should be a divorce, there would be nothing to prevent our marrying.

AGNES. Our—marrying!

LUCAS [*sitting, not looking at her, as if discussing the matter with himself*]. It might be to my advantage to settle again in London some day. After all, scandals quickly lose their keen edge. What would you say?

AGNES. Marriage—

LUCAS. Ah, remember, we're rational beings for the future. However, we needn't talk about it now.

AGNES. No.

LUCAS. Still, I assume you wouldn't oppose it. You would marry me if I wished it?

AGNES [*in a low voice*]. Yes.

LUCAS. That's a sensible girl! By Jove, I *am* hungry!

> [*He lights a cigarette, as she walks slowly to the door, then throws himself idly back on the settee.*

AGNES [*to herself, in a whisper*]. My old life—my old life coming all over again!

> [*She goes out. He lies watching the wreaths of tobacco smoke. After a moment or two,* FORTUNÉ *enters, closing the door behind him carefully.*

LUCAS. Eh?

FORTUNÉ [*after a glance round, dropping his voice*]. Ze Duke of Saint Olphert 'e say 'e vould like to speak a meenit alone.

> [LUCAS *rises, with a muttered exclamation of annoyance.*

LUCAS. Priez Monsieur le duc d'entrer.

> [FORTUNÉ *goes to the door and opens it. The* DUKE OF ST. OLPERTS *enters; he is in evening dress.* FORTUNÉ *retires.*

ST. OLPHERTS. Quite alone?

LUCAS. For the moment.

ST. OLPHERTS. My excuse to Mrs. Ebbsmith for not dining at the Grünwald—it was a perfectly legitimate one, dear Lucas. I was really expecting visitors.

LUCAS [*wonderingly*]. Yes?

ST. OLPHERTS [*with a little cough and a drawn face*]. Oh, I am not so well to-night. Damn these people for troubling me! Damn 'em for keeping me hopping about! Damn 'em for every shoot I feel in my leg. Visitors from England—they've arrived.

LUCAS. But what—?

ST. OLPHERTS. I shall die of gout some day, Lucas. Er—your wife is here.

LUCAS. Sybil!

ST. OLPHERTS. She's come through with your brother. Sandford's a worse prig than ever—and I'm in shockin' pain.

LUCAS. This—this is your doing!

ST. OLPHERTS. Yes. Damn you, don't keep me standing!

> [AGNES *enters, with* LUCAS's *hat and coat. She stops abruptly on seeing* ST. OL-PHERTS.

ST. OLPHERTS [*by the settee—playfully, through his pain*]. Ah, my dear Mrs. Ebbsmith, how can you have the heart to deceive an

invalid, a poor wretch who begs you [*sitting on the settee*] to allow
him to sit down for a moment?

[AGNES *deposits the hat and coat.*

AGNES. Deceive?—

ST. OLPHERTS. My friends arrive, I dine scrappily with them, and
hurry to the Grünwald thinking to catch you over your Zabajone.
Dear lady, you haven't been *near* the Grünwald.

AGNES. Your women faint sometimes, don't they?

ST. OLPHERTS. My—? [*In pain.*] Oh, what *do* you mean?

AGNES. The women in your class of life?

ST. OLPHERTS. Faint? oh yes, when there's occasion for it.

AGNES. I'm hopelessly low-born; I fainted involuntarily.

ST. OLPHERTS [*moving nearer to her*]. Oh, my dear, pray forgive me.
You've recovered? [*She nods.*] Indisposition agrees with you, evidently.
Your colouring to-night is charming. [*Coughing*]. You are—delightful
—to—look at.

> [GERTRUDE *enters, carrying a tray on which
> are a bowl of soup, a small decanter
> of wine, and accessories. She looks at
> ST. OLPHERTS unconcernedly, then turns
> away and places the tray on a table.*

ST. OLPHERTS [*quietly to* AGNES]. Not a servant?

AGNES. Oh, no.

ST. OLPHERTS [*rising promptly*]. Good God! I beg your pardon. A
friend?

AGNES. Yes.

ST. OLPHERTS [*looking at* GERTRUDE, *critically*]. Very nice. [*Still
looking at* GERTRUDE, *but speaking to* AGNES *in undertones*]. Married
or—? [*Turning to* AGNES]. Married or—?

[AGNES *has walked away.*

GERTRUDE [*to* LUCAS, *looking round*]. It is draughty at this table.

LUCAS [*going to the table near the settee and collecting the writing
material*]. Here—

[AGNES *joins* GERTRUDE.

ST. OLPHERTS [*quietly to* LUCAS].   Lucas— [LUCAS *goes to him*].
Who's that gal?

LUCAS [*to* ST. OLPHERTS]. An hotel acquaintance we made in Florence
—Mrs. Thorpe.

ST. OLPHERTS. Where's the husband?

LUCAS. A widow.

ST. OLPHERTS. You might—

[GERTRUDE *advances with the tray.*

LUCAS. Mrs. Thorpe, the Duke of St. Olpherts asks me to present
you to him.

[GERTRUDE *inclines her head to the* DUKE.
LUCAS *places the writing materials on
another table.*

ST. OLPHERTS [*limping up to* GERTRUDE *and handling the tray*]. I
beg to be allowed to help you. [*At the table*]. The tray here?

GERTRUDE. Thank you.

ST. OLPHERTS. Ha, how clumsy I am! We think it so gracious of you to look after our poor friend here who is not quite herself to-day. [*To* AGNES]. Come along, dear lady—everything is prepared for you. [*To* GERTRUDE.] You are here with—with your mother, I understand.

GERTRUDE. My brother.

ST. OLPHERTS. Brother. Now, do tell me whether you find your— your little hotel comfortable.

GERTRUDE [*looking at him steadily*]. We don't stay at one.

ST. OLPHERTS. Apartments?

GERTRUDE. Yes.

ST. OLPHERTS. Do you know, dear Mrs. Thorpe, I have always had the very strongest desire to live in lodgings in Venice?

GERTRUDE. You should gratify it. Our quarters are rather humble; we are in the Campo San Bartolomeo.

ST. OLPHERTS. But how delightful!

GERTRUDE. Why not come and see our rooms?

ST. OLPHERTS [*bowing*]. My dear young lady! [*producing a pencil and writing upon his shirt-cuff*]. Campo San Bartolomeo—

GERTRUDE. Five—four—nought—two.

ST. OLPHERTS [*writing*]. Five—four—nought—two.   To-morrow afternoon? [*She inclines her head*]. Four o'clock?

GERTRUDE. Yes; that would give the people ample time to tidy and clear up after us.

ST. OLPHERTS. After you—?

GERTRUDE. After our departure. My brother and I leave early to-morrow morning.

ST. OLPHERTS [*after a brief pause, imperturbably.*] A thousand thanks. May I impose myself so far upon you as to ask you to tell your landlord to expect me? [*Taking up his hat and stick*]. We are allowing this soup to get cold. [*Joining* LUCAS]. Dear Lucas, you have something to say to me—?

LUCAS [*opening the door*]. Come into my room.

[*They go out. The two women look at each other significantly.*

AGNES. You're a splendid woman.

GERTRUDE. That's rather a bad man, I think. Now, dear—

[*She places* AGNES *on the settee and sets the soup, etc., before her.* AGNES *eats.*

GERTRUDE [*watching her closely*]. So you have succeeded in coming to close quarters, as you expressed it, with him.

AGNES [*taciturnly*]. Yes.

GERTRUDE. His second visit here to-day, I gather?

AGNES. Yes.

GERTRUDE. His attitude towards you; his presence here under any circumstances—it's all rather queer.

AGNES. His code of behaviour is peculiarly his own.

GERTRUDE. However, are you easier in your mind?

AGNES [*quietly, but with intensity*]. I shall defeat him. I shall defeat him.

GERTRUDE. Defeat him? You will succeed in holding Mr. Cleeve, you mean?

AGNES. Oh, if you put it in that way—

GERTRUDE. Oh, come, I remember all you told me this afternoon. [*With disdain.*] So it has already arrived, then, at a simple struggle to hold Mr. Cleeve?

> [*There is a pause.* AGNES, *without answering, stretches out her hand to the wine. Her hand shakes—she withdraws it helplessly.*

GERTRUDE. What do you want—wine?

> [AGNES *nods.* GERTRUDE *pours out wine and gives her the glass.* AGNES *drains it eagerly and replaces it.*

GERTRUDE. Agnes—

AGNES. Yes?

GERTRUDE. You are dressed very beautifully.

AGNES. Do you think so?

GERTRUDE. Don't you know it? Who made you that gown?

AGNES. Bardini.

GERTRUDE. I shouldn't have credited the little woman with such excellent ideas.

AGNES. Oh, Lucas gave her the idea when he—when he—

GERTRUDE. When he ordered it?

AGNES. Yes.

GERTRUDE. Oh,—the whole thing came as a surprise to you?

AGNES. Er—quite.

GERTRUDE. I noticed the box this afternoon, when I called.

AGNES. Mr. Cleeve wishes me to appear more like—more like—

GERTRUDE. An ordinary smart woman. [*Contemptuously.*] Well, you ought to find no difficulty in managing that. You can make yourself very charming, it appears.

> [AGNES *again reaches out a hand towards the wine.* GERTRUDE *pours a very little wine into the wine-glass and takes up the glass;* AGNES *holds out her hand to receive it.*

GERTRUDE. Do you mind my drinking from your glass?

AGNES [*staring at her*]. No.

> [GERTRUDE *empties the glass and then places it in a marked way, on the side of the table furthest from* AGNES.

GERTRUDE [*with a little shudder*]. Ugh! Ugh! [AGNES *moves away from* GERTRUDE, *to the end of the settee, her head bowed, her hands clenched*]. I have something to propose. Come home with me to-morrow.

AGNES [*raising her head*]. Home?—

GERTRUDE. Ketherick. The very spot for a woman who wants to shut out things. Miles and miles of wild moorland! For company, purple heath and moss-covered granite, in summer; in winter, the moor-fowl and the snow glistening on top of the crags. Oh, and for open-air music, our little church owns the sweetest little peal of old bells!—[AGNES *rises, disturbed.*] Ah, I can't promise you *their* silence! Indeed, I'm very much afraid that on a still Sunday you can even hear the sound of the organ quite a long distance off. I am the organist when I'm at home. That's Ketherick. Will you come?

> [*The distant tinkling of mandolin and guitar is again heard.*

AGNES. Listen to that. The mandolinisti! You talk of the sound of your church-organ—and I hear *his* music.

GERTRUDE. His music?

AGNES. The music he is fond of; the music that gives him the thoughts that please him, soothe him.

GERTRUDE [*listening—humming the words of the air, contemptuously*].
> "Bell' amore deh! porgi l' orecchio,
> Ad un canto che parte dal cuore. . . ."

Love-music!

AGNES [*in a low voice, staring upon the ground*]. Yes, love-music.

> [*The door leading from* LUCAS'S *room opens and* ST. OLPHERTS *and* LUCAS *are heard talking.* GERTRUDE *hastily goes out.* LUCAS *enters; the boyishness of manner has left him—he is pale and excited.*

AGNES [*apprehensively*]. What is the matter?

LUCAS. My wife is revealing quite a novel phase of character.

AGNES. Your wife—?

LUCAS. The submissive mood. It's right that you should be told, Agnes. She is here, at the Danieli, with my brother Sandford. [ST. OLPHERTS *enters slowly*]. Yes, positively! It appears that she has lent herself to a scheme of Sandford's [*glancing at* ST. OLPHERTS] and of—and of—

ST. OLPHERTS. Of Sandford's.

LUCAS [*to* AGNES]. A plan of   reconciliation. [*To* ST. OLPHERTS.] Tell Sybil that the submissive mood comes too late, by a year or so!

> [*He paces to and fro.* AGNES *sits, with an expressionless face.*

AGNES [*quietly to* ST. OLPHERTS]. The "friends" you were expecting, duke?

ST. OLPHERTS [*meekly*]. Yes. [*She smiles at him scornfully.*

LUCAS. Agnes, dear, you and I leave here early to-morrow.

AGNES. Very well, Lucas.

LUCAS [*to* ST. OLPHERTS]. Duke, will you be the bearer of a note from me to Sandford?

ST. OLPHERTS. Certainly.

LUCAS [*going to the door of his room*]. I'll write it at once.

ST. OLPHERTS [*raising his voice*]. You won't see Sandford then, dear Lucas, for a moment or two?

LUCAS. No, no; pray excuse me.

> [*He goes out.* ST. OLPHERTS *advances to* AGNES. *The sound of the music dies away.*

ST. OLPHERTS [*slipping his cloak off and throwing it upon the head of the settee*]. Upon my soul, I think you've routed us!

AGNES. Yes.

ST. OLPHERTS [*sitting, breaking into a laugh*]. Ha, ha! he, he, he! Sir Sandford and Mrs. Cleeve will be so angry. Such a devil of a journey for nothing! Ho! [*Coughing.*] Ho, ho, ho!

AGNES. This was to be your *grand coup.*

ST. OLPHERTS. I admit it—I *have* been keeping this in reserve.

AGNES. I see. A further term of cat-and-dog life for Lucas and this lady—but it would have served to dispose of me, you fondly imagined. I see.

ST. OLPHERTS. I knew your hold on him was weakening. [*She looks at him.*] You knew it too. [*She looks away.*] He was beginning to find out that a dowdy demagogue is not the cheeriest person to live with. I repeat, you're a dooced clever woman, my dear. [*She rises, with an impatient shake of her body, and walks past him, he following her with his eyes.*] And a handsome one, into the bargain.

AGNES. Tsch!

ST. OLPHERTS. Tell me, when did you make up your mind to transform yourself?

AGNES. Suddenly, after our interview this afternoon; after what you said—

ST. OLPHERTS. Oh!—

AGNES [*with a little shiver*]. An impulse.

ST. OLPHERTS. Impulse doesn't account for the possession of those gorgeous trappings.

AGNES. These rags? A surprise gift from Lucas, to-day.

ST. OLPHERTS. Really, my dear, I believe I've helped to bring about my own defeat. [*Laughing softly.*] Ho, ho, ho! How disgusted the Cleeve family will be! Ha, ha! [*Testily.*] Come, why don't you smile—laugh? You can afford to do so! Show your pretty white teeth! laugh!

AGNES [*hysterically*]. Ha, ha, ha! Ha!

ST. OLPHERTS [*grinning*]. That's better!

> [*Pushing the cigarette-box towards him, she takes a cigarette and places it between her lips. He also takes a cigarette gaily.*

They smoke—she standing, with an elbow resting upon the top of the stove, looking down upon him.

ST. OLPHERTS [*as he lights his cigarette*]. This isn't explosive, I hope? No nitric and sulphuric acid, with glycerine, eh? [*Eyeing her wonderingly and admiringly.*] By Jove! Which is *you?* The shabby, shapeless rebel who entertained me this afternoon, or—[*kissing the tips of his fingers to her*] or *that?*

AGNES. This—this. [*Seating herself, slowly and thoughtfully, facing the stove, her back turned to him.*] My sex has found me out.

ST. OLPHERTS. Ha! tsch! [*Between his teeth.*] Damn it, for your sake I almost wish Lucas was a different sort of feller!

AGNES [*partly to herself, with intensity*]. Nothing matters now—not even that. He's mine. He would have died but for me. I gave him life. He is my child, my husband, my lover, my bread, my daylight—all—everything. Mine, mine.

ST. OLPHERTS [*rising and limping over to her*]. Good luck, my girl.

AGNES. Thanks!

ST. OLPHERTS. I'm rather sorry for you. This sort of triumph is short-lived, you know.

AGNES [*turning to him*]. I know. But I shall fight for every moment that prolongs it. This is my hour.

ST. OLPHERTS. Your hour—?

AGNES. There's only one hour in a woman's life.

ST. OLPHERTS. One—?

AGNES. One supreme hour. Her poor life is like the arch of a crescent; so many years lead up to that hour, so many weary years decline from it. No matter what she may strive for, there is a moment when Circumstance taps her upon the shoulder and says, "Woman, this hour is the best that Earth has to spare you." It may come to her in calm or in tempest, lighted by a steady radiance or by the glitter of evil stars; but however it comes, be it good or evil *it is her hour*—let her dwell upon every second of it!

ST. OLPHERTS. And this little victory of yours—the possession of this man; you think this is the best that earth can spare you? [*She nods, slowly and deliberately, with fixed eyes.*] Dear me, how amusin' you women are! And in your dowdy days you had ambitions! [*She looks at him suddenly.*] They were of a queer, gunpowder-and-faggot sort—but they were ambitions.

AGNES [*starting up*]. Oh!— [*Putting her hands to her brows.*] Oh!— [*Facing him.*] Ambitions! Yes, yes! You're right! Once, long ago, I hoped that my hour would be very different from this. Ambitions! I have seen myself, standing, humbly clad, looking down upon a dense, swaying crowd—a scarlet flag for my background. I have seen the responsive look upon thousands of white, eager, hungry faces, and I've heard the great, hoarse shout of welcome as I have seized my flag and hurried down amongst the people—to be given a place with their leaders! I! With the leaders, the leaders! Yes, that is what I once hoped would be my hour! [*Her voice sinking—weakly.*] But this *is* my hour.

ST. OLPHERTS [*after a brief pause*]. Well, my dear, when it's over, you'll have the satisfaction of counting the departing footsteps of a ruined man.

AGNES. Ruined—!

ST. OLPHERTS. Yes, there's great compensation in that—for women.

AGNES [*sitting*]. Why do you suggest he'll be ruined through me? [*Uneasily.*] At any rate, he'd ended his old career before we met.

ST. OLPHERTS. Pardon me; it's not too late now for him to resume that career. The threads are not quite broken yet.

AGNES. Oh, the scandal in London—

ST. OLPHERTS. Would be dispelled by this sham reconciliation with his wife.

AGNES [*looking at him*]. Sham—?

ST. OLPHERTS. Why, of course. All we desired to arrange was that for the future their household should be conducted strictly *à la mode*.

AGNES. *À la mode*?

ST. OLPHERTS [*behind the settee, looking down upon her*]. Mr. Cleeve in one quarter of the house, Mrs. Cleeve in another.

AGNES. Oh, yes.

ST. OLPHERTS. A proper aspect to the world, combined with freedom on both sides. It's a more decorous system than the aggressive Free Union you once advocated; and it's much in vogue at my end of the town.

AGNES. Your plan was a little more subtle than I gave you credit for. This was to be your method of getting rid of me!

ST. OLPHERTS. No, no. Don't you understand? With regard to yourself, we could have arrived at a compromise.

AGNES. A compromise?

ST. OLPHERTS. It would have made us quite happy to see you placed upon a—upon a somewhat different footing.

AGNES. What kind of—footing.

ST. OLPHERTS. The suburban villa, the little garden, a couple of discreet servants—everything *à la mode*.

> [*There is a brief pause. Then she rises and walks across the room, outwardly calm, but twisting her hands.*

AGNES. Well, you've had Mr. Cleeve's answer to *that*.

ST. OLPHERTS. Yes.

AGNES. Which finally disposes of the whole matter—disposes of it—

ST. OLPHERTS. Completely. [*Struck by an idea.*] Unless *you*—!

AGNES [*turning to him*]. Unless I—!

ST. OLPHERTS. Unless you—

AGNES [*after a moment's pause*]. What did Lucas say to you when you—?

ST. OLPHERTS. He said he knew you'd never make that sacrifice for him—[*She pulls herself up rigidly.*] So he declined to pain you by asking you to do it.

AGNES [*crossing swiftly to the settee and speaking straight into his face*]. That's a lie!

ST. OLPHERTS. Keep your temper, my dear.

AGNES [*passionately*]. His love may not last—it won't!—but at this moment he loves me better than that! He wouldn't make a mere light thing of me!

ST. OLPHERTS. Wouldn't he! You try him!

AGNES. What!

ST. OLPHERTS. You put him to the test!

AGNES [*with her hands to her brows*]. Oh—!

ST. OLPHERTS. No, no—don't!

AGNES [*faintly*]. Why?

ST. OLPHERTS. I like you. Damn *him*— you deserve to live your hour!

> [LUCAS *enters, with a letter in his hand.*
> AGNES *sits.*

LUCAS [*giving* ST. OLPHERTS *the letter*]. Thanks.

> [ST. OLPHERTS *pockets the letter and picks up his cloak;* LUCAS *assisting him.*

AGNES [*outwardly calm*]. Oh—Lucas—

LUCAS. Yes?

AGNES. The duke has been—has been—telling me—

LUCAS. What, dear?

AGNES. The sort of arrangement proposed for your going back to London.

LUCAS. Oh, my brother's brilliant idea!

AGNES. Acquiesced in by your wife.

> [ST. OLPHERTS *strolls away from them.*

LUCAS. Certainly; as I anticipated, she has become intensely dissatisfied with her position.

AGNES. And it would be quite possible, it seems, for you to resume your old career?

LUCAS. Just barely possible—well, for the moment, quite possible.

AGNES. Quite possible.

LUCAS. I haven't, formally, made a sign to my political friends yet. It's a task one leaves to the last. I shall do so now, at once. My people have been busying themselves, it appears, in reporting that I shall return to London directly my health is fully re-established.

AGNES. In the hope?— Oh, yes.

LUCAS. Hoping they'd be able to separate us before it was too—too late.

AGNES. Which hope they've now relinquished?

LUCAS. Apparently.

AGNES. They're prepared to accept a—a compromise, I hear?

LUCAS. Ha, yes!

AGNES. A compromise in my favour?

LUCAS [*hesitatingly*]. They suggest—

AGNES. Yes, yes, I know. After all, your old career was—a success. You made your mark, as you were saying the other day. You did make your mark. [*He walks up and down, restlessly, abstractedly, her eyes following him.*] You were generally spoken of, accepted, as a Coming Man. *The* Coming Man, often, wasn't it?

LUCAS. [*with an impatient wave of the hand*]. That doesn't matter!

AGNES. And now you are giving it up—giving it all up.

> [*He sits on the settee, resting his elbow on his knee, pushing his hand through his hair.*

LUCAS. But—but you believe I shall succeed equally well in this new career of mine?

AGNES [*looking at him stonily*]. There's the risk, you must remember.

LUCAS. Obviously, there's the risk. Why do you say all this to me now?

AGNES. Because *now* is the opportunity to—to go back.

LUCAS [*scornfully*]. Opportunity—?

AGNES. An excellent one. You're so strong and well now.

LUCAS. Thanks to you.

AGNES [*staring before her*]. Well—I did nurse you carefully, didn't I?

LUCAS. But I don't understand you. You are surely not proposing to—to—break with me?

AGNES. No—I—I—I was only thinking that you—you might see something in this suggestion of a compromise.

> [LUCAS *glances at* ST. OLPHERTS, *whose back is turned to them, but who instinctively looks round, then goes and sits by the window.*

LUCAS [*looking at her searchingly*]. Well, but—you—!

AGNES [*with assumed indifference*]. Oh, I—!

LUCAS. You!

AGNES. Lucas, don't—don't make *me* paramount.

> [*He moves to the end of the settee, showing by a look that he desires her to sit by him. After a moment's hesitation she takes her place beside him.*

LUCAS [*in an undertone*]. I do make you paramount, I do. My dear girl, under any circumstances you would still be everything to me—always. [*She nods with a vacant look.*] There would have to be this pretence of an establishment of mine— that would have to be faced; the whited sepulchre, the mockery of dinners and receptions and so on. But it would be to you I should fly for sympathy, encouragement, rest.

AGNES. Even if you were ill again—?

LUCAS. Even then, if it were practicable—if it could be—if it—

AGNES [*looking him in the face*]. Well—?

LUCAS [*avoiding her gaze*]. Yes, dear?

AGNES. What do you say, then, to asking the duke to give you back that letter to your brother?

LUCAS. It wouldn't settle matters, simply destroying that letter. Sandford begs me to go round to the Danieli to-night, to—to—

AGNES. To see him? [LUCAS *nods.*] And her? [*He shrugs his shoulders.*] At what time? Was any time specified?

LUCAS. Half-past nine.

AGNES. I—I haven't my watch on.

LUCAS [*referring to his watch*]. Nine twenty-five.

AGNES. You can almost manage it—if you'd like to go.

LUCAS. Oh, let them wait a few minutes for me; that won't hurt them.

AGNES [*dazed*]. Let me see—I did fetch your hat and coat—

> [*She rises and walks mechanically, stumbling against a chair.* LUCAS *looks up, alarmed;* ST. OLPHERTS *rises.*

AGNES [*replacing the chair*]. It's all right; I didn't notice this. [*Bringing* LUCAS's *hat and coat, and assisting him with the latter.*] How long will you be?

LUCAS. Not more than half an hour. An hour at the outside.

AGNES [*arranging his neck-handkerchief*]. Keep this so.

LUCAS. Er—if—if I—if we—

AGNES. The duke is waiting.

> [LUCAS *turns away, and joins* ST. OLPHERTS.

LUCAS [*to him, in a low voice*]. I am going back to the hotel with you.

ST. OLPHERTS. Oh, are you?

> [*The door opens and* FORTUNÉ *enters,. followed by* AMOS WINTERFIELD. FORTUNÉ *retires.*

AMOS [*to* LUCAS, *sternly*]. Is my sister still here, may I ask?

> [LUCAS *looks to* AGNES *interrogatively. She inclines her head.*

AMOS. I should like her to know that I am waiting for her.

> [AGNES *goes out.*

LUCAS [*to* AMOS]. Pray excuse me.

> [AMOS *draws back.* ST. OLPHERTS *passes out. At the door,* LUCAS *pauses, and bows slightly to* AMOS, *who returns his bow in the same fashion, then* LUCAS *follows* ST. OLPHERTS. *Then* GERTRUDE *enters, wearing her hat and mantle.* AGNES *follows; her movements are unsteady, and there is a wild look in her eyes.*

GERTRUDE. You've come to fetch me, Amos?

> [*He assents by a nod.*

AMOS [*to* AGNES]. I'm sorry to learn from Dr. Kirke that you've been ill. I hope you're better.

AGNES. Thank you, I am quite well.

[*Turning away,* GERTRUDE *watching her.*

AMOS [*gruffly*]. Are you ready, Gertrude?

GERTRUDE. No, dear, not yet. I want you to help me.

AMOS. In what way?

GERTRUDE. I want you to join me in persuading Mrs. Ebbsmith—*my friend,* Mrs. Ebbsmith—to come to Ketherick with us.

AMOS. My dear sister—!

GERTRUDE [*firmly*]. Please, Amos!

AGNES. Stop a moment! Mr. Winterfield, your sister doesn't in the least understand how matters are with me. I am returning to England —but with Mr. Cleeve. [*Recklessly.*] Oh, you'd hear of it eventually! He is reconciled to his wife.

GERTRUDE. Oh—! Then, surely, you—

AGNES. No. The reconciliation goes no further than mere outward appearances. [*Turning away.*] He relies upon me as much as ever. [*Beating her hands together passionately.*] He can't spare me— can't spare me!

AMOS [*in a low voice to* GERTRUDE]. Are you satisfied?

GERTRUDE. I suspected something of the kind. [*Going to* AGNES, *gripping her wrist tightly.*] Pull yourself out of the mud! Get up—out of the mud!

AGNES. I have no will to—no desire to!

GERTRUDE. You mad thing!

AGNES [*releasing herself, facing* GERTRUDE *and* AMOS.] You are only breaking in upon my hour!

GERTRUDE. Your hour—?

AGNES [*waving them away*]. I ask you to go! to go!

[GERTRUDE *returns to* AMOS.

AMOS. My dear Gertrude, you see what our position is here. If Mrs. Ebbsmith asks for our help, it is our duty to give it.

GERTRUDE. It is especially *my* duty, Amos.

AMOS. And I should have thought it especially mine. However, Mrs. Ebbsmith appears to firmly decline our help. And at this point, I confess, I would rather you left it—*you,* at least.

GERTRUDE. You would rather *I* left it—I, the virtuous, unsoiled woman! Yes, I am a virtuous woman, Amos; and it strikes you as odd, I suppose—my insisting upon friendship with her. But, look here, both of you! I'll tell you a secret. You never knew it, Amos, my dear; I never allowed anybody to suspect it—

AMOS. Never knew—what?

GERTRUDE. The sort of married life *mine* was. It didn't last long, but it was dreadful, almost intolerable.

AMOS. Gertrude!

GERTRUDE. After the first few weeks—weeks, not months! after the first few weeks of it, my husband treated me as cruelly—[*turning to* AGNES] just as cruelly, I do believe, as your husband treated *you.*

[AMOS *makes a movement showing consternation.*] Wait! Now, then! There was another man—one I loved—one I couldn't help loving! I could have found release with him, perhaps happiness of a kind. I resisted, came through it. They're dead—the two are dead! And here I am, a virtuous reputable woman; saved by the blessed mercy of Heaven! There, you are not surprised any longer, Amos! [*Pointing to* AGNES.] "My friend, Mrs. Ebbsmith!" [*Bursting into tears.*] Oh! Oh, if my little boy had been spared to me, he should have grown up tender to women—tender to women! he should, he should—!

> [*She sits upon the settee, weeping. There is a short silence.*

AMOS. Mrs. Ebbsmith, when I came here to-night I was angry with Gertrude—not altogether, I hope, for being in your company. But I was certainly angry with her for visiting you without my knowledge. I think I sometimes forget that she is eight and twenty, not eighteen. Well, now I offer to delay our journey home for a few days—if you hold out the faintest hope that her companionship is likely to aid you in any way.

> [AGNES, *standing motionless, makes no response.* AMOS *crosses to her and, as he passes* GERTRUDE, *he lets his hand drop over her shoulder; she clasps it, then rises and moves to a chair where she sits, crying silently.*

AMOS [*by* AGNES's *side—in a low voice*]. You heard what she said. Saved by the mercy of Heaven.

AGNES. Yes, but she can feel that.

AMOS. You felt so once.

AGNES. Once—!

AMOS. You have, in years gone by, asked for help upon your knees.

AGNES. It never came.

AMOS. Repeat your cry.

AGNES. There would be no answer.

AMOS. Repeat it!

AGNES [*turning upon him*]. If miracles *could* happen! If "help," as you term it, *did* come! Do you know what "help" would mean to *me?*

AMOS. What—!

AGNES. It would take the last crumb from me!

AMOS. This man's—protection?

AGNES [*defiantly*]. Yes!

AMOS. Oh, Mrs. Ebbsmith—!

AGNES [*pointing to the door*]. Well, I've asked you both to leave me, haven't I! [*Pointing at* GERTRUDE *who has risen.*] The man *she* loves is dead and gone! She can moralize—! [*Sitting, beating upon the settee with her hands.*] Leave me!

> [AMOS *joins* GERTRUDE.

GERTRUDE. We'll go, Amos.

> [*He takes from his pocket a small leather-bound book; the cover is well-worn and shabby.*

AMOS [*writing upon the fly-leaf of the book with a pencil*].   I am writing our address here, Mrs. Ebbsmith.

AGNES [*in a hard voice*].   I already have it.

> [GERTRUDE *glances at the book, over* AMOS's *shoulder, and looks at him wonderingly.*

AMOS [*laying the book on the settee by* AGNES's *side*].   You might forget it.

> [*She stares at the book with knitted brows for a moment, then stretches out her hand and opens it.*

AGNES [*withdrawing her hand sharply*].   No—I don't accept your gift.

AMOS.   The address of two friends is upon the fly-leaf.

AGNES.   I thank both of you—but you shall never be troubled again by me. [*Rising, pointing to the book.*] Take that away! [*Sitting facing the stove, the door of which she opens, replenishing the fire—excitedly.*] Mr. Cleeve may be back soon; it would be disagreeable to you all to meet again.

> [GERTRUDE *gently pushes* AMOS *aside, and picking up the book from the settee, places it upon the table.*

GERTRUDE [*to* AGNES—*pointing to the book*].   This frightens you. Simple print and paper, yet you pretend to regard it—but *it frightens you.* [*With a quick movement,* AGNES *twists her chair round and faces* GERTRUDE *fiercely.*] I called you a mad thing just now. A week ago I did think you half-mad—a poor, ill-used creature, a visionary, a moral woman living immorally; yet, in spite of all, a woman to be loved and pitied. But now I'm beginning to think that you're only frail—wanton. Oh, you're not so mad as not to know you're wicked! [*Tapping the book forcibly.*] And so this frightens you!

AGNES.   You're right! Wanton! That's what I've become! And I'm in my right senses, as you say. I suppose I *was* mad once for a little time, years ago. And do you know what drove me so? [*Striking the book with her fist.*] It was *that—that!*

GERTRUDE.   That!

AGNES.   I'd trusted in it, clung to it, and it failed me. Never once did it stop my ears to the sound of a curse; when I was beaten it didn't make the blows a whit the lighter; it never healed my bruised flesh, my bruised spirit! Yes, that drove me distracted for a while; but I'm sane now—*now* it is *you* that are mad, mad to believe! You foolish people, not to know [*beating her breast and forehead*] that Hell or Heaven is here and here! [*Pointing to the book.*] Take it!

> [GERTRUDE *turns away and joins* AMOS, *and they walk quickly to the door.*

AGNES [*frantically*].   I'll not endure the sight of it—!

> [*As they reach the door,* GERTRUDE *looks back and sees* AGNES *hurl the book into the fire. They go out.* AGNES *starts to*

her feet and stands motionless for a
moment, her head bent, her fingers
twisted in her hair. Then she raises her
head; the expression of her face has
changed to a look of fright and horror.
Uttering a loud cry, she hastens to the
stove and, thrusting her arm into the
fire, drags out the book. GERTRUDE and
AMOS re-enter quickly in alarm.

GERTRUDE. Agnes—!

[They stand looking at AGNES, who is kneeling upon the ground, clutching the charred
book.

END OF THE THIRD ACT.

THE FOURTH ACT.

The scene is an apartment in the Campo San Bartolomeo. The walls are of plaster; the ceiling is frescoed in cheap modern-Italian fashion. An arch spans the room, at the further end of which is a door leading to Agnes's bedroom; to the left, and behind the support of the arch, is an exit on to a landing, while a nearer door, on the same side, opens into another room. The furniture, and the few objects attached to the walls, are characteristic of a moderate-priced Venetian lodging. Placed about the room, however, are photographs in frames, and pretty knick-knacks personal to GERTRUDE, *and a travelling trunk and bag are also to be seen. The shutters of the two nearer windows are closed; a broad stream of moonlight, coming through the further window, floods the upper part of the room.*

HEPHZIBAH, *a grey-haired north-country-woman dressed as a lady's maid, is collecting the knick-knacks and placing them in the travelling-bag. After a moment or two,* GERTRUDE *enters by the further door.*

GERTRUDE [*at the partly closed door, speaking into the further room*]. I'll come back to you in a little while, Agnes. [*Closing the door and addressing* HEPHZIBAH.] How are you getting on, Heppy?

HEPHZIBAH. A 'reet, Miss Gerty. I'm puttin' together a' the sma' knick-knacks, to lay them wi' the claes i' th' trunks.

GERTRUDE [*taking some photographs from the table and bringing them to* HEPHZIBAH]. We leave here at a quarter to eight in the morning; not a minute later.

HEPHZIBAH. Aye. Will there be much to pack for Mistress Cleeve?

GERTRUDE. Nothing at all. Besides her hand-bag, she has only the one box.

HEPHZIBAH [*pointing to the trunk*]. Nay, nobbut that thing!

GERTRUDE. Yes, nobbut that. I packed that for her at the Palazzo.

HEPHZIBAH. Eh, it won't gi' us ower much trouble to maid Mistress Cleeve when we get her hame.

GERTRUDE. Heppy, we are not going to call—my friend— "Mrs. Cleeve."

HEPHZIBAH. Nay! what will thee call her?

GERTRUDE. I'll tell you—by and by. Remember, she must never, never be reminded of the name.

HEPHZIBAH. Aye, I'll be maist carefu'. Poor leddy! After the way she tended that husband o' hers in Florence neet and day, neet and day!

GERTRUDE. The world's full of unhappiness, Heppy.

HEPHZIBAH. The world's full o' husbands. I canna' bide 'em. They're true eneugh when they're ailin'—but a lass can't keep her Jo always sick. Hey, Miss Gerty! Do forgie your auld Heppy!

GERTRUDE. For what?

HEPHZIBAH. Why, your own man, so I've heerd, ne'er had as much as a bit headache till he caught his fever and died o't.

GERTRUDE. No, I never knew Captain Thorpe to complain of an ache or a pain.

HEPHZIBAH. And *he* was a rare, bonny husband to thee, if a' tales be true.

GERTRUDE. Yes, Heppy. [*Listening, startled.*] Who's this?

HEPHZIBAH [*going and looking*]. Maister Amos.

> [AMOS *enters briskly.*

AMOS [*to* GERTRUDE]. How is she?

GERTRUDE [*assisting him to remove his overcoat*].   More as she used to be; so still, so gentle. She's reading.

AMOS [*looking at her significantly*]. Reading?

GERTRUDE. Reading.

> [*He sits humming a tune, while* HEPPY *takes off his shoes and gives him his slippers.*

HEPHZIBAH. Eh, Maister Amos, it's good to see thee sae glad-some.

AMOS. Home, Heppy, home!

HEPHZIBAH. Aye, hame!

AMOS. With our savings!

HEPHZIBAH. Thy savings—!

AMOS. Tsch! get on with your packing.

> [HEPHZIBAH *goes out, carrying the travelling-bag and* AMOS's *shoes. He exchanges the coat he is wearing for a shabby little black jacket which* GERTRUDE *brings him.*

GERTRUDE [*filling* AMOS's *pipe*]. Well, dear! Go on!

AMOS. Well, I've seen them.

GERTRUDE. Them—?

AMOS. The duke and Sir Sandford Cleeve.

GERTRUDE. At the hotel?

AMOS. I found them sitting together in the hall, smoking, listening to some music.

GERTRUDE. Quite contented with the arrangement they believed they had brought about.

AMOS. Apparently so. Especially the baronet—a poor cadaverous creature.

GERTRUDE. Where was Mr. Cleeve?

AMOS. He had been there, had an interview with his wife, and departed.

GERTRUDE. Then by this time he has discovered that Mrs. Ebbsmith has left him?

AMOS. I suppose so.

GERTRUDE. Well, well! the duke and the cadaverous baronet?

AMOS. Oh, I told them I considered it my duty to let them know that the position of affairs had suddenly become altered. [*She puts his pipe in his mouth and strikes a match.*] That, in point of fact, Mrs. Ebbsmith had ceased to be an element in their scheme for re-establishing Mr. Cleeve's household.

GERTRUDE [*holding a light to his pipe*]. Did they inquire as to her movements?

AMOS. The duke did—guessed we had taken her.

GERTRUDE. What did they say to that?

AMOS. The baronet asked me whether I was the chaplain of a Home for—[*angrily*] ah!

GERTRUDE. Brute! And then?

AMOS. Then they suggested that I ought hardly to leave *them* to make the necessary explanations to their relative, Mr. Lucas Cleeve.

GERTRUDE. Yes—well?

AMOS. I replied that I fervently hoped I should never set eyes on their relative again.

GERTRUDE [*gleefully*]. Ha!

AMOS. But that Mrs. Ebbsmith had left a letter behind her at the Palazzo Arconati, addressed to that gentleman, which I presumed contained as full an explanation as he could desire.

GERTRUDE. Oh! Amos—!

AMOS. Eh?

GERTRUDE. You're mistaken there, dear; it was no letter.

AMOS. No letter—?

GERTRUDE. Simply four shakily written words.

AMOS. Only four words!

GERTRUDE. "My—hour—is—over." [HEPHZIBAH *enters with a card on a little tray.* GERTRUDE *reads the card and utters an exclamation. Taking the card—under her breath.*] Amos!

> [*He goes to her; they stare at the card together.*

AMOS [*to* HEPHZIBAH]. Certainly.

> [HEPHZIBAH *goes out, then returns with the* DUKE OF ST. OLPHERTS, *and retires.* ST. OLPHERTS *bows graciously to* GERTRUDE, *and, more formally to* AMOS.

AMOS. Pray sit down.

> [ST. OLPHERTS *seats himself on the settee.*

ST. OLPHERTS. Oh, my dear sir! If I may use such an expression in your presence—here is the devil to pay!

AMOS [*to* ST. OLPHERTS]. You don't mind my pipe? [ST. OLPHERTS *waves a hand pleasantly.*] And I don't mind your expression. [*Sitting by the table.*] The devil to pay?

ST. OLPHERTS. This, I daresay well-intentioned, interference of yours has brought about some very unpleasant results. Mr. Cleeve returns to the Palazzo Arconati and finds that Mrs. Ebbsmith has flown.

AMOS. That result, at least, was inevitable.

ST. OLPHERTS. Whereupon he hurries back to the Danieli and denounces us all for a set of conspirators.

AMOS. Your Grace doesn't complain of the injustice of that charge?

ST. OLPHERTS [*smilingly*]. No, no, I don't complain. But the brother— the wife! Just when they imagined they had bagged the truant— there's the sting!

GERTRUDE. Oh, then Mr. Cleeve now refuses to carry out his part of the shameful arrangement?

ST. OLPHERTS. Absolutely. [*Rising, taking a chair, and placing it by the settee.*] Come into this, dear Mrs. Thorn—!

AMOS. Thorpe.

ST. OLPHERTS. Come into this! [*Sitting again.*] *You* understand the sort of man we have to deal with in Mr. Cleeve.

GERTRUDE [*sitting*]. A man who prizes a woman when he has lost her.

ST. OLPHERTS. Precisely.

GERTRUDE. Men don't relish, I suppose, being cast off by women.

ST. OLPHERTS. It's an inversion of the picturesque; the male abandoned is not a pathetic figure. At any rate, our poor Lucas is now raving fidelity to Mrs. Ebbsmith.

GERTRUDE [*indignantly*]. Ah—!

ST. OLPHERTS. If you please, he cannot, will not, exist without her. Reputation, fame, fortune, are nothing when weighed against—Mrs. Ebbsmith. And we may go to perdition, so that he recovers—Mrs. Ebbsmith.

AMOS. Well—to be plain—you're not asking us to sympathize with Mrs. Cleeve and her brother-in-law over their defeat?

ST. OLPHERTS. Certainly not. All I ask, Mr. Winterfield, is that you will raise no obstacle to a meeting between Mrs. Cleeve and—and—

GERTRUDE. No!

[ST. OLPHERTS *signifies assent;* GERTRUDE *makes a movement.*

ST. OLPHERTS [*to her*]. Don't go.

AMOS. The object of such a meeting?

ST. OLPHERTS. Mrs. Cleeve desires to make a direct, personal appeal to Mrs. Ebbsmith.

GERTRUDE. Oh, what kind of woman can this Mrs. Cleeve be?

ST. OLPHERTS. A woman of character, who sets herself to accomplish a certain task—

GERTRUDE. Character!

AMOS. Hush, Gerty!

ST. OLPHERTS. And who gathers her skirts tightly round her and gently tip-toes into the mire.

AMOS. To put it clearly—in order to get her unfaithful husband back to London, Mrs. Cleeve would deliberately employ this weak, unhappy woman as a lure.

ST. OLPHERTS. Perhaps Mrs. Cleeve is an unhappy woman.

GERTRUDE. What work for a wife!

ST. OLPHERTS. Wife—nonsense! She is only married to Cleeve.

AMOS [*walking up and down*]. It is proposed that this meeting should take place—when?

ST. OLPHERTS. I have brought Sir Sandford and Mrs. Cleeve with me. [*Pointing toward the outer door.*] They are—

AMOS. If I decline?

ST. OLPHERTS. It's known you leave for Milan at a quarter to nine in the morning; there might be some sort of foolish, inconvenient scene at the station.

AMOS. Surely your Grace—?

ST. OLPHERTS. Oh, no, I shall be in bed at that hour. I mean between the women, perhaps—and Mr. Cleeve. [*Going to* AMOS.] Come, come, sir, you can't abduct Mrs. Ebbsmith—nor can we. Nor must you gag her. [AMOS *appears angry and perplexed*.] Pray be reasonable. Let her speak out for herself, here, finally, and settle the business. Come, sir, come!

AMOS [*going to* GERTRUDE, *and speaking in a low voice*]. Ask her. [GERTRUDE *goes out*.] Cleeve! Where is he while this poor creature's body and soul are being played for? You have told him that she is with us?

ST. OLPHERTS. No, I haven't.

AMOS. He must suspect it.

ST. OLPHERTS. Well, candidly, Mr. Winterfield, Mr. Cleeve is just now employed in looking for Mrs. Ebbsmith elsewhere.

AMOS. Elsewhere?

ST. OLPHERTS. Sir Sandford recognized that, in his brother's present mood, the young man's presence might be prejudicial to the success of these delicate negotiations.

AMOS. So some lie has been told him, to keep him out of the way?

ST. OLPHERTS. Now, Mr. Winterfield—!

AMOS. Good heavens, duke—forgive me for my roughness—you appear to be fouling your hands, all of you, with some relish!

ST. OLPHERTS. I must trouble you to address remarks of that nature to Sir Sandford Cleeve. I am not longer a prime mover in the affair; I am simply standing by.

AMOS. But how can you "stand by"!

ST. OLPHERTS. Confound it, sir—if you will trouble yourself to rescue people—there is a man to be rescued here as well as a woman; a man, by-the-way, who is a—a sort of relative of mine!

AMOS. The woman first!

ST. OLPHERTS. Not always. You can rescue this woman in a few weeks' time; it can make no difference.

AMOS [*indignantly*]. Ah—!

ST. OLPHERTS. Oh, you are angry!

AMOS. I beg your pardon. One word! I assure your Grace that I truly believe this wretched woman is at a fatal crisis in her life; I believe that if I lose her now there is every chance of her slipping back into a misery and despair out of which it will be impossible to drag her. Oh, I'll be perfectly open with you! At this moment we—my sister and I—are not sure of her. Her affection for this man may still induce her to sacrifice herself utterly for him; she is still in danger of falling to the lowest depth a woman can attain. Come, duke, don't help these people! And don't "stand by"! Help me and my sister! For God's sake!

ST. OLPHERTS. My good Mr. Winterfield, believe me or not, I—I positively like this woman.

AMOS [*gladly*]. Ah!

ST. OLPHERTS. She attracts me curiously. And if she wanted assistance—

AMOS. Doesn't she?

ST. OLPHERTS. Money—

AMOS. No, no.

ST. OLPHERTS. She should have it. But as for the rest—well—

AMOS. Well?

ST. OLPHERTS. Well, sir, you must understand me. It is a failing of mine; I can't approach women—I never could—in the Missionary spirit.   [GERTRUDE *re-enters; the men turn to face her.*

AMOS [*to* GERTRUDE]. Will she—?

GERTRUDE. Yes. [ST. OLPHERTS *limps out of the room, bowing to* GERTRUDE *as he passes.*] Oh, Amos!

AMOS. Are we to lose the poor soul after all, Gerty?

GERTRUDE. I—I can't think so—oh, but I'm afraid.

> [ST. OLPHERTS *returns, and* SIR SANDFORD CLEEVE *enters with* SYBIL CLEEVE. SANDFORD *is a long, lean, old-young man with a pinched face.* SYBIL *is a stately, handsome young woman, beautifully gowned and thickly veiled.*

ST. OLPHERTS. Mrs. Thorpe—Mr. Winterfield.

> [SANDFORD *and* SYBIL *bow distantly to* GERTRUDE *and* AMOS.

AMOS [*to* SANDFORD *and* SYBIL, *indicating the settee*]. Will you—? [SYBIL *sits on settee;* SANDFORD *takes the chair beside her.*] Gertrude—

> [GERTRUDE *goes out.*

SIR SANDFORD [*pompously*]. Mr. Winterfield, I find myself engaged upon a peculiarly distasteful task.

AMOS. I have no hope, Sir Sandford, that you will not have strength to discharge it.

SIR SANDFORD. We shall object to loftiness of attitude on your part, sir. You would do well to reflect that we are seeking to restore a young man to a useful and honourable career.

AMOS. You are using very honourable means, Sir Sandford.

SIR SANDFORD. I shall protest against any perversion of words, Mr. Winterfield—

> [*The door of* AGNES'S *room opens, and* GERTRUDE *comes in, then* AGNES. *The latter is in a rusty, ill-fitting, black, stuff dress; her hair is tightly drawn from her brows; her face is haggard, her eyes are red and sunken. A strip of linen binds her right hand.*

ST. OLPHERTS [*speaking into* SYBIL'S *ear*]. The lean witch again! The witch of the Iron Hall at St. Luke's!

SYBIL [*in a whisper*]. Is *that* the woman?

ST. OLPHERTS. You see only one of 'em—there are *two* there.

> [SANDFORD *rises as* AGNES *comes slowly forward, accompanied by* GERTRUDE. AMOS *joins* GERTRUDE, *and they go together into an adjoining room,* GERTRUDE *giving* AGNES *an appealing look.*]

SIR SANDFORD [*to* AGNES]. I—I am Mr. Lucas Cleeve's brother; [*with a motion of the hand towards* SYBIL] this is—this is—

> [*He swallows the rest of the announcement, and retires to the back of the room where he stands before the stove.* ST. OLPHERTS *strolls away and disappears.*]

SYBIL [*to* AGNES, *in a hard, dry, disdainful voice*]. I beg that you will sit down. [AGNES *sits, mechanically, with an expressionless face.*] I—I don't need to be told that this is a very—a very unwomanly proceeding on my part.

SIR SANDFORD. I can't regard it in that light, under the peculiar circumstances.

SYBIL. I'd rather you wouldn't interrupt me, Sandford. [*To* AGNES.] But the peculiar circumstances, to borrow my brother-in-law's phrase, are not such as develop sweetness and modesty, I suppose.

SIR SANDFORD. Again I say you wrong yourself there, Sybil—

SYBIL [*impatiently*]. Oh, please let me wrong myself, for a change. [*To* AGNES.] When my husband left me, and I heard of his association with you, I felt sure that his vanity would soon make an openly irregular life intolerable to him. Vanity is the cause of a great deal of virtue in men; the vainest are those who like to be thought respectable.

SIR SANDFORD. Really, I must protest—!

SYBIL. But Lady Cleeve—the mother—and the rest of the family have not had the patience to wait for the fulfillment of my prophecy. And so I have been forced to undertake this journey.

SIR SANDFORD. I demur to the expression "forced," Sybil—

SYBIL. Cannot we be left alone? Surely—! [SANDFORD *bows stiffly and moves away, following* ST. OLPHERTS.] However—there's this to be said for them, poor people—whatever is done to save my husband's prospects in life must be done *now*. It is no longer possible to play fast and loose with friends and supporters—to say nothing of enemies. His future now rests upon a matter of days, hours almost. [*Rising and walking about agitatedly.*] That is why I am sent here—well, why I *am* here.

AGNES [*in a low, quavering voice*]. What is it you are all asking me to do now?

SYBIL. We are asking you to continue to—to exert your influence over him for a little while longer.

AGNES [*rising unsteadily*]. Ah—! [*She makes a movement to go, falters, and irresolutely sits again.*] My influence! mine!

SYBIL [*with a stamp of the foot*]. You wouldn't underrate your power if you had seen him, heard him, about an hour ago [*mockingly*], after he had discovered his bereavement.

AGNES. He will soon forget *me*.

SYBIL. Yes, if you don't forsake him.

AGNES. I am going to England, into Yorkshire; according to your showing, that should draw him back.

SYBIL. Oh, I've no doubt we shall hear of him—in Yorkshire! You'll find him dangling about your skirts, in Yorkshire!

AGNES. And *he* will find that I am determined, strong.

SYBIL. Ultimately he will tire, of course. But when? And what assurance have we that he returns to us when he has wearied of pursuing you? Besides, don't I tell you that we must make sure of him *now?* It's of no use his begging us, in a month's time, to patch up home and reputation. It must be *now*—and *you* can end our suspense. Come, hideous as it sounds, this is not much to ask.

AGNES [*shrinking from her*]. Oh—!

SYBIL. Oh, don't regard me as the wife! That's an unnecessary sentiment, I pledge you my word. It's a little late in the day, too, for such considerations. So, come, help us!

AGNES. I will not.

SYBIL. He has an old mother—

AGNES. Poor woman!

SYBIL. And remember, *you* took him away—!

AGNES. I!

SYBIL. Practically you did—with your tender nursing and sweet compassion. Isn't it straining a point—to shirk bringing him back?

AGNES [*rising*]. I did not take him from you. You—you sent him to me.

SYBIL. Iio, yes! that tale has been dinned into your ears often enough, I can quite believe. *I* sent him to you—my coldness, heartlessness, selfishness sent him to you. The unsympathetic wife, eh? Yes, but you didn't put yourself to the trouble of asking for *my* version of the story before you mingled your woes with his. [AGNES *faces her suddenly*.] You know him now. Have I been altogether to blame, do you still think? Unsympathetic! Because I've so often had to tighten my lips, and stare blankly over his shoulder, to stop myself from crying out in weariness of his vanity and pettiness? Cruel! Because, occasionally, patience became exhausted at the mere contemplation of a man so thoroughly, greedily self-absorbed? Why, *you* married miserably, the Duke of St. Olpherts tells us! Before you made yourself my husband's champion and protector, why didn't you let your experience speak a word for *me?* [AGNES *quickly turns away and sits upon the settee, her hands to her brow*.] However, I didn't come here to revile you. [*Standing by her*.] They say that you're a strange woman—not the sort of woman one generally finds doing such things as you have done; a woman with odd ideas. I hear—oh, I'm willing to believe it!— that there's good in you.

> [AGNES *breaks into a low peal of hysterical laughter*.

AGNES. Who tells you—that?

SYBIL. The Duke.

AGNES. Ha, ha, ha! A character—from him! ha, ha, ha!

SYBIL [*Her voice and manner softening*]. Well, if there *is* pity in you, help us to get my husband back to London, to his friends, to his old ambitions.

AGNES. Ha, ha, ha, ha! your husband!

SYBIL. The word slips out. I swear to you that he and I can nevei be more to each other than companion figures in a masquerade. The same roof may cover us; but between two wings of a house, as you may know, there often stretches a wide desert. I despise him, he hates me. [*Walking away, her voice breaking.*]   Only—I did love him once . . . I don't want to see him utterly thrown away—wasted . . . I don't quite want to see that . . .

[AGNES *rises and approaches* SYBIL, *fearfully.*

AGNES [*in a whisper*]. Lift your veil for a moment. [SYBIL *raises her veil.*] Tears—tears—[*with a deep groan.*]—Oh—! [SYBIL *turns away.*] I— I'll do it . . . I'll go back to the Palazzo . ·. . at once . . . [SYBIL *draws herself up suddenly.*] I've wronged you! wronged you! oh! God! oh, God!

> [*She totters away and goes into her bed-room. For a moment or two* SYBIL *stands still, a look of horror and repulsion upon her face. Then she turns and goes towards the outer door.*

SYBIL [*calling*]. Sandford! Sandford!

> [SIR SANDFORD CLEEVE *and the* DUKE *of* ST. OLPHERTS *enter.*

SIR SANDFORD [*to* SYBIL]. Well—?

SYBIL. She is going back to the Palazzo.

SIR SANDFORD. You mean that she consents to—?

SYBIL [*stamping her foot*]. I mean that she will go back to the Palazzo. [*Sitting and leaning her head upon her hands.*] Oh! oh!

SIR SANDFORD. Need we wait longer, then?

SYBIL. These people—these people who are befriending her! Tell them.

SIR SANDFORD. Really, it can hardly be necessary to consult—

SYBIL [*fiercely*]. I will have them told! I will have them told!

> [SANDFORD *goes to the door of the other room and knocks, returning to* SYBIL *as* GERTRUDE *and* AMOS *enter.* SYBIL *draws down her veil.*

GERTRUDE [*looking round*]. Mrs. Ebbsmith—? Mrs. Ebbsmith—!

SIR SANDFORD. Er—many matters have been discussed with Mrs. Ebb-smith. Undoubtedly she has, for the moment, considerable influence over my brother. She has consented to exert it, to induce him to return, at once, to London.

AMOS. I think I understand you!

[AGNES *appears at the door of her room dressed in bonnet and cloak.*

GERTRUDE. Agnes—!

[AGNES *comes forward, stretches out her hand to* GERTRUDE, *and throws herself upon the settee.*

SYBIL [*to* SANDFORD, *clutching his arm*]. Take me away.

[*They turn to go.*

GERTRUDE [*to* SYBIL]. Mrs. Cleeve—! [*Looking down upon* AGNES.] Mrs. Cleeve, we—my brother and I—hoped to save this woman. She was worth saving. You have utterly destroyed her.

[SYBIL *makes no answer, but walks slowly away with* SANDFORD, *then stops and turns abruptly.*

SYBIL [*with a gasp*]. Oh—! No—I will not accept the service of this wretched woman. I loathe myself for doing what I have done. [*Coming to* AGNES.] Look up! Look at me! [*Proudly lifting her veil.*] I decline your help—I decline it. [*To* GERTRUDE *and* AMOS.] You hear me—you—and you? I unsay all that I've said to her. It's too degrading, I will not have such an act upon my conscience. [*To* AGNES.] Understand me! If you rejoin this man I shall consider it a fresh outrage upon me. I hope you will keep with your friends.

[GERTRUDE *holds out her hand to* SYBIL; SYBIL *touches it distantly.*

AGNES [*clutching at* SYBIL'S *skirts*]. Forgive me! forgive—!

SYBIL [*retreating*]. Ah, please—! [*Turning and confronting* SANDFORD.] Tell your mother I have failed. I am not going back to England.

[LUCAS *enters quickly; he and* SYBIL *come face to face. They stand looking at each other for a moment, then she sweeps past him and goes out.* SANDFORD *follows her.*

LUCAS [*coming to* AGNES]. Agnes—[*To* AGNES, *in rapid, earnest undertones.*] They sent me to the railway station; my brother told me you were likely to leave for Milan to-night. I ought to have guessed sooner that you were in the hands of this meddling parson and his sister. Why has my wife been here—?

AGNES [*in a low voice, rocking herself gently to and fro*]. Your wife— your wife—!

LUCAS. And the others? What scheme is afoot now? Why have you left me? Why didn't you tell me outright that I was putting you to too severe a test? You tempted me, you led me on, to propose that I should patch up my life in that way. [*She rises, with an expressionless face.*] But it has had one good result. I know now how much I depend upon you. Oh, I have had it all out with my-self, pacing up and down that cursed railway station. [*Laying his hand upon her arm and speaking into her ear.*] I don't deceive my-self any longer. Agnes, *this* is the great cause of the unhappiness I've experienced of late years—I am not fit for the fight and press of life. I wear no armour; I am too horribly sensitive. My skin

bleeds at a touch; even flattery wounds me. Oh, the wretchedness
of it! But *you* can be strong—at your weakest, there is a certain
strength in you. With you, in time, I feel I shall grow stronger.
Only I must withdraw from the struggle for a while; you must take
me out of it and let me rest—recover breath, as it were. Come!
Forgive me for having treated you ungratefully, almost treacherously.
Tomorrow we will begin our search for our new home. Agnes!

AGNES. I have already found a home.

LUCAS. Apart from me, you mean?

AGNES. Apart from you.

LUCAS. No, no. You'll not do that!

AGNES. Lucas, this evening, two or three hours ago, you planned out
the life we were to lead in the future. We had done with "madness,"
if you remember; henceforth we were to be "mere man and woman."

LUCAS. You agreed—

AGNES. Then. But we hadn't looked at each other clearly then, as mere
man and woman. You, the man—what are you? You've confessed—

LUCAS. I lack strength; I shall gain it.

AGNES. Never from me—never from me. For what am I? Untrue to
myself, as you are untrue to yourself; false to others, as you are false
to others; passionate, unstable, like yourself; like yourself, a coward.
A coward. I—I was to lead women! I was to show them, in your company, how laws—laws made and laws that are natural—may be set
aside or slighted; how men and women may live independent and
noble lives without rule, or guidance, or sacrament. I was to be the
example—the figure set up for others to observe and imitate. But
the figure was made of wax—it fell away at the first hot breath that
touched it! You and I! What a partnership it has been! How base
and gross and wicked almost from the very beginning! We know
each other now thoroughly— how base and wicked it would remain!
No, go your way, Lucas, and let me go mine.

LUCAS. Where—where are you going?

AGNES. To Ketherick—to think. [*Wringing her hands.*] Ah, I have to
think, too, now, of the woman I have wronged.

LUCAS. Wronged?

AGNES. Your wife; the woman I have wronged, who came here to-night,
and—spared me. Oh, go!

LUCAS. Not like this, Agnes! not like this!

AGNES [*appealingly*]. Gertrude! [LUCAS *looks round—first at* GERTRUDE
then at AMOS—*and, with a hard smile upon his face, turns to go.
Suddenly* AGNES *touches his sleeve*]. Lucas, when I have learnt to pray
again, I will remember you every day of my life.

LUCAS [*staring at her*]. Pray! . . . you! . . .

> [*She inclines her head twice, slowly; with-
> out another word he walks away and goes
> out.* AGNES *sinks upon the settee;* AMOS
> *and* GERTRUDE *remain, stiffly and silently,
> in the attitude of people who are waiting
> for the departure of a disagreeable person.*

ST. OLPHERTS [*after watching* LUCAS's *departure*]. Now, I wonder whether, if he hurried to his wife at this moment, repentent, and begged her to relent—I wonder whether—whether she would—whether —[*looking at* AMOS *and* GERTRUDE, *a little disconcerted*]—I beg your pardon—you're not interested?

AMOS. Frankly, we are not.

ST. OLPHERTS. No; other people's affairs are tedious. [*Producing his gloves.*] Well! A week in Venice—and the weather has been delightful. [*Shaking hands with* GERTRUDE, *whose expression remains unchanged.*] A pleasant journey! [*Going to* AGNES, *offering his hand.*] Mrs. Ebbsmith—? [*She lifts her maimed hand.*] Ah! An accident! [*She nods.*] I'm sorry . . . I . . .

> [*He turns away and goes out, bowing to*
> AMOS *as he passes.*

THE END